Books are to be returned on or before
the last date below

0415080231

The uncertain science

This book argues that sociology has not freed itself from the influence of philosophy, and specifically from the search for certainty. This 'foundationalism', which is characteristic of Western thought, has influenced both the method adopted by sociologists, and their research practices. The authors criticize sociology for its formalism, arguing that this blunts the radicalism of its project. To regain the radical and critical edge implicit in sociology, it is necessary to return to and develop the comparative and historical approach which interprets social science as part of societal learning.

In the first part of the book, the authors trace formalism to central positions in Western philosophy and examine its impact on historiography, evolutionary social thought and positivist sociology. In Part II, the authors examine the tensions between formalism and social theory in the work of Lévi Strauss and Habermas. In Part III, they compare modernization theory to the more recent discussions of 'modernity' and 'postmodernity', and show the elements of continuity between these apparently contrary positions. The book closes with a discussion of alternative, more sociological accounts of rationality and scientific knowledge which form the basis of a non-formalist, comparative and historical sociology.

Well informed and cogently argued, this book will be of interest to students of Sociology and Philosophy.

Ahmed Gurnah formerly taught Sociology at Sheffield Polytechnic, and **Alan Scott** teaches Sociology at the University of East Anglia.

The uncertain science

Criticism of sociological formalism

Ahmed Gurnah and Alan Scott

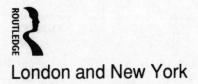

London and New York

First published in 1992
by Routledge
11 New Fetter Lane, London EC4P 4EE

Simultaneously published in the USA and Canada
by Routledge
a division of Routledge, Chapman and Hall, Inc.
29 West 35th Street, New York, NY 10001

Typeset in Baskerville by LaserScript, Mitcham, Surrey
Printed and bound in Great Britain by
Mackays of Chatham PLC, Chatham, Kent

British Library Cataloguing in Publication Data
A catalogue record for this book is available from the British Library

Library of Congress Cataloging in Publication Data
Gurnah, Ahmed, 1947–
    The uncertain science: criticism of sociological formalism/Ahmed
    Gurnah & Alan Scott
        p. cm.
    Includes bibliographical references and index.
    1. Sociology – Philosophy. 2. Sociology – History. I. Scott, Alan,
1956–   . II. Title.
HM26.G876   1992
    301–dc20   91-34727
                                                                           CIP

ISBN 0–415–04136–8 (hbk)
        0–415–08023–1 (pbk)

Contents

Introduction

SOCIOLOGY: A SUBVERTED PROJECT

We shall argue here that the continued interlacing of philosophy and sociology distorts sociology and limits its critical impact. We make this argument not in the name of objectivism or of a 'positivist' science of society, but rather as a comparative and interpretative understanding of history and of other societies. The rationale of sociology has the capacity for a radical critique of 'foundationalist' and absolutist modes of inquiry, or what Mannheim calls 'static thought'. Nevertheless, it is our contention that both the originators of sociology and its contemporary practitioners have hesitated in seizing the opportunity to offer a radical programme because of their anxiety to ground sociology itself in some ultimate and immutable sphere.

The tension between sociology as an empirical investigation of the culturally and historically specific and philosophy as a reflection on the constant and universal, has haunted sociology from the start. Marx's critique of the static and fetishized character of liberal thought is key to the development of sociology. For him, rather than lay claim to a limited historical validity, liberalism presumptuously assumes for itself a permanent and central place in the *structure* of thought as such.

Our thesis is anti-philosophical. It starts with the view that social research is limited if it is structured by philosophical concerns. But we are not narrowly defending the discipline-base of sociology. Our concern is rather to counter philosophers' inflexible defence of universal standards, because we believe that sociology's modest and essentially historical approach to everyday problems is its strength. Sociology at its core is concerned with understanding contemporary societies in their historical context. It is not pre-occupied with final truths, or with the attempt to settle epistem-ological 'puzzles' once and for all. This comes under threat, however, when sociologists themselves subordinate their research programme to traditional philosophical concerns, in which case they undermine the sociological project. Ironically, the sociological challenge to apodictic modes of reasoning was weakened by its originators' ambiguous attitude towards a philosophical and scientific certainty and the subsequent re-incorporation of philosophy into sociology by contemporary theorists like Lévi-Strauss and Habermas.

A sociological understanding of social life which is divorced from the philosophical project has, however, yet to be pro-fessionally secured. Philosophers have continued to argue, and argue with some effect not least on sociologists themselves, that social sciences generally are in need of conceptual clarification (cf. Bernstein 1979); or even that sociology is 'misbegotten epistem-ology' (Winch 1958). The declining influence of positivism, and the *official* ideology of the social sciences has spurred on the search for alternative epistemologies with reference to which the scientificity of social science can be vindicated. Both philosophical realism and idealism have been called into play in the search for a philosophical underpinning. Those who have rejected these attempts to ground sociology in a theory of knowledge have largely been content, or forced, to comment from the sidelines. In contrast, we shall argue that a radical anti-philosophical and anti-epistemological approach lies at the heart of the sociological enterprise.

The demand for a clear division between sociology and phil-osophy has wrongly become closely associated with the more vigorous forms of positivism. The sociological critique of phil-osophy has come to be equated all too easily with objectivism; that is, with the denial of the normative basis of sociology as a human enterprise and, more precisely, with the attempt to disguise norms behind the assumption of sociological objectivity. We do not believe that the rejection of the rationale of philosophical rationalism must always lead sociologists to embrace naturalism.

THE EFFECTS OF 'FORMALISM' ON SOCIOLOGY

The philosophical grounding of sociology, rather than secure its foundations, tends to render its project abstract, superficial and ethnocentric. It is in fact our view that even that positivism which most loudly calls for a 'scientific' method – as opposed to 'philosophical speculation' – is moulded by traditional 'philosophical' concerns. It engages in the search for certain foundations for knowledge secured through categories that are culturally and temporally universal. In this respect positivists are formalists.

Perhaps this would be of little significance to practising sociologists if sociology's commitment to a foundationalist project did not have substantive implications for sociological research. We argue that it does. Therefore, not only does foundationalism blunt the critical edge of the sociological enterprise, it also distorts its understanding of that sphere over which it lays claim: social relations and human cultural arrangements. Foundationalism in sociology leads to what we have chosen to call 'formalism', and formalism inhibits processes of understanding. What Gadamer has vividly called the 'fusion of horizons' becomes problematic not only because of the inherent difficulty of understanding other cultural 'texts', not merely by the 'fact' that our own understanding cannot be presuppositionless, but also because of the formalistic character of those presuppositions.

'Formalism' in the sense we give the term, refers to the substantive consequences of foundationalism in the social sciences. Among the components of sociological formalism the following are particularly significant: (i) the placing of empirical or pseudo-empirical methods at the service of the quest for certitude in knowledge in which normative systems or ideologies can be grounded; (ii) the reduction of the sociological enterprise to a set of methodological and formal procedures used in that search; (iii) the vindication of that methodology and its results in 'naturalism' (philosophical realism), intuition (a philosophical anthropology), logic (conceptual universals), or the formal characteristics of language or communication. We shall argue that this approach is itself formed by historically specific concerns, namely those of Western rationalism.

Despite the earlier disclaimer, it might appear that our argument is a conventional and familiar one. We may appear to be saying that empirical investigation ought to be categorically distinct from philosophical investigation, with the former being confined to the realm of the 'is' and the latter the 'ought'. This is not, however, the proposition we wish to defend in the following pages. There are two crucial differences between our position and the idea that sociology can distance itself from all value questions, relegating the latter to some pre-scientific sphere. First, we think that philosophy enters sociology *through science*, or, more precisely, through particular conceptions of scientific method. Rather than science exhibiting its famed value-neutral judgements, it colludes with the ideology of the search for certitude. We therefore wish to defend a broadly 'conventionalist' view of science against those who insist that science is not so much about what people do, have done, or are likely to do in the future in the interests of improving their lives and understanding, but pertains to logical standards of coherence internal to its practice, or corresponds to reason itself. In that defence, we reject both the related formalism of scientific naturalism and philosophical foundationalism.

The way we wish to differentiate sociology from philosophy forms the second distinction between our case and the traditional positivist one. For us, sociology is distinct from philosophy, or ethics or political theory, not because of its disregard for evaluative or normative issues, but rather because sociology tackles these issues in a different way. A consistent sociological approach to 'philosophical' questions must be conducted through cultural and comparative analysis, and not by identifying the essence of human rationality in itself; as a separate entity which is a culture-free and history-free reason. Sociological analysis can best be understood as a learning process akin to learning a new language or culture. It is not the accretion of discrete pieces of information or knowledge, but the slow acquisition of skills, including skills of interpretation, understanding and acting, which constitute sociology's claim to be a cognitive activity. Winch made this point some time ago when he compared social scientific knowledge not to the technical knowledge of an engineer, but to the engineer's practical knowledge of the social behaviour associated with the 'profession' – form of life – of engineers (Winch 1958: 88).

SOCIOLOGY'S CHALLENGE TO FOUNDATIONALISM

We have spoken of the challenge sociology poses to philosophical modes of thought. But wherein lies this challenge? Sociology is the product of developments internal to philosophy, but developments which indicate the limitations of philosophy's ambition to act as an ethical and cognitive broker. Sociology came into being with the realization that our natures were not immutably fixed, and with the consequent recognition that philosophical reflection must defer to the historical and empirical investigation of social relations and structures. It was then recognized that philosophy is not, as Richard Rorty puts it, 'a name for a discipline which confronts permanent issues, and unfortunately keeps misstating them . . . [but rather is a] cultural genre, a "voice in the conversation of mankind" ' (Rorty 1979: 264).

Kant's arguments against naïve realism and rationalism, that nature was neither static metaphysics nor external to the knowing subject, perhaps provided the starting point for all sociological insights. But it was an insight further radicalized by Hegel's critique of Kant in which the subject that knows itself becomes historically variable. For Hegel, reason resides neither in nature nor in the fixed categories of a transcendental subject, but in history.

It is in the work of Marx that the implications of these arguments are developed into something like their full sociological conclusions. Marx abandons the last vestiges of absolutism in recognizing that there is no cunning of reason which works behind the back of acting subjects. Knowledge becomes both practical and contingent upon humanity as a species being:

> It is therefore in his fashioning of the objective that man really proves himself to be a *species being*. Such production is his active species life. Through it nature appears as *his* work and his reality. The object of labour is therefore the *objectification of the species life of man*: for man reproduces himself not only intellectually, in his consciousness, but actively and actually, and he can therefore contemplate himself in a world he himself has created.
>
> (Marx 1975 [1844]: 329)

Yet in Marx too there is an ambiguity which de-radicalizes this sociological understanding of knowledge. For while in a vital sense he initiated the sociological project through his critique of the ahistorical assumptions of liberal thought, his own anxiety to identify general historical laws, knowledge of which distinguishes communism from utopian socialism (essentially an example of the tendency to disguise a normative standpoint behind assumed universals), in some ways drags him back towards the very ahistorical and de-contextual assumptions of which he, in his critique of political economy, was most damning. Engels's later much maligned argument in the *Anti-Düring* that dialectics were a scientific discovery in much the same way as natural selection may well be a caricature of Marx's scientific ambitions, but it is a caricature which accurately reflects aspects of the original. The search for certitude disguised as scientific method, even if it is an aberration, has in Marx's work substantive consequences similar to those it has in sociology generally. Marx's historical equation of capitalism with the highest – pre-communist – stage of human development is the central substantive ethnocentric consequence.

The pressure to institutionalize sociology in a university context provided a further stimulation to the process of making its mode of argument subservient to formalism. It is not merely Weber's and Durkheim's flirtations with positivism, nor their incipient philosophical liberalism, which led them to formalize sociological method, but also their understandable desire to secure a place for the new discipline in the academy. They hoped that the controlled use of philosophical categories and modes of argument would identify the framework of sociology, differentiate it from the competing claims of psychology and economics, and place it on the road to becoming a scientific discipline. The real effect is different: the sociological project becomes less radical and less 'sociological'. Its distinctive character becomes more, not less, difficult to distinguish.

When Weber and Durkheim systematically developed their sociological method, they not only popularized, professionalized, increased the precision and raised the standards of sociological thought, they also introduced a formality bound to reintroduce philosophy into the discipline. Both Weber's discussion of *Verstehen* and Durkheim's search for the 'rules' of sociological method, formalized their projects to the extent that it conflicts with their objectives. They introduced methodologies which in some hands are merely alternative tools for liberal epistemology.

After Durkheim and Weber a study in methodology becomes not a critical process of evaluation of empirical and theoretical research in a contemporary international setting, but a process of building newer and more limiting systems which will permanently guide social research. We thus agree with Berger and Offe's observation that 'methodological debates remain unsound so long as they remain strictly methodological' (1982: 521).

There are a number of standard objections to the interpretation of social science which we are proposing. These criticisms will be considered in greater detail later, but here we shall briefly mention the most common: (i) there is a categorical opposition between empirical and conceptual questions, and a comparative sociological approach to ethical and philosophical problems is simply inappropriate. Existing views and prejudices are not, it is argued, relevant in adjudicating on ethical or epistemological questions since we can only start discussing such issues, let alone resolve them, if we are clear that our aim is to identify standards which are quite independent of any given contingent human context.

As Rorty has again pointed out, the confidence with which this case can be made has been undermined by developments *within* philosophy. Much recent philosophy, both 'Anglo-Saxon' and 'Continental', subverts the traditional philosophical project of laying bare the universal ethical and cognitive truths which underlie, indeed may be distinguished by, the variety of actually existing ideologies and cultures.

Developments within philosophy which undermine its claim to be a suitable arbiter to true knowledge may also make the second criticism less fearful for the comparatively minded sociologist: (ii) sociology is relativist, and relativism is self-contradictory. As our argument takes the form of a critique of Western rationalism, the relativist objection will probably take the following form: Western thought, and Western science in particular, simply is less ridden with contradiction that non-Western or pre-scientific Western thought (cf. Gellner 1970). Although it does not answer the objection, it may be worth making one initial observation here too. Ethnocentrism is a real danger in this argument, even if not actually entailed by it. Gellner points out the danger of excessive charity in the argument that all forms of life are cognitive equals. In Gellner's response there is another danger, namely selective charity. If we wish to retain the idea that Western thought, or at least Western science, is cognitively privileged, it becomes all too easy to treat beliefs as rational *because they are Western*. We are thus inclined to treat someone who believes that bread and wine *are* the body and blood of Christ with rationality, while denying this to someone who believes that twins *are* birds. This error of judgement is one into which formalistic sociology has often fallen. Our fuller response to the objections of relativism will be that relativism, in the sense of generalized scepticism, is not entailed by a comparative sociology.

Before going on to outline the organization of our argument, one final general comment. In identifying sociology as a subverted project we are not merely saying that there are aspects of the project which are not, or not as yet, fully realized. Sociology is 'subverted' and self-contradictory because it is philosophized. Kolakowski (1972) argues that the 1917 Revolution schismatized Marxism into social democracy and Leninism, and effectively made any accommodation of revisionism and revolution impossible. Similarly, sociology's failure to develop its critique of formalism has schismatized the discipline into theoreticism and empiricism. It will be a central feature of our argument that 'grand theory' and 'abstract empiricism' are caught in the same set of contradictions as rationalistic approaches, and that even what is taken to be 'empiricism' is better understood as formalism.

ORGANIZATION OF THE ARGUMENT

Part I examines formalism as a formative influence in sociology. In Chapter 1 we discuss some of the substantive and methodological manifestations of formalism in various human sciences: historiography, evolutionary thought and positivist sociology. Here we shall be particularly concerned to show that the common criticism that sociology is empiricist is misleading. We argue that both 'empiricism' and positivism are formalist in their conception of knowledge.

In Chapter 2 we first specify more closely what we mean by formalism and then examine two central examples of formalistic projects in philosophy, namely Plato's theory of forms and Kant's transcendental arguments for a knowing subject. We shall not argue that sociology is either strictly 'Platonic' or 'Kantian', but rather, using examples of the formative figures in sociology, we argue that formalism in philosophy has set the boundaries of the debate in which sociology, in its anxiety to establish itself as a respectable scientific and academic discipline, has remained trapped.

Part II. Our aim here is to demonstrate the influence of formalism on more recent sociological thought. In Chapter 3 we discuss Lévi-Strauss and in Chapter 4 Habermas. We argue that despite differences in the influences and intentions of the work of these two authors, they are caught in a similar contradiction. On the one hand Lévi-Strauss, in his critique of evolutionism, and Habermas, in his critique of technological reductionism in the social and cultural sphere, make arguments which subvert formalist assumptions and which assert a radically sociological perspective. On the other hand, both authors are compelled towards a search for universals in the structures of human society (Lévi-Strauss), or in human cognition, communication and action (Habermas). Here we see once more the foreclosure of the possibility of a radical sociological critique by a philosophical attitude towards social life.

Part III. In Chapter 5 we examine two, we argue related, debates: from the 1960s sociological theories of modernization and from the 1980s the 'modernity' versus 'postmodernity' debate. While some of the claims of the postmodernists appear similar to our critique of formalism, we wish to resist the assimilation of our arguments into the postmodernist camp. There are two reasons for this: first, postmodernists have the tendency to reduce social practices to 'discourse', and treat each discourse as if it was closed from other discourses.[1] In contrast, while we have criticized the 'grand narrative' of sociological formalism, we have done so assuming that communication between forms of life is possible and desirable, and that a comparative sociology can aid this process. As we see it, the challenge for sociology is to work the ground between the Habermasians and the postmodernists: to hold out the possibility of negotiation and communication between social forms of life – 'discourses' – without the need to identify formal and universal conditions for the possibility of such communications. Secondly, we are sceptical about the possibility of a *sociology* of postmodernity. Such a project appears highly paradoxical and contradictory because it works at such a level of generality that it is difficult to resist the view that a sociology of postmodernity is yet another grand narrative little different in its explanatory structure from the theories which preceded it. Thirdly, we are committed to *empirical* sociology, to the view that sociology cannot be conducted in a self-referenial mode, but must posit an object outside its own discourse. Both the modernists and, paradoxically, the postmodernists seek a coherent, self-contained, and totalizing picture of social 'condition'. A more empirically and historically sensitive sociology is more awake to the fractured nature of reality than are the all-encompassing theories of 'modernity' or those of 'post- modernity' which seek to supplant them.

Thus, in Chapter 5 we examine both theories of modernization from the 1950s and 1960s and the more recent debate about 'postmodernity' which in many respects reproduces the assumptions of its predecessor. While we share Habermas's desire to resist the relativism and potentially elitist implications of 'post-structuralism', we do not believe that this can be achieved through the attempt to defend unreconstructed Enlightenment notions against their critics. Even modernized Enlightenment notions of reason grounded in a theory of communicative competence do not adequately address the problems of contemporary society. With regard to its approach to racism, we argue that sociology is not merely limited, but also distorted, by the ethnocentric assumptions which are consequent upon its formalism.

It is thus vital to our argument that there is some substantive 'pay-off' for sociology in abandoning the secure and homely citadel of universal rationality and an ethic grounded in science or human nature. We trust that the reward for this loss of *Gemütlichkeit* (security, comfort and familiarity) might in any case be a greater sense of risk and intellectual excitement, and ultimately of a truer, more 'open-minded' and informed understanding of our world and ourselves.

The final chapter, Chapter 6, will address two related issues in the attempt to make explicit some of the positive implications of our argument. The final topics discussed are the questions of rationality and science. Since we are critical of notions of rationality which generalize from historically specific cases, usually that of Western society, we think it necessary to offer some indication of what a *sociological* conception of rationality might look like. We argue for a conception of rationality as institutionalized social knowledge and experience. By treating rationality as a learning process we argue that it is possible to retain a notion of reason grounded in the pragmatic concerns of social life, and even in part in trial and error, while not implying relativism. At the same time we wish to avoid teleological and quasi-evolutionary conceptions: it is, after all, as possible for society not to learn from experience, or to draw the wrong conclusions, as it is for individuals. Universalized conceptions of rationality inhibit societal learning because they close off paths of cross-cultural and historical understanding and thus, paradoxically, further irrationality. Human rationality cannot be guaranteed, but we can at least minimize such barriers to societal learning. Thus rationality is, in our view, intimately bound up with an historical and cross-cultural consciousness. Finally, we discuss the application of such an argument to our conception of science.

In our opinion, unless sociology rids itself of its formalism and once again turns to its historical and contextual project, our political and moral outlook will lag behind international social and political struggles. Instead of social scientific work responding to and guiding the enlightened social and political initiatives taken to achieve liberation, it will detain, confuse and negatively label those struggles and the people involved in them. This is indeed what science is about: continued emancipation and enlightenment and empowerment. This, and the formalism in which it is grounded, will not be a problem for those comfortable in the role of a ruling intelligentsia, or aspiring to that role. However, at a time when the influence of philosophy on sociology is if anything growing, if we are to take our own rhetoric about the truth-seeking and liberating potential of the social sciences seriously, then we have no alternative but to eliminate those philosophical and foundationalist elements from our discipline.

NOTE

1 Ingram, following Habermas, traces this to the onesidedness of postmodernist analysis which, over-eager to abandon the claims of the Enlightenment *in toto*, perceives only fragmentation: 'they neglect to situate surface phenomenon indicative of actual fragmentation against the background of a distorted lifeworld whose ideal presuppositions, when understood from the perspective of the actor rather than the scientific observer, include solidarity and wholeness' (1987: 187).

Part I

Formalism and the formation of sociological discourse

Chapter 1

Empiricism and positivism in history and sociology

INTRODUCTION

The topic of this chapter is the nature of empiricism and its effects on research, particularly research into other societies. We shall both describe empiricist history and philosophy, and trace its influence. Our overriding purpose here is to question the common assumption that sociological analysis is empiricist,[1] and to argue that its rationalism is its more central characteristic. Empiricism, we argue, is more influential in historiography than in sociology. Where true empiricism is found in sociology, it typically originates from historical or statistical sources. The stronger tradition in sociology stems from German idealism and leads to treating theory as prior to, not part of, knowledge production.

While conceding that there is some imported empiricist influence in sociology, towards the end of the chapter we will argue that in fact the mainstream of sociological analysis is positivist (cf. Bernstein 1979 and Winch 1958). The influence of empiricist philosophy in sociology is quite marginal, especially once we clear up the confusion between 'empiricism' and 'empirical', and when we remember that positivism is not the same as empiricism, even if they share some common assumptions.

By identifying sociology as formalist, then, in no way do we exclude its identification as positivist. To be sure, both formalism and positivism are perched on an idealist framework of reference. Nevertheless, our emphasis will be on the rationalist rather than idealistic or empiricist influences on sociology. This will give more room for the argument that as a discipline influenced by rationalism, sociology is also formalist. This suggests that many of the difficulties in sociology may actually have little to do with its being either empiricist or positivist.

EMPIRICISM AND SEVENTEENTH-CENTURY SCIENCE: A DEATHBLOW TO METAPHYSICS?

Standard sociological criticisms of empiricism fail to recognize its rationale and the challenge it represented to aprioristic conceptions of knowledge. They fail too to recognize the contribution of empiricism in the development of modern science.

Empiricist philosophies self-consciously set out to justify empirically based science, and to aid the development of cognitive practices towards that ideal. They both described and desired a shift in the conception of what constituted truth-generating activity from 'being a means of reconciling of man and the world as it is, was, and ever will be, come doomsday, to one controlling nature through knowledge of its eternal laws' (Bernal 1969: 375).

Above all, their campaign took the form of a critique of metaphysics. For empiricists and seventeenth-century philosophy generally, every metaphysical system 'conceives of the world as something finished and thereby leaves the will with nothing to do' (Kroner 1956: 27). In the place of authoritative wisdom, empiricists demanded proof. In this secular and sceptical demand lay empiricism's challenge to medieval knowledge. It confronted clerical and feudal institutions head on and aided the development of constitutional government, the rule of law and mature capitalism with its technical benefits and liberalism.

The challenge that empiricism presented is to be found in three main areas: (i) Locke's critique of innate ideas; (ii) Hume's scepticism; and (iii) the critique of metaphysics developed by, above all, Kant. Since we wish to suggest that in this broad sense sociology, like other 'scientific' disciplines, is empiricist, it is worth discussing these briefly.

In *An Essay Concerning Human Understanding,* John Locke states that his purpose is 'to inquire into the original, certainty, and extent of human knowledge, together with the grounds and degree of belief, opinion, and assent' (Bk 1-1-2: 63). The aim is epistemological: to secure rational means for evaluating truth and falsity. In Locke's case, the critique of the notion of 'innate ideas' is central to this evaluation:

If truth can be imprinted on the understanding without being perceived, I can see no difference there can be between any truths the mind is capable of knowing in respect of their original: they must all be innate, or all adventitious.

(Locke Bk 1-2-5: 69)

In Locke's view, the presence of innate ideas would render learning redundant and presuppose consent. Since there is learning, but not consent, the notion of innate ideas is a nonsense. Furthermore, as 'soon as men come to use reason these supposed native inscriptions come to be known and observed by them' (Bk 1-2-7: 70). But how can we use reason to discover innate ideas, when reason is 'the faculty of deducing unknown truths from principles or presuppositions that are already known' (Bk 1-2-9: 70)?

The types of arguments which Locke employed against innatism may caricature rationalism. Nevertheless, they were vital in embarrassing metaphysical dogmatism. Besides, these arguments served merely as a preamble to his exposition of empiricism in which he attempts to show that knowledge derives through our sensual capacities from our familiarity with empirical things. This is the starting point of Hume's sceptical arguments.

In the *Enquiries* David Hume muses about the value of an enquiry into 'the nature of that evidence which assures us of any real existence and matter of fact, beyond the present testimony of our senses . . . [and] memory' (ss22m: 26). But is it only in an understanding of cause and effect, rather than knowledge of the inner nature of things, that we can hope to go beyond immediate sense experience? Knowledge of cause and effect itself arises out of experience:

If we would satisfy ourselves, therefore, concerning the nature of evidence, which assures us of matters of fact, we must enquire how we arrive at the knowledge of cause and effect.

The knowledge of this relation is not, in any instance, attained by reasoning *a priori*; but arises entirely from experience.

(Hume ss23: 27)

For Hume, all knowledge is constituted in *perception*, which is part sense *impression* and part *idea*. By 'idea' Hume means representations or images, not innate idea. The creative power of the mind is 'no more than the faculty of compounding, transposing, augmenting, or diminishing the material afforded us by the sense and experience' (ss13: 19). No room here for metaphysical reflection on the necessary and the eternal.

Hume takes his objections to any form of metaphysical realism to their logical and sceptical conclusions. Not only does sense experience fail to give us knowledge of the world 'as it really is', as opposed to how it appears to us, but he also questions whether we can have knowledge of the existence of other minds or of causal relations, as opposed to regular conjunctions between items of sense experience:

> No object ever discovers, by the qualities which appear to the senses, either the causes which produce it, or the effects which will arise from it; nor can our reason, unassisted by experience, ever draw any inference concerning real existence and matter of fact.
>
> (Hume ss23: 27)

Hume challenged the arrogance of wide-ranging knowledge claims, particularly those which thought themselves unbound by the strict limitations of what our senses can tell us, in a radical and uncompromising fashion. The critique of metaphysics which runs through the work of the empiricists finds echoes in the arguments of other Enlightenment philosophers, notably Kant for whom 'we have no knowledge antecedent to experience, and with experience all our knowledge begins' (*CPR*: 41). Kant, who differs from Hume in that he argues that experience is not sufficient condition for knowledge, nevertheless shares with the former a deep suspicion of the claims of metaphysics.

In contrast to standard sociological objections to empiricism, we would wish to claim that sociology is, and ought to be, placed on the empiricist side of the divide between empiricism and metaphysics. It remains critical of notions of innate ideas, and opposed to methods of investigation which are exclusively contemplative; or at least it ought to do these things. Furthermore, and this is the argument to which we shall now turn, not sociology but historiography is empiricist in the narrower methodological sense which sociologists have in mind when they accuse their own discipline of empiricism.

In sum, we assume that sociologists fail to recognize the contribution of empiricism while at the same time over-estimating its influence in sociology. Where sociology ought to be criticized, we suggest, is in its proximity to that which empiricism criticizes: aprioristic wisdom.

EMPIRICISM IN HISTORIOGRAPHY

In the demonology of recent sociology 'empiricism' is but a pale shadow of the arguments of Locke, Hume et al. Lost is empiricism's critical edge: its critique of metaphysics. In its place we find a number of simple, even simple-minded, principles: a naïve trust in facts; a distrust of 'theory'; an unshakeable faith in inductive methods; a hard-nosed no-nonsense approach to investigation, etc. This degeneration of complex arguments into cliché is the result of their absorption into 'common sense' and translation of argument into methodology. It is thus not the fault of empiricism's sociological critics that the term, like positivism, has become little more than a sign of general approbation.

This transformation has important implications for the kind of connection we wish to posit between social scientific practices and philosophical arguments. The connection between methodological approaches in the social sciences and the philosophies which inspire them is a loose one. There is no logical or necessary connection between, say, empiricist philosophy and empiricist historiography. Often the methodology contradicts the strict principles of the philosophy which inspires or justifies it. Thus, for example, empiricist historiography adheres to a naïve realism which empiricist philosophy itself rejects. Philosophical arguments are translated, in both senses of the term, when they are taken up in research practices.

We neither wish to argue that the connection is a strong one of logical entailment, nor do we believe it is no more than an 'elective affinity' or 'family resemblance'. These terms suggest nothing stronger than a fortuitous similarity, and this is too weak. The connection is provided neither by logic nor by chance, but rather by the practice of sociologists and historians who are occasionally forced to look up from their research activity and ask questions about 'why', and with what warrant, as well as 'how'. When they do look up, what they see is philosophy and what they seek is philosophy's benediction upon their humble activities. But this is not a passive activity.

The interest of the researcher is not in philosophy as a critical debate which is to be understood only in the context of the ideas with which it engages, but philosophy as wisdom; as a set of incorrigible and context-independent principles to which the anxious researcher can appeal. This is quite a different orientation towards argument analogous to the transformation which occurs in social-scientific arguments when they are taken up by politicians or journalists. The critical edge is lost because the content is removed from its discursive context and because the intention towards the argument is different. Thus the social-scientific version of empiricism, and so on, is both the same as and different from the ideas to which it appeals. But this is stronger than mere elective affinity in Weber's sense. It is more like the transformation of Calvinist doctrine into social ethic which Weber describes in *The Protestant Ethic* where esoteric beliefs are, Weber implies, necessarily transformed when they become adopted by communities of practically oriented actors. The connection we posit is thus found in the *usage* to which arguments are put in different contexts rather than in the structure of the ideas and arguments themselves. It is the intention and orientation of the actor which is the key connecting factor.

Where we depart from the critique of empiricism found in sociological literature is its assumption that empiricist principles, even in this attenuated form, are found primarily in sociology. They dominate, we argue, not in sociology but in history.

Having denied the possibility of innate ideas, Locke supposed that the mind was void; a *tabula rasa*. Experience writes ideas in the mind:

> First, *our senses*, conversant about particular sensible objects, do convey *into the mind* several distinct perceptions of things . . .
> And thus we come by those *ideas* we have of *yellow, white, heat, cold, soft, hard, bitter, sweet.*
>
> (Locke Bk 2-1-3: 90)

Reflection, or 'inner sense', teaches us 'the perception of the operations of our mind within us'. Such reflection is, however, no more than the making of connections between ideas arising out of experience. Sense perception, not reflection and contemplation, is the basis of all knowledge.

Not sociology, but history has taken up this conception of knowledge with respect to a number of themes: (i) facticity; (ii) induction; (iii) solipsism/individualism.

Facticity and data collection

Empiricist historians seek to collect, sort and establish facts from the past using 'reliable' epistemological standards. 'Facts' are the desirable base for historical research because they are void of cultural content; uncontaminated by interest, emotion and prejudice. For the empiricist historian they are the equivalent of the 'brute fact' so beloved of the empiricist philosophy of science. Such historians are more at home with the hard data of archaeology or numismatics than they are with the 'soft' data of oral history or the self-understandings of actors:

> Let us now attempt to draw the archaeological picture . . . [and] consider this material evidence independently of the history with which it must in the event be reconciled. I hope in this way to, so far as is possible, avoid, the danger of seeing the archaeological evidence through eyes already conditioned by the historical sources as to what they should see.
>
> (Chattick 1965: 283)

Such suspicion can be seen at its most explicit in the case of historians examining the histories of societies other than their own. The especially 'dubious' nature of indigenous interpretations leads the Western historian consciously to restrict his/her sources and to treat oral or literary evidence with special caution. In his study of East Africa, A.H.J Prins makes this quite explicit:

> I have endeavoured in the following account to use the primary sources whenever available, to admit the use of secondary ones with caution, and to avoid the use of tertiary.
>
> (Prins 1961: 40)

By no means all historians accept the trenchant empiricist assumptions of this approach with its naïve faith in hard, uncontaminated facts. E.H. Carr, famously, is fully aware of the theory-saturated nature of 'raw' data, including historical data: 'Caesar crossed the Rubicon and the fact there is a table in the middle of the room are facts . . . [But] not all facts about the past are historical facts' (Carr 1961: 10). For Carr, while accuracy remains the duty of the historian, he/she must recognize the necessary role of interpretation in the selection of what counts as an historical event, and the ascription of a specific type of significance to that event. Carr questions the 'bruteness' of all historical facts and the implausibility of the view that the historian's mind is a *tabula rasa* while that of the subject is imbued with prejudice and interest.

The worship of facts makes it possible for the historian to ignore crucial aspects of social reality until a coin or a piece of broken pottery is found. The predilection for uncontaminated evidence leads to the ascription of 'pre-historical' status to those societies where such hard evidence is lacking. In the history of 'pre-colonial' and colonial societies, 'history' automatically becomes the documentation of Western history abroad since local history cannot be got at in any sense acceptable to the historian.

Induction

If, as empiricists believe, experience of isolated sensations is the basis of knowledge, how is generalization possible? The answer, briefly, is through induction. G.H. von Wright observes that when some members of a class are true, we can assume the rest to be:

> induction has led to the establishment of a generalization . . . the process by which we proceed from particular to general propositions . . . from old particulars to a new particular . . . reasoning from known to the unknown . . . from the past to the future.
>
> (Von Wright 1941: 1)

Thus, the historian's collection of fact is not motivated merely by the acquisitiveness of a Victorian palaeontologist, nor by a will to taxonomy, but rather by a desire to create a picture of the whole while remaining closely bound to the parts.

As elsewhere, the 'empiricism' of historians is only very loosely connected to the empiricist philosophy which inspires it. Ironically, Hume had already undermined the philosophical justification for induction by insisting that what we learn from experience cannot be rationally justified:

> nature . . . has afforded us only the knowledge of a few superficial qualities of objects, while she conceals from us those powers and principles on which the influence of these objects entirely depends.
>
> (quoted in Nagel and Brandt 1965: 226)

For Hume, induction is a psychological inference, and not, as it is for the historian, a reliable method of investigation. Their unreflective faith in the power of inductive method again leads historians towards conservative and ethnocentric methodologies.

Solipsism and individualism

Solipsism – i.e. scepticism about the existence of other minds – is the conclusion drawn by Hume from the individualist starting point of empiricism. Although not strictly solipsistic, historiography frequently shares the individualism of the empiricist methodology which underpins it.

In historiography, individualism manifests itself as, firstly, a view of history as the outcome of the actions and beliefs of a few key actors (the great 'man' view); and, secondly, as psychologism.

Strictly individualist histories are the legacy of nineteenth-century historiography. Witness the comment of Charles Kingsley in 1861:

> the new science of little men can be no science at all; because the average man is not a normal man, and never yet has been; because the great man is rather the normal man, as approaching more nearly than his fellows . . . [the] standard of a complete human character . . . to turn to the mob for your theory of humanity . . . is about as wise as to ignore the Apollo and Theseus, and to determine the propositions of the human figure from a crowd of dwarfs and cripples.
>
> (quoted in Stedman Jones 1972: 98)

The language and the confidence of the Victorian *Weltanschauung* underlying this judgement would hardly be repeated today. But despite the efforts of historians such as Christopher Hill, Eric Hobsbawm or E.P. Thompson, the individualist assumptions behind this statement are not as outmoded as the form in which they were expressed by Kingsley. In his history of Zanzibar, E.B. Martin ascribes the course of the country's recent history, up to 1972, largely to the will of its leader, Karume. In doing so he avoids addressing the vital social questions which underlie absolute rule:

> How such a man came to wield complete control over the lives of 350,000 people will perhaps never be fully understood. His prime concern appears to have been to create safeguards for his own preservation as Head of State.
>
> (Martin 1978: 62)

Having attributed social change to the will of one man, Martin abandons any hope of explaining why people are so passive in such circumstances.

Martin's type of analysis also illustrates the psychologism of much historiography. Individuals' predilections and prejudices are ascribed a central causal role within individualist history: 'many of Karume's edicts stemmed from his own prejudices against the Arabs, Asian and Persian minorities' (p. 68). Where such 'prejudices' may have come from, what their public rationale might have been, lies beyond the scope of individualist historiography. Probing the inner workings of an individual's mind is permissible; interrogating public morality, social structure or class relations is not.

Paralleling individualism, but actually in contradiction to it, is the view of history as a moral tale, a 'scientific sermon' (Stedman Jones 1972: 98). Liberal historians seem to feel the need to deduce some form of public morality to counter-balance the image of individuals as self-seeking rational actors. Isaiah Berlin, for example, ascribes the following duty to the historian: 'to judge Charlemagne or Napoleon or Genghis Khan or Hitler or Stalin for their massacres' (Carr 1961: 78). Such a duty is often executed from Olympian heights. The historian sits in judgement and, like the judge, is not to be challenged by those against whom the judgement is made. Thus we are told that for British public opinion the strongest reason for retaining colonial policies in East Africa was 'to put down the slave traffic, to substitute a mellower trade and civilization' (Robertson et al. 1974: 50).

EVOLUTIONARY THEORY AND ETHNOCENTRISM IN HISTORIOGRAPHY

Empiricist historians have often too readily adopted evolutionary theory as part of their culture, and linked it to their own notions of morality. Evolutionary theory is theoretically connected to Aristotelian, Judaeo-Christian notions of being and becoming. Aristotle thought that change in nature is continuous and teleological (see Bock 1979). Other Greeks constructed 'conceptual cultural series that were taken to represent time sequences in abstract cultural history' (Bock 1979: 45).

Having adopted some of these views, philosophers in the early modern period linked them to the empiricist notion of fact collection, and developed their methodology of science through such arguments:

> since nature is regular and uniform in her working, men of equal ability must have been produced in all ages; and that, by sheer accumulation of equal products of equal resources, there must have been an advance or progress in knowledge.
>
> (Bock 1979: 47)

There is an uncanny logic to this view, especially if linked to Spencerian or Darwinian notions. Herbert Spencer stresses the *necessary* superiority of Western science over rival cognitive systems:

> All sensible existence *must* in some way or other and at some time or other reach their concrete shapes through process of concentration; and such facts as have been named have been named merely to clarify the perception of this necessity.
>
> (Andreski (ed.) 1971: 60)

In Spencer this idea is linked to notions of being and becoming both in knowledge and human achievement. Knowledge is strictly empiricist in character. It is 'limited to the phenomenal' (Andreski (ed.) 1971: 53). At the same time, knowledge is tied to technical, economic and political advancement:

> As in the changed impression on the wax, we read the change in the seal; so in the integrations of advancing language, science and art, we see reflected certain integrations of advancing human structure, individual and social.
>
> (Andreski (ed.) 1971: 70)

The 'impression in the wax' can be traced in the evolution from homogeneity to heterogeneity in both human society and its material expressions, particularly its art. Human groups grew, both in size and complexity, as 'weaker races' were absorbed by the 'superior races' (see Andreski (ed.) 1971: 98). Similarly, artistic expression became more differentiated:

> Rhythm in speech, rhyme in sound, and rhythm in motion were in the beginnings part of the same thing, and have only in process of time become separate things. Among various existing barbarous tribes we find them still united.
>
> (Andreski (ed.) 1971: 87)

These homogeneity/heterogeneous, undifferentiated/differentiated dualisms betray not only an ignorance of 'primitive' art, but an exaggeration of the degree of institutional differentiation of Western art by implying, for example, a greater autonomy of art from, say, religion than is in fact the case. But Spencer's rather simplistic evolutionism is open to other familiar objections: 'Can we predict the course of progress in human society?', 'Can it be measured against the single yardstick of Western science?', etc. By assuming an affirmative answer to such questions, evolutionary thinkers not only judge Western society by its own standards, they expect others to judge their own societies by those standards also.

Though such simple unilinear theories of evolution may be passé, some of the assumptions with which they are associated live on in historiographical writings. Empiricist historians are not immune to assessing other societies by their military prowess or the approximation of their institutions to those of Westminster. The search for an East African 'middle ages' or some equivalent of Magna Carta; the expression of bewilderment at finding incomprehensible social behaviour in wretched conditions, etc., are the expression of unexpressed, but still powerful, evolutionary ideas and prejudices.

POSITIVISM IN SOCIOLOGY

Sociology too is built on an empirical tradition: that *is* its main strength. As we have seen, it enters this tradition not through empiricism, but through positivism. But via positivism, sociology acquires idealist assumptions which have had a most important formative influence in the discipline. It incorporates the later tradition directly from philosophy.

Habermas identifies positivist philosophy as that theoretical perspective which abandons the German critical philosophy of later Kant: 'Positivism marks the end of theory of knowledge. In its place emerges the philosophy of science.' It is neither interested in the 'transcendental-logical inquiry' about the possibility of knowledge, nor is it concerned with the meaning of knowledge: 'Knowledge is implicitly defined by the achievement of the sciences' (Habermas 1971b: 67). Meaningful and secure knowledge is itself defined exclusively by scientific rules. Positivism conceives of science:

not so much as eliminating the question of meaning of knowledge in general but as prejudging its answer ... But by marking a dogma of sciences' belief in themselves, positivism assumes the prohibitive function of protecting scientific inquiry from epistemological self-reflection.

(Habermas 1971b: 76)

Therefore, according to Habermas, positivism is not philosophical in the sense of being critical. For positivists the meaning of knowledge is understood by what science does and is capable of doing, and is 'explicated through the methodological analysis of scientific procedure' (1971b: 67). Thus, positivists shift 'the system of reference' for knowledge and what makes knowledge away from the individual, the mind or history, away from consciousness, in the fashion of Enlightenment liberalism, by investing it in a system of scientific rules and procedures. Furthermore, this transference only makes subjects insignificant.

Their deeds and destinies belong at best to the psychology of empirical persons to whom the subjects of knowledge have been reduced ... The obverse of this restriction is the development through which logic and mathematics become independent, self-sufficient formal sciences, so that henceforth the problems of their formation are no longer discussed in connection with the problem of knowledge. As a method of research the philosophy of science presupposes the validity of formal logic and mathematics.

(Habermas 1971b: 68)

Kolakowski adds meat to this critical skeleton of positivist philosophy. He itemizes four fundamental rules with which positivism defines knowledge (1972: 11): phenomenalism, nominalism, the non-empirical base of value-judgement, and the unity of the scientific method.

Phenomenalism posits no difference between 'essence' and 'phenomenon', unlike metaphysical doctrines which assume phenomena to be a manifestation of underlying reality.

Positivists do not object to inquiry into the immediately invisible causes of any observed phenomenon, they object only to any accounting for it in terms of occult entities that are by definition inaccessible to human knowledge.

(Kolakowski 1972: 12)

Humean scepticism is resolved here in a general theory of induction, where observable facts add up to a general theory. Now, regardless of whether this rule of nominalism works or not, it *aims* to transcend Humean scepticism. By this rule, any abstractions used to order experience only serve to organize experience and 'are not entitled to lay claim to any separate existence' (Kolakowski 1972: 15). Here, there are no 'universals'.

The rule of *value-judgement* insists that experience cannot vindicate value-judgements:

> We are entitled to express value judgements on the human world, but we are not entitled to assume that our grounds for making them are scientific; in other words, the only grounds for making them are our own arbitrary choices.
>
> (Kolakowski 1972: 17)

Finally, *the unity of science* hypothesis accords method a central role in knowledge-generating activity, and assumes that the most successful such activity, science, is characterized, indeed defined, by a unified methodology. Differences of content between sciences constitutes no barrier to their uniformity, they only exhibit 'characteristics of a particular historical stage in the development of science' (Kolakowski 1972: 18). When all the particular sciences become mature, these qualitative differences will disappear and 'reduce all domains of knowledge to a single' system, like physics.

The extent of positivism's influence in sociology is well known[2] and there is no need for us to go over the same ground. But most discussions about positivism tend to emphasize its empiricism. However, according to Habermas, Comtean positivism is at least as much influenced by rationalism as it is by empiricism. Comte removes the question of meaning from knowledge acquisition and from science, making the latter irrational. Since the intention of early positivism was not to do that, but to extend 'the cognitive monopoly of science', meaning was re-established by Comte, in terms of philosophy of history, by constructing the three stages of scientific-technical progress. Thus, early positivism 'justifies sciences' scientistic belief in themselves by constructing the history of the species as the realisation of the positive spirit' (Habermas 1971b: 72).

Now, observation and fact accumulation are made purposeful in the process of human development from pre-scientific and pre-technical to the scientific and the technical; but also gain meaning by developing from the purposeless relationship with the natural world to the purposeful manipulation of it. What was accidental to empiricism – the appropriation of evolutionary theory in the process of fact collection – now becomes incorporated in positivistic methodology. This both emphasizes the similarities between empiricism and positivism and distinguishes their differences. For Habermas, this combination is the result of an eclectic fusion of frameworks by Comte:

> the methodological ideas of his philosophy of science are more or less commonplaces of the empiricist and rationalist traditions.
>
> (Habermas 1971b: 73)

Accordingly, the introduction of scientific laws in sociology imply the appropriation of rationalist 'methodological principles, which have been isolated from their epistemological contexts', and were applied to a scientific schema. Thus, contrary to belief, positivism needs more than sense certainty to validate scientific knowledge, even if 'sense experience defines access to the domain of facts' (Habermas 1971b: 74).

> *Methodological certainty* is just as important as sense certainty. While the reliability of metaphysical knowledge was based on unity and interconnectedness of being as a whole, the reliability of scientific knowledge is guaranteed by unity of method . . . Science asserts the priority of method over substance, because we can reliably inform ourselves about substance only with the aid of the scientific modes of procedure.
>
> (Habermas 1971b: 74–5)

Habermas quotes Comte who insists that scientific theories consist 'essentially of laws and not facts', but facts are 'indispensable for their justification and confirmation'. Comte states:

> no isolated fact, no matter of what sort, can really be incorporated into science before it is at least correctly connected with other conception through the aid of a rational hypothesis.
>
> (quoted in Habermas 1971b: 75)

Though Habermas does not remark on it, there appears to be a conflict between this view and induction. The inductive method supposes that theory is the outcome of the accumulation of discrete facts. Now, Comte suggests that discrete facts cannot be incorporated into science without prior theory. Positivists would deal with this problem in two ways: firstly, they would argue that a 'rational hypothesis' is not the same as scientific laws. Secondly, they would suggest that *new* facts will be incorporated by old generalizations, which are the consequence of previous fact accumulation. Science is evolutionary: if the laws are inadequate, factual data will make that obvious, and lead to better covering laws.

Of course, Habermas's argument is strengthened when we remember not only the great importance that positivists, including contemporary positivists, put on 'covering laws' and the significance they attach to 'unity of sciences'. In both these ways, they not only exhibit their rationalist origins, but also the way that they dissociate themselves from British empiricism.

According to Habermas, Comte not only compares his thoughts on the positive method to Descartes' *Discourse*, but also suggests that progress in science takes place when particular laws give way to more general laws, when theory is unified.

Thus, in spite of some common characteristics between classical empiricism and positivism, there are a good many differences between them. The similarities include their common rejection of the *noumena* and their affirmation that knowledge can only be phenomenal. That is, experience has to be the basis for knowledge, and that knowledge has to be of observable phenomena of objects. However, though both are also naturalistic, they are so in different ways. Empiricists are naturalistic in their belief that dependable knowledge is the outcome of human sensual experience, which is not mediated by consciousness. But such knowledge is available to us merely because of the fact that we possess sensual faculties. Positivists are naturalistic in the sense that they believe in a correspondence between our scientific knowledge and the physical world. Indeed, knowledge is said to be scientific *because* it corresponds to that world. In short, empiricism is anthropological and positivism is 'physical', but both bind security of knowledge to naturalism.

The distinctions between positivism and empiricism become more obvious when we bear in mind that the former is a self-confessed *a priori* theoretical system while the latter is *a posteriori*. Positivism is not only *influenced* by rationalism, but its cosmic 'laws' show a similar metaphysical inter-connectedness to rationalism; empiricism has no such system. The attempt to resolve Hume's scepticism via a general theory of factual information is more apparent in positivism than it is in empiricism. Finally, positivism intrinsically incorporates a philosophy of history – an evolutionary theory – and empiricism comes upon it accidentally through Western culture.

We pursue this line of argument in order that we may understate the rationalist critique of sociology as empiricist, and the Frankfurt School critique of positivist sociology. The tendency here is to place most of the blame for the attack on human reflection and action on a positivist theory of science, forgetting that rationalist influences may *effectively* have the same consequence. For in spite of the fact that Habermas recognizes both the general influence of rationalism and that of Kant on Comte and positivist sociology, he eventually views that influence either as being merely legitimizing, eclectic, or ineffectual. He does that so he may polarize the methodological distinctions between positivism and German idealism, and contradictorily understate their joint parentage he had helped to establish.

Thus, apart from Habermas's explicit discussion of the philosophical-scientistic paradox in Comte, he is unaware of a deeper German idealist influence in social theory, even in positivism. Which is why, in his own work, he sets out to build a Kantian, Freudian and linguistic rationalism, which he dilutes with a theory of action from phenomenology. Then, his powerful and legitimate criticism of scientism is mixed up with and reduced to a critique of positivism. Richard Bernstein, an admirer of Habermas, discusses how mainly through the agency of linguistic philosophy, phenomenology and critical theory (in the way that Habermas has reconstructed them), contemporary 'mainstream' 'empirical social science' has been salvaged from scienticism by:

> the new understanding of the complexity of language, especially language of action, challenges the pretentious claims made by social scientists about the nature, description, and explanation of action.
>
> (Bernstein 1979: xvi)

According to Bernstein, linguistic philosophy shows social scientists that they are 'conceptually confused', phenomenologists teach them more complex appreciation of social interaction (1979: xvi–xvii), and Habermas 'sought to develop a comprehensive social theory which is dialectical synthesis of empiricist, phenomenological, hermeneutic, and Marxist–Hegelian themes' (1979: xviii), and attempts to elaborate 'an alternative to a naturalistic understanding of social sciences'.

These interventions, as Bernstein claims, clearly appeared partly as a response to positivism. Bernstein also correctly describes some of the recent developments in social sciences. But in his presentation he makes one crucial error by assuming that no aspects of phenomenology, hermeneutics, language awareness, dialectics, and Hegelianism were present in sociology before there was this recent intervention of these various frameworks in what he calls 'empirical theory'. In fact, it is precisely the *combination* of empiricism, positivism and idealism of various kinds, and Marxism in the nineteenth and early twentieth centuries, which brought about the mature existence of the social sciences, especially sociology. The synthesis, as is well-known, took place at two levels: first, in the work of specific classical sociologists like Marx, Weber, Durkheim, Simmel, Tönnies and Spencer, etc.; secondly, at a disciplinary level, where students simply learn the work of these sociologists, as if they are all complementing each other or where each is thought to make a discrete contribution to specific sociological problems. In his keenness to polarize the 'before' and 'after' of this recent intervention in positivist sociology, Bernstein understates the *pre-existence* of these frameworks in the earlier periods. By that error, we believe, he wrongly identifies the central difficulties of sociology (as do Habermas, the Frankfurt School and some idealists) with the preponderance of positivism and empiricism. Positivism is preponderant in sociology and it has created its difficulties.[3] But this idealist critique of positivism plays down pre-existing idealist influences in sociology and in positivism. They underrate the *central* role that Kantian thought plays in contemporary sociology. By this error, critics of positivist sociology misunderstand the nature of sociological limitations by entirely identifying them with positivism. Thus, in the last analysis by their critique, rationalists not only wrongly subjugate the 'empirical' rather than the 'empiricist' in sociology, but by arguing that we must outline rational 'human interests' or 'theoretical practices' before we can examine any 'facts', their critique leads to a gross misunderstanding of important limitations in sociology. Sociology is in fact manifestly theoretical. Unlike empiricist history, it approaches its 'facts' with an *a priori* frame of reference, be it positivist or phenomenological. As Habermas shows through

Comte, sociologists are only interested in *interpreting* 'facts' and do not wish to get bogged down by them. This is implied as strongly in positivism as it is in existential phenomenology. Contrary to Bernstein's arguments, it was in fact the functionalist, through Durkheim, who reified language and culture in sociology and not Wittgenstein and Chomsky. It was Weber who introduced Dilthey and Ricket to sociology and not Habermas. *In fact*, positivist sociology greatly reduces the distance between empiricism and rationalism and German idealism. In sociology there is an old *a priori* tradition, incorporated from German idealism. By this tradition, sociology habitually assumes theory not to be part of the construction of knowledge but to be prior to it.

In subsequent chapters we shall examine the complexity of the relationship between positivism, rationalism and influential sociological theories.

NOTES

1 A tendency to equate sociology with empiricism can be found in Smart 1976; Filmer et al. 1972; Lessnoff 1974; Ryan 1970; and Hindess and Hirst 1975.
2 See, among others, Giddens 1979; Halfpenny 1982, Adorno et al. (eds) 1976; Hindess 1973; Benton 1977; Fay 1975; Keat and Urry 1982; and Bernstein 1979.
3 See Fay 1975 and the writings of the Frankfurt School generally, especially Habermas.

Chapter 2

Philosophical formalism and the development of sociology

Although liberal doctrines have not been proved to be true principles of political practice it has been the objective of many liberal writers to demonstrate that their political conclusions logically follow from either incontestable metaphysical foundations or indisputable factual evidence . . . Although developments . . . have defied liberal expectations, leading liberal thinkers to abandon old opinions in favour of new ones, this has not deterred them from the search for certainty.

(D.J. Manning *Liberalism*: 119)

As a fledgling science, sociology set itself a daring goal, the attainment of a unified scientific theory of human behaviour. In formulating this goal, the founders of sociology gave the discipline a static, metaphysical cast that it has never been able to shed.

(Daniel W. Rossides *The History and Nature of Sociological Theory*: xviii)

INTRODUCTION

The Kantian idealist influence in sociology, contrary to the common view, becomes strongest when the discipline attempts to attain a scientific status. This influence was invited into the social sciences by positivists and rationalists for the *same* reasons. Consequently, we shall argue, in the same way that positivists assume that their efforts will bring to an end all critical enquiries, so too do their rationalist counterparts. As Habermas notes in the case of positivism, rationalistic attempts to construct social epistemologies *likewise* empty analysis of meaning. Despite his criticisms of Comte,

Habermas is similarly forced to depend on an evolutionary scheme in his theory of communicative action to re-establish meaning in his research. If the philosophy of history looks uncomfortable when juxtaposed to a theory of science, rationalistic 'cognitive interests', 'universal pragmatics', 'savage minds', etc., appear no less unresolved when they tie a theory of history to a context-specific sociology.

The need to create formal grounds for securing knowledge goes back a long way. Sociology has thus not only consistently dipped into the Western historical reserve for inspiration, but has often lifted ideas wholesale from it. This makes a comparison between Platonic, Kantian and sociological formalism quite instructive. The task of a methodological study is to help sociologists reflect upon their discipline, so they may periodically break-out of their historic casts. To achieve this both the self-image of sociology and its actual achievements need to be considered.

In this chapter we hope to identify sociology as formalist and its theoretical status as ambiguous. It is ambiguous because it is formalist: it is abstract and aprioristic while at the same time it clings to an historical and contextual view of social entities. Since it is ambiguous, it also fails to be consistently self-critical. Sociology becomes formalist when it confuses the study of empirical social entities with the metaphysical study of *nature* and essential social reality. But more importantly, sociology becomes formalist because, unable to have an intuitive passage from analysis to these natures, sociologists confuse their *theories* of nature with history. In other words, having identified their views of history as correct, they turn to interpret history accordingly.

Contemporary formalism, both philosophical and sociological, is an historical development. As Nisbet observes:

> If one looks at the two revolutions [industrial and democratic] from the point of view of the most fundamental and widespread processes they embodied in common, three are especially striking . . . *individualization, abstraction,* and *generalization.*
>
> (Nisbet 1967: 42)

By 'individualization' is meant here individuals' distancing of themselves from their communal structures, while 'generalization' concerns the spreading of individual interests to national and international spheres. What is of greater interest for us is the process of 'abstraction', which may be seen as the secularization of

values, making them utilitarian and separating them from their
'concrete and particular roots'. Previously, according to Nisbet,
honour, loyalty and friendship had their symbolic distinctiveness
tied to their particular context. The change came when they were
separated by technology from their link to the direct experience of
nature 'of its rhythms and cycles of growth and decay, of cold and
warmth, of light and dark' (Nisbet 1967: 43). Values which were
previously based on familial and economic social relations in the
feudal period have given way to the technological, scientific and
political demands of emerging capitalism. They have become
'abstract': removed from 'the particular and the concrete'. For
formalists, this putative historical development is at the same time
the methodological prerequisite of social scientific discourse.
These epistemic developments, though radically challenged by
Marx's sociologism, still play a central part in sociology; but not for
the same historic reasons. But why did sociology become formalist?

WHY FORMALISM?

There are two types of reasons why formalism was adopted: psychological and philosophical. Psychological insecurity forced philosophers in the eighteenth century, who were faced with a fast
changing world of developing capitalism, to seek to establish
secure grounds for knowledge. They thought that these grounds
depended on the fact that humans had a rational capacity to sense,
comprehend and adhere to rational standards. Subsequently
positivists shifted the reference point from the natural human to
the natural world. They argued that true knowledge is possible
through the distillation and formalization of fundamental principles of the workings of that world.

By the mid-nineteenth century, the psychological and theoretical insecurity caused by consolidating capitalism drove classical
sociologists to seek similar security in the steadier 'forms'. Though
clearly aware of the difficulties of eighteenth-century philosophy
and nineteenth-century positivism, these sociologists, being keen
to construct a truth-seeking science, built a pragmatic compromise
from these two formalist perspectives. Weber thought that even if
the mind and science cannot give us truthful classifications of our
ever-shifting social world and of the physical world, the subjective
meaning that we attach to objects and events in that world, plus the
scientific organization of the phenomenal data we collect from it,

would make aspects of its reality comprehensible to us. Thus, any method we use will ensure that knowledge is accrued; but for the best results we shall need the scientific method.

Beyond these psychological grounds, there were also philosophical reasons connected to what is known as 'the problem of knowledge'. In traditional philosophy, this problem is usually posed in terms of a number of standard questions. First, how can we have true dependable knowledge, regardless of historical context or interest? Secondly, where can we find incontestable moral standards to guide our actions through all our social and individual interactions in spite of the limitations imposed on us by social conventions, personal and social histories and lust? In both cases, furthermore, how can we identify the correct standards for knowledge and morality in the relative world of cultures, religions, languages, nationalities, habitat, power-relations and status?

Western philosophers had tried to answer these questions by deriving the answers from the essential nature of humans and of the physical world. They thought that by identifying human and physical nature from that they can derive how both work. The problem of what constitutes truthful knowledge and correct morality, then, becomes relatively easy.

While recognizing the dead-end that this type of enquiry may lead to, Weber as a philosophical liberal was not sufficiently troubled by its implications to abandon formalism. For he was well aware that human nature is not essential but existential. Yet the need for scientific security troubled him sufficiently to abandon what he knew was problematic. Contemporary sociologists like Habermas and Lévi-Strauss, while even more aware of these negative implications of liberalism, similarly refuse to give up formalism's structuring rationality. Thus, sociology is unreflectively conducted within these philosophical perimeters to the extent that 'various studies of the development of sociological theory distort our view of the past by their failure to recognise the metaphysical and ideological nature of that theory, they also distort our view of the present' (Rossides 1978: xviii).

These sociologists would have then only partially absorbed Marx's socialization of the problem of knowledge. Marx removes this problem of knowledge acquisition from the realms of the philosophical discourse of essential human and physical nature and places it firmly within the historical construction of knowledge through human understanding and human consciousness.

Consequently, he thus further develops this Kantian insight by mediating knowledge and physical natures, and places them firmly within the historical construction of human societies. Like modern phenomenologists, then, Marx avoids a forced naturalism or scientism and places both the possibility of knowledge and the soundness of morality within human discourse and struggle. Marx does not deny that human and physical natures constitute, as a Kantian would argue, a limit to both human comprehension and morality. But reality is socially and not naturally or philosophically defined. We cannot adhere to some lasting notions, or even merely 'limiting notions' of nature – physical or human – or link our comprehension of both to their lasting 'characteristics', without freezing social reality and natural processes. 'Reality' can only be glimpsed at as it really is, from time to time, when we come to understand the particular social relationships, theorized in their historical context.

Then we can comprehend its epistemic source, comprehend its concerns and needs, sense its purpose, recognize its achievements, while we see through its little deceptions, without resorting to metaphysics. Then we would have solved 'the problem of knowledge'. We can come upon *dependable* knowledge around which we can construct our moral theory of action, without any need for metaphysical reinforcement. Our grounds, then, are to be understood in the context of continuing social struggles and class relationships.

Classical and modern sociologists, and indeed Marxists themselves, are only selectively persuaded by this thorough-going sociologism, which needs no assurances from metaphysics of nature or of science. But then this leaves sociology to occupy a paradoxical crevice between Marx's social pragmatism and traditional liberal philosophy. Classical and contemporary sociologists live in a post-Hegelian, post-Marxian age and are fully briefed about problems of analysing the social world by abstract, non-temporal philosophy. Having constructed it *a priori*, classical sociologists took their formal method *back* to history. This dilemma of sociology eventually either forces sociologists into abstract theorizing *or* non-theorized (unreflective) empirical work.

THE STRUCTURE OF FORMALISM

Formalism is characterized by three assumptions: (i) the search for certitude; (ii) the use of formal theoretical procedure; which is

(iii) guaranteed by naturalism or logic. In the eighteenth century these classical formalist arguments were used and developed. It was thought that 'truth' was somehow linked to the workings of our minds, our intuition and our sense experience and the workings of the physical world. Through its discovery, it was believed, we shall lay bare all the secrets of human and social nature. The problematic character of human existence will be resolved through enlightenment and justice.[1] Thus, the first assumption of formalism is the search for unified, dependable, truthful knowledge.

The second assumption is that certitude can be procured by a formal theoretical procedure or a scientific method. Even when declared just an entrée or an 'ideal type', such a formal procedure cannot be so modest. Instead, whether the formalists like it or not, it becomes an *a priori* cast in which scientific knowledge or truth about empirical reality is moulded. After all, formal procedures always give formalized processed answers. The limits of the procedures, in the end, dictate both the theoretical limits for the analyst, as much as the legitimate objects of analysis. Under the guise of clarifying their concepts, methodologists universalize them. This formalization of theoretical procedures encourages speculative dogmatism rather than empirical studies. It also allows liberal metaphysical notions, which give priority of theory over empirical entities, to be imported to sociology. Furthermore, such a methodological reduction is common not only among positivists, but also among Marxists.

Thirdly, sociology becomes formalistic when this theoretical procedure is thought to be vindicated by human and physical nature, or by the logical sciences. In short, sociologists are formalist when they search for the ultimate truth by the formal theoretical procedure and validate that procedure by eighteenth-century epistemological findings; believing that these findings to be concomitant with the universal structure of thought, as such.

In the same way that sociologists are not empiricists, they are also not simply formalists. At the same time as searching for sure foundations, sociology attempts *to make sense* of history and social context. The problem arises because it is assumed that in order to make history and society intelligible, we need to discover juridical and anthropological constants, through the philosophical method, while at the same time we can use science, logic and mathematics to identify physical constants. Sociological formalism is essentially an argument for a construction of a social epistemology.

The search for certitude: Plato, Kant and sociology

In Plato we find an ancient 'paradigm' articulation of a search for certitude. Though clearly modern formalism is different from Plato's, it has borrowed enough from him for his thought to interest us. For Plato, knowledge is possible when entities do not change but remain permanent (see Staniland 1972: 6). As no such entities exist in the ordinary world of changing objects, he sought their essence. He thought a 'form' or 'idea' would capture the universal characteristic in thought, language and science. These forms, he thought, were more real than objects:

> They *are* what particulars merely strive to be in vain. Also, they have greater reality because they are independent, eternal, and changeless, whereas particulars are dependent, transient, and in a state of control.
>
> (Staniland 1972: 5)

But forms are not dependent on objects for their existence; and objective changes do not affect the forms.

Plato was convinced that changing objects were not a reliable source of genuine knowledge, because they could not be fully real if they were not permanent. Genuine knowledge is of the 'essential natures of things' (Staniland 1972: 5) and therefore forms are more real than particulars. He finally concludes that these independent forms are both manifestations of objects and of human minds. Thus, a form is 'neither an idea . . . nor a concept'; it 'exists actually, substantially and in its own right' is 'fully real' and 'cannot be apprehended by . . . human senses, but only by the intellect in complete isolation from any kind of sensory interference' (Garforth 1971: 43–4).

For Plato, then, forms are not concepts, they are not linguistic constructions or theories: they actually exist. As peculiar as this notion may sound, we do meet it in sociology – as we shall see. The use of general words for different things, therefore, does not refer to a loose classification: it indicates participation in the same form (see Staniland 1972: 7).

For a long time after Plato, metaphysics was highly regarded for its truth content. It was thought that propositions could not be denied because it was scrupulous (see Walsh 1963: 11). Plato represented his ideas metaphysically, no doubt to ensure their truthfulness. In his search for certitude, Plato characterizes his views in the following five points. *Firstly*, the philosopher or metaphysician prefers clear, connected knowledge to fragmentary, confused opinions (Walsh 1963: 34). *Secondly*, the philosopher has access to real, unchanging, stable things, which are for that reason knowable (Walsh 1963: 35). *Thirdly*, the philosopher not only avoids appearances, but reaches behind them 'to explain them in the light of first principles'. *Fourthly*, philosophy being fully sceptical is also fully intellectual and universal in its scope. *Finally*, philosophy enlightens, 'by revealing the truth about things, which is very different from what is commonly thought' (Walsh 1963: 35). These Platonic fundamental conditions for the search for certitude, holds Walsh, have constantly recurred in the history of metaphysics, where sense data are suspected of inconsistency, contradiction and transience. This necessitates that people should use thought to look behind 'appearances', at a deeper reality, in accordance with a 'single synoptic science' (Walsh 1963: 36–7). Metaphysics was thought to be entirely self-critical. It 'left nothing unquestioned and proceeded entirely without assumptions' (Walsh 1963: 11). Under the influence of Kant and Hegel, Habermas is still in search of such magical powers.

But the similarities between some of these metaphysical fundamentals and sociological analysis is quite striking. Except for some phenomenologists, many sociologists constantly seek for clear, connected knowledge in opposition to general belief. They feel they can attain such knowledge because they are scientific. They suppose that their search is for 'real' entities not ideologies or beliefs. They often hold, that intellectual and analytical realms must be settled first, before we can turn to data, if at all. For it is only by that kind of 'theoretical practice' that we can avoid error. Finally, sociology does aim to change people's lives through science, theory, analysis and political action. But then political action appears merely as the translation of analysis and not as an independent response: theory is not a form of reflection here, but a programme.

This comparison between Plato and sociological thought is clearly illegitimate as it stands. It is meant to be indicative rather than evidence. For by reproducing some of these principles of metaphysics, it does not make sociologists metaphysicians. What might make a sociological project metaphysical, however, depends on whether it accepts not just some of these ancient insights, but also the rationale of the package. That is, when sociologists accept its theory of knowledge.

But apart from his metaphysical search for truth, Plato is said to have used 'form' philosophically as a limiting concept. Philosophically, forms can be conceived of as permanent, changeless, genuinely known, non-transient frameworks, without a further need to imply their existence beyond the empirical world:

> In so far as he conceived of Forms as standards, it seems that Plato thought of them as lying beyond the familiar world . . . To pass from the state of belief to that of knowledge is . . . to move to another and better world.
>
> (Walsh 1963: 28)

Apparently he uses form metaphorically, to explain what occurs structurally, rather than outline metaphysical concepts in the beyond (Walsh 1963: 29). In other words, Plato could be said to be giving theoretical explanations for obvious but not easily understandable events. For Plato, to comprehend the world involves an understanding of the forms. If he is ambiguous on this issue about whether forms are metaphysical entities in the beyond, or are merely conceptual limits, Kant is not.

Kant was not opposed to the search for certitude or to idealism: only to the means that Plato used. He starts by dissociating his own idealism from Plato's, which he thought was visionary. Kant embraced idealism in order to raise the hitherto ignored problem of the 'possibility of our knowledge *a priori* of the objects of experience', rather than to isolate metaphysical forms. He thought this visionary idealism 'inferred from our knowledge *a priori* . . . another intuition than that of the senses (namely intellectual intuition), because it never occurred to anyone that the senses should also intuit *a priori*' (*Prolegomena*: 146).

Like many of his contemporaries, Kant thought that Plato's forms, as his metaphysics generally, depended for their security on the abstract and the 'beyond'. In any case, Kant thought that Plato's notion of intuitive, intellectual understanding was parasitic on the senses. But, as a philosophical liberal, Kant identifies the source of true knowledge not in metaphysical forms, but in the rational individual (*CPR*: 10 and 25; also footnote xxii). Thus, he shifts the search for truth from the nature of forms out there to sensual experience and the formal structuring of the mind of the individual. In that sense, Kantianism truly does represent what J.N. Finley has called 'a permanent thought bastion' (1970: 145) against all extreme objectivist theories. Following the Stoics, Kant links his search to the individual. Ernst Cassirer pithily represents this shift from Platonic objectivism to humanism by his translation of Montaigne. 'We must try to break the chain connecting us with outer world in order to enjoy true freedom.' Then, Cassirer adds, a person's essence does not depend on the environment, but entirely:

> on the value he gives to himself. Riches, rank, social distinction, even health or intellectual gifts – all this becomes indifferent. What matters alone is the tendency, the inner attitude of the soul; and this inner principle cannot be disturbed.
>
> (Cassirer 1944: 7)

But empiricists also anthropologized knowledge through sensual experience. However, Kant was not satisfied by the impending scepticism and what he thought was irrationalism that went with empiricism. He thought while certainty of experience tells us:

> what is, but not that it must necessarily be so, and not otherwise. It therefore gives us not true universality . . . Such universal modes of knowledge, which at the same time passes the character of inner necessity, must in themselves, independently of experience be clear and certain.
>
> (Cassirer 1944: 7)

So, while Kant was not against metaphysics or science, he wanted them to be able to construct knowledge 'according to a sure plan', 'completely and according to universal principles, in its boundaries as well as in its content' (*Prolegomena*: 10). There are many such references to apodeictic knowledge all through his first and second *Critiques* and in the *Prolegomena*: 'As regards the *form* of our enquiry, *certainty* and *clearness* are two essential requirements' (*CPR*: 11). Opinions are not allowed in a scientific enquiry. In the first preface to the first *Critique* he says:

> Everything, therefore, which bears any manner of resemblance to an hypothesis is to be treated as contraband; it is not to be put

up for sale even at the lowest price, but forthwith confiscated, immediately upon detection. Any knowledge that professes to hold *a priori* lays claim to be regarded as absolutely necessary.

(*CPR*: 11)

He presses home this point in his second preface by castigating philosophy in this famous phrase:

it still remains a scandal to philosophy and to human reason in general that the existence of things outside us (from which we derive the whole material of knowledge, even for our inner sense) must be accepted merely on *faith*, and that if anyone thinks good to doubt their existence, we are unable to counter his doubts by any satisfactory proof.

(*CPR*: 34, footnote)

He believes he would have rendered 'a service to reason' should he find a path which 'it can securely travel', even if he later had to give up all his other ideas (*CPR*: 17).

For Kant, logic exemplifies such a search, because since Aristotle 'it has not required to retrace a single step', except for those 'features which concern the elegance rather than the certainty of the science' (*CPR*: 17). After all, his objective is methodological and not theoretical. He wishes to mark out 'the whole plan of the science, both as regards its limits and as regards its entire internal structure'. For that, he would need a formal theoretical procedure.

In the *Prolegomena* Kant offers a new science which will provide us with a pilot: 'who will be able to sail the ship safely wherever he will, using sure principles of navigation drawn from knowledge of the globe, and equipped with a complete set of charts and a compass' (*Prolegomena*: 11). His critique is not opposed to the 'dogmatic procedure' itself, but to dogmatism which presumes 'it is possible to make progress with pure knowledge, according to principles, from concepts alone' (*CPR*: 32). The dogmatic procedure must address empirical reality and be self-critical.

Kant represents an extremely important shift of emphasis for both liberal thought and sociology; not merely a shift from rationalist idealism to the reconstruction of empirical data. It is a shift from the extension of a *possible* method, at the start of the enquiry, to the establishment of a *dependable* method. It is a shift away from an enquiry into method to the refinement of method.

It is true that Hegel was later to expose the static nature of Kantian formalism, and propose a *dynamic* form of internal criticism and Marx further sociologized the insights of both. But Kant remains important for his synthesis of the major trends in the modern period, which begins to approach important philosophical and sociological preoccupations about thought, experience, and action; and about method and history. The significance of Kant for the development of sociology arises from (i) his insistence on the role of experience; and (ii) his argument for the necessity of fixed laws.

With respect to experience, at the very beginning of the First Critique Kant insists that all knowledge begins with experience, which stimulates the mind 'to compare these representations, and, by combining or separating them, work up the raw material . . . [into] knowledge of objects' (*CPR*: 41). Balancing this, in his comments about the synthetic *a priori*, Kant ascribes a central position to human consciousness and judgement. Like Galileo, Torricelli and Stahl, Kant thought that reason should not be kept in 'nature's leading-strings, but must itself show the way with principles of judgement based upon fixed laws, containing nature to give answers to questions of reason's own determining' (*CPR*: 20). We should learn from nature, but not 'in the character of a pupil who listens to everything that the teacher chooses to say, but of an appointed judge who compels the witness to answer questions which he has himself formulated'.

In short, theoretical understanding of both our rational capacities and, more importantly, the formal theoretical procedures of science, arise from those rational capacities, is prior to any research. If research is not to be undirected, fanciful and false, we require the 'clear determination of concepts, insistence upon strictness of proof, and avoidance of venturesome, nonconsecutive steps in our inferences'. This places the scientist in a good position to raise 'metaphysics to the dignity of science' (*CPR*: 33).

Contemporary sociology clearly does not conspicuously set out to search for certitude; its general commitment to history and social structure would see to that. Curiously, however, there is a way in which both Plato's *metaphysical* forms and Kant's philosophical or *conceptual* forms find their way into the knowledge-seeking social sciences. The point is made when social scientists and philosophers set out to find the real 'democracy' or 'equality' or 'justice' or 'communism' or 'revolution' or 'socialism' or 'class', etc. For while engaged in that project, they utilize their concepts as if they represent at least four different things: (1) they are descriptions of substantive entities; (2) they are descriptions of abstract entities; (3) they are cognitive; (4) they are psychological feelings.

To take one typical example from political philosophy, in the following quote we see Jean Faurot equivocating as to whether freedom is a metaphysical abstraction, a philosophical concept or merely a state of mind:

> The practical problem of freedom, how to get freedom and how to keep it, is based on the assumption that everyone knows what freedom is and considers it desirable . . . Is the proverbial un-spoiled savage free, and does a man lose his freedom when he is prevented from keeping pigs in his yard and is compelled to pay taxes? . . . it [cannot] be resolved by factual investigation because this problem has to do with the state of mind, not with a state of affair. The philosopher's problem is to unravel the confusions that result when men talk about such matters as freedom and justice without having thought through what they are.
>
> (Faurot 1970: 3)

For example, when people ask 'what is democracy?' Do they as good sociologists or social scientists mean democracies? Or do they, like philosophers, imply *the* democracy. Alternatively, are they trying to identify an ideal type of democracy? If they mean the ideal type, does this imply abstract existence or merely a generalization, a cognitive democracy? If it is a generalization, should this be taken as an *average* of many democracies? Does it mean comparative democracies? It is not clear what that could possibly be, for democracies compared remain as such and do not change into an abstract ideal democracy. Similarly 'freedom' is treated as though it pertained to the abstract individual, as if our desire to be free had to be checked against the abstraction of an ideal freedom.[2] The possibility that the search for freedom may be so closely related to the character of the present circumstances that individuals and groups may mean quite distinct things by the term is rarely considered.

But this view is not restricted to analytic philosophers. Many sociologists, totally convinced of the importance of empirical data also, adopt such views. For example, in a discussion of Marx's theory of class, Stuart Hall suggests that it was 'tantalisingly in-complete' (Hall 1977: 3). Vic Allen, in his reasonable attempt to identify the 'working class', muses that:

the question of differentiation amongst people in contem-porary capitalist societies has been treated in class terms but without any agreement about the meaning of class. Indeed class is one of the most confused and confusing of major sociological terms.

(Allen 1977: 61)

Allen seems to slip down from the worthy activity of identifying the working class into the philosophical abyss of the meaning or nature of *the* class, right down to conceptual limitations of the word class, in two sentences, without being aware he is doing it.

The same type of ambiguity between the empirical class and the ideal class appears in Alan Hunt's article:

Despite the central role of class and classes in Marxist theory and political strategy, there are important respects in which it has remained under developed and unexplored.

(Hunt 1977: 82)

This implies that not only 'classes' are collapsible to the theory of class, but that 'class' is existent: for only empirical or theoretical existents can have teleological notions of 'underdeveloped' or 'unexplored' applied to them. Since by all these accounts class is not just an empirical existent, it must also be a theoretical one, which may imply metaphysics.

Furthermore, these ambiguities are not only found in Marxism. For as Faurot did, non-Marxist sociologists Kingsley Davis and Wilbert E. Moore indicate a similar confusion, except in their case it is quite explicit:

The present task requires two different lines of analysis – one to understand the universal, the other to understand the variable features of stratification.

(Davis and Moore 1969: 403)

They are unaware, it would seem, that these are not comple-mentary but contradictory approaches to the problem; and also unaware that universal categories are philosophical reductions, and variables are sociological generalizations, and cannot just be linked as if they were complementary.

Thus, while sociology is carrying out its classical and worthy task of describing and explaining the social context and even propagating change, it often also juxtaposes this task next to the older philosophical one. It confronts its historical and social structural analysis with a philosophical rationale by adopting indigestible formalist notions. By assuming a variant of Platonic formalism, sociologists operate with their concepts as if they represent 'real' things, that exist out there, which are sometimes more real than what does exist, which is confusing and confused, to be evaluated scientifically only in their ideality. Their adopted philosophical formalism imposes on their discipline standards of coherence possible *only* in a definition or in abstract forms. Then science becomes suspicious of belief; knowledge becomes ignorant of contingencies; truth or clarity of perception demands the avoidance of confusions exacted on us by our daily circumstances. Not realizing that belief as much as science, knowledge as well as ignorance, clarity as significantly as confusion, are all human characteristics which *actually* define people. Thus science cannot just explain these things, but it must presume them in analysis. For whether we like them or not, our ignorance, belief and confusions, as much as our enlightenment and clarity of thought, are what constitute our knowledge of ourselves and of the world around us. They all predominate in our analysis and theorizing.

This criticism must not imply that we favour methodological anarchism or that we are sceptics. We certainly do not believe any view or method is as good as any other, or we would not be making criticisms of formalism. We hope only to point out the difficulties accrued from a search for certitude. After all, as we shall see later, knowledge does not need to be metaphysically certain for it to be knowledge, even dependable knowledge. Furthermore, we wish to register the absurdity and the unethical presumptions which prompt people to universalize regional concepts of, say, democracy, and apply them analytically to other societies. The ambiguity between concepts about empirical relationships and abstract universal ones – say of democracy or class – allows that to happen.

The search for certitude at socially unstable periods justifiably drove Plato and Kant to forms. But when modern sociologists become suspicious of all common-sense explanations, they are unjustified twice over. They are unjustified for reasons that Plato and Kant were not, because they believed that 'rational' knowledge was the only viable form of knowledge. But they are also unjustified because they do not realize that for rational standards to remain so, they must respond to changing circumstances. For not to do that, will make these standards irrational because they will lead to irresponsible political decisions and trite social analyses. But this puts formalists in a difficult position. For to *change* the rational standards for them would also imply relativism and irrationality. But to remain stalwart defenders of dogmatic formal standards, by our account, would also invariably make them relativistic and irrational; for they will be defending standards which are historically dated and pertain to a particular social group in a particular region of the world.

Methodological reduction and theoretical security

Plato's search for truth leads him to reduce his formal theoretical procedure to intellectual intuitionism and to science. The metaphysical notion of form provided him with universal standards for identifying empirical objects. To make sense of either universals or objects depended almost entirely upon the power of the intellect.

Plato takes the link between intellectual activity and the 'real' very seriously. He separates knowledge and truth, which are the outcome of intellectual activity, from belief and habitual practice. Knowing is intuitive and infallible, while belief is less secure. Know- ledge liberates not only from mere belief, but also from 'bodily appetites'. Reality is assimilated through the intellect.

Plato was greatly impressed by another formal theoretical procedure: Pythagoras's mathematics. In it he saw the solution to the general problem of universals. He uses mathematics to link intelligibility to reality through the translation of the knowledge of forms into mathematical terms: defined, precise, universal, 'complete and perfect'.

Sociology is still 'Platonic' in the categorical distinctions it is occasionally tempted to draw between beliefs and science – think here of Althusser's battle cry 'epistemological break' so eagerly taken up by sociologists in the 1970s – and in the still pervasive assumption that the understanding of social life can be formalized methodologically and, occasionally at least, mathematically. No more than Plato is sociology in such a mode able to say why these particular forms have been chosen.

We do not suggest that sociology is strictly Platonic, but rather that there is a long tradition specifying what real knowledge consists in and how it is to be ascertained which sociology has absorbed both wittingly and unwittingly. Another dominant figure in this tradition, and one who exercises a clearer and more explicit influence on sociology, is Kant. His path to conceptual forms is through philosophy, modelled on scientific analogies. But even more than Plato, Kant thought that such truth can be reached only through formal theoretical procedures.

Kant is important to sociological analysis both because he synthesized the major trends of the modern period and because that synthesis begins to approach important philosophical and sociological preoccupations about thought and experience, thought and action, knowledge and morality, method and history. In short, Kant begins to address the relationship between formal theory and formal method and history.

The *Critique of Pure Reason* commences with the insistence that knowledge begins with experience which stimulates the mind to 'compare these representations, and, by combining or separating them, work up the raw material of sensible impressions into knowledge of objects' (*CPR*: 41). This notwithstanding, Kant also insists that science 'must first be capable of being determined exactly; otherwise the boundaries of all the sciences run into one another and none of them can be treated soundly according to its own nature' (*Prolegomena*: 15). It is here that the *a priori* preconditions of the possibility of knowledge which can be rationally reconstructed through philosophical reflection are of central significance. They define not only the limits of rationality and science, but also vindicate the latter. Kant's search for a 'synthetic *a priori*' grounded in pure intuition is necessitated by this desire to find the rational basis of knowledge.

For Kant, while experience is essential, we can only make sense of the objects of experience through universal and *a priori* categories which act as the necessary and transcendental condition of experience. These categories are built into the structure of (human) consciousness itself. It is that which consciousness brings to bear on experience which makes knowledge possible. Thus the human subject is brought firmly in to the knowledge-generating process, but primarily in order to serve the function of guaranteeing knowledge through the universality of its categories of thought:

experience is itself a species of knowledge which involves understanding; and understanding has rules which I must presuppose
as being in me prior to objects being given to me, and therefore
as being *a priori*. They find expression in *a priori* concepts to
which all objects of experience necessarily conform, and with
which they must agree.

(*CPR*: 22–3)

Similarly, formal logic is also appointed the task of being the
'vestibule' for science, which is concerned with 'objective' and not
analytical definitions. It defines the limitations of possible knowledge, of the 'sure path to science', which is presupposed in it.

Unlike strict rationalists, Kant was convinced that method had
to refer to empirical reality and history. But he did not believe
that this could be done in a naïve correspondence, but instead
tried to demonstrate through philosophical argument, as he conceived it, the 'necessary' relations underpinning knowledge. To be
necessary, these relations had to exist outside history, in the pure
intuition of the isolated individual subject.[3] In the Kantian world,
knowledge is not merely decontextualized, but decontextualiza-
tion is a condition for the possibility of truth.

What is the lasting relevance of this decontextualized conception of truth for sociology? One of Marx's contributions to
sociology is that he contradicted Kant's view of science. He insisted
that experience does not just provide the data for theoretical
construction, but constitutes a part in it, which may and often does
come before scientific understanding. Most sociologists still
believe this Marxian shift to be correct. However, as with Kant,
their *intention* internally to link experience to theory is made
ambiguous by the *method* they adopt. Their *intention* as sociologists
is to explain empirical social reality. Their *method*, however, reflects
both the historic anxiety and influence of liberal epistemology,
which in the end becomes a barrier to such an explanation. Their
methodological reduction competes with their historicity. Rather
than resolving this very difficult problem, in the end sociologists
juxtapose its constituents and hope for the best.

But, after examining numerous books on sociological theory,
we are left in no doubt that its self-identified project is not philosophical but empirical. That is, thanks to Marx, most sociologists
are engaged in theory not *necessarily* to track down irreducible
characteristics of the natural or human world, but so that their

theories may be reliably used to study the empirical world.[4] Even when they do engage in the said philosophical project of identifying the essential nature of things, they also do it with policy intent in mind. But, as we have already seen, sociologists are bad empiricists. Therefore, Raymond Aron speaks for many sociologists when he insists that sociological knowledge cannot be defined as the 'ability to understand the diversity of social phenomena', for this 'could just as easily be a definition of historical knowledge' (Aron 1967: 26). For him, the historian is like a botanist who collects rare species. The sociologist, on the other hand, 'takes note of this diversity, but he would like to understand it and grasp its implicit logic'. Now what we need to find out is: where does *de facto* place itself, between these two extremes of philosophical idealism and historical empiricism? In other words, where does the ambiguity finally land sociology?

As far as Aron is concerned, he celebrates Lévi-Strauss's work on kinship as a model for scientific sociology because, while recognizing social diversities, it also insists on an underlying logical unity of 'fundamental themes'. 'This constancy of the themes, and the diversity of their manifestations in various societies, is what the sociologist is trying to understand' (Aron 1967: 26). So whatever the approach or philosophical assumptions, few sociologists would deny that, at some level, sociological theory is trying to explain the empirical world of social relations. Aron's comments, however, are not merely a plea for comparative studies, they affirm universal similarities between people. The justification for the need for universal theoretical categories, which apply as easily to Russia as they do to the USA, is the same as that one given by philosophers. Universals are necessary if we want to make comparisons and they are always theoretical. Aron again:

> we are necessarily led, finally, to attempt to establish, as a final term of supreme hope, types of global structure. Going beyond the analysis and definition of social facts, sociology attempts to determine the fundamental types of social organisation, *the underlying logic of community life*.
>
> (Aron 1967: 26)

The argument is that comparisons can only be made when the same assumptions can be presumed; which probably makes any form of communication between strangers or even friends impossible. However, this view is not peculiar to Aron: it was also held by the classical sociologists of the nineteenth century including Durkheim, Tönnies, Pareto and Simmel. Aron is also fully aware that this view may imply that one abandons 'science and return(s) to philosophy'.

However, if we accept this definition of the sociological project, we may very well be arguing that sociological theory is prior to experience. But Aron is explicitly anti-metaphysical and is opposed to Weberian scepticism as much as he condemns holistic sociologies. And yet he is still unclear about what his alternative is to be and ends up in a void:

> Social reality is neither completely integrated whole nor an incoherent mass, and so it is impossible to be dogmatic either about universal validity of social types, or about the relativism of every theory.
>
> (Aron 1967: 27)

However, Aron's reasons for rejecting both Weber and metaphysicians are quite legitimate. For him, social reality is neither incoherent nor completely ordered:

> it contains innumerable semi-organised parts, but not obvious total order. The sociologist does not arbitrarily create the logic of the social behaviour which he analyses. When one examines an economic system . . . one brings to light an order which is written into the system, not superimposed by the observer.
>
> (Aron 1967: 28)

But the ordering is diverse and the sociologist has a choice between different orderings and categories.

What Aron does not seem quite clear about is how he might conceive of the relationship between the enquirer and the object of enquiry, or how theory interacts with history. But he quite rightly emphasizes the independence of historical existence from our minds, and ambiguously insists that our theories or concepts are independent of history. However, the *relationship* between theory and history is not reflected upon: in this case, too, the two are merely juxtaposed.

The reason for the juxtaposition is clear enough. Sociologists are entirely convinced that their project deals with empirical human realities and human histories. At the same time, sociologists aim to carve out a science, or even just a discipline, for themselves, one which can authoritatively pronounce on its material. For that to happen, it is believed, we need the independence of con- cepts. But Aron laments that 'we are still a long way from having a system of sociological concepts which would enable us to represent the whole society with accuracy'. Of course, he suspects that this may be even useless:

> Nevertheless, the development of sociology and the resulting aims of present-day sociologists cannot be ignored: their desire to know things with increasing precision, to go on asking new questions, and to refine and make more rigorous the con- ceptual systems which they use to interpret the facts.
>
> (Aron 1967: 29)

But it is clear from this comment that even if Aron is confused about the placement of sociological theory, he is not confused about its role, which is to make sense of social relationships. Nor is Aron equivocal about how to attain that empirical knowledge: the 'conceptual systems' will 'interpret the facts'. Thus, this un- resolved difficulty about the nature of sociological theory and its relationship to history and social context leads to the unintended over-emphasis of theory over history and context. It is unintended because priority of theory mostly expands on the nature of theory and not of the empirical reality. For empirical reality to be richly known, theories have to be less imperialistic.

In so far as there is a relationship between theory and social historical reality, theory explains, orders and selects the relevant data from reality. This view is stated implicitly or explicitly.[5] At its most extreme crudeness, but also most illustrative confidence, Lewis A. Coser designated to sociological classics the task of a 'tool kit', from which we can take out various concepts, different major sociologists, for specific application; without worry that they may be contradictory or of mixed assumptions and usefulness.

Sociological theory, as it is, is confused and conflict-ridden. It fails to achieve its stated need to explain social (empirical) rela- tions, because in its confusion it contradictorily opts for abstract *a priori* theory. This sociological tendency can best be summarized by Lukács's notorious classic statement:

> Let us assume for the sake of argument recent research had disproved once and for all every one of Marx's individual theses ... every serious 'orthodox' Marxist would still be able to accept all such modern findings without reservation and hence dismiss

all of Marx's theses *in toto* – without having to renounce his orthodoxy for a single moment. Orthodox Marxism therefore does not imply the uncritical acceptance of the results of Marx's investigations. It is not the 'belief' in this or that thesis, nor the exegesis of a 'sacred' book . . . Orthodoxy refers exclusively to *method*. It is the scientific conviction that dialectical materialism is the road to truth and that its methods can be developed, expanded and deepened . . . All attempts to surpass or 'improve' it have led and must lead to over-simplification, triviality and eclecticism.

(Lukács 1971: 1)

This notion of method is not so different from Kant's (see below). In brief, no sociologist would willingly adopt a metaphysical stance, but a search for certitude by the reductive method, validated by naturalism or logic, leads to that stance.

The point here is not that formal methods should not be allowed in scientific work: that would be an absurd restriction. In any case the formal approach in the search for knowledge has not only been historically valuable, but continues to be so. Our concern is not so much that the formal method is used as an aid in the search for knowledge, but that when used, people who use it believe that not only is it the road to truth but that it is the royal road to truth, or perhaps the only road to truth.

FORMALISM AND COGNITION

But formalism has often been intimately linked to the possibility of knowledge. In his book *An Essay on Man*, Ernst Cassirer makes this point most intelligently. He insists that through the symbolic system, people have escaped the reactive attitude towards the environment found in animals and started living in 'a new *dimension* of reality'. People's responses to stimuli are reflected upon by them, and are 'interpreted and retarded by a slow complicated process of thought' (Cassirer 1944: 24). It becomes our inescapable fate to shun naturalism:

Language, myth, art, and religion are parts of this universe. They are the varied threads which weave the symbolic net, the tangled web of human experience. All human progress in thought and experience refines upon and strengthens this net. No longer can man confront reality immediately; he cannot see it, as it were face to face. Physical reality seems to recede in proportion as man's symbolic activity advances. Instead of dealing with the things themselves man is in a sense constantly conversing with himself.

(Cassirer 1944: 25)

Cassirer's point is as clear as it is powerful. Human nature is constituted not only by its biological and vital characteristic, but also by its symbolic formalism. People are so wrapped up in their 'linguistic forms, in artistic images, in mythical symbols or religious rites', that they 'cannot see or know anything except by the interposition of this artificial medium'. They live 'in the midst of imaginary emotions, in hopes and fears, in illusions and disillusions, in . . . [their] fantasies and dreams. "What disturbs and alarms man" said Epictetus, "are not the things, but his opinions and fantasies about the things"' (Cassirer 1972: 25).

In short, what constitutes human nature is social mediation; and what makes human knowledge, appreciation, morality, affectivity, etc., possible is reflection through formal cultural symbols. *Animal symbolicum* described by Cassirer is no threat to our critique of formalism, for it is an entirely different kind of formalism from the one we are criticizing. Cassirer's description is entirely sociological, and merely calls for the identification of profound human characteristics through their cultural production. As cultural production is never static, his conception of human nature and search for knowledge has a distinctive pragmatist logic about it.

John Dewey, in his book *Logic*, observes that all logical forms 'arise within the operation of inquiry and are concerned with control of inquiry so that they may yield warranted assertions'. Logical standards are then determined on the basis of the failure or success of the enquiry. Successful enquiry is assessed by its longevity and its continued yield of results, 'that are either confirmed in further inquiry or that are corrected by the use of the same procedures'. In this scheme, an enquiry has no need for rationalistic foundation, it only needs a successful tradition (Dewey 1983: ch. 1).

Implied in both views is the assumption that what makes human nature human and human knowledge dependable, are not rules and standards developed in antiquity or in eighteenth-century Europe, but is due to the cultural activity of humans at any time. Both undermine the notion that there is a qualitatively different, more rational form of knowledge which was developed in the enlightened Europe. People everywhere are humans and scientists because they produce successful cultures and live in them. Thus, the formalism we are criticizing is one connected with liberal/ capitalist abstraction as described by Nisbet, which was exalted by the eighteenth-century epistemologists. Furthermore, as Bronowski and Mazlish observe, 'just as the changes in outlook since the Renaissance have affected the content of what men think and write, so they have affected the manner in which they think and write' (1963: 552). But they also articulate another very common view thus:

> This idea of human self-fulfilment has also inspired scientific and technical progress . . . The purpose and the effect has been to liberate men from the exhausting drudgeries of earning their living, in order to give them the opportunity to live.
>
> (Bronowski and Mazlish 1963: 556)

This further implies the sociological motive force of science. The point is again emphasized by another scientist when he insists that mathematics became 'especially prominent in modern times . . . to provide a rational organisation of natural phenomena' (Kline 1954: 5). Implying that contrary to belief mathematical explanatory power is not just logical, but is also aesthetic and psychological.

> On the one hand, the conviction that nature is lawful has stimulated man to keep a close watch on natural phenomena, to observe and to experiment, in order to see in what manner she repeats herself . . . On the other hand, it has stimulated men to think behind the practical pattern, to analyse and to reason, in order to find its simple and rational organisation in order to find intelligible laws.
>
> (Bronowski and Mazlish 1963: 548)

At this point of the argument, therefore, the success of science need not necessarily signal its truth content, but merely its organized persistence. If we are to believe Kuhn, as we shall see later, the consistent change of these laws most definitely encourages the assumption that there are no internally accumulating coherent laws. Any accumulation of scientific knowledge we experience is cultural accumulation.

The picture that emerges is that aesthetic and symbolic formalism, which are either arbitrary or sociological, may still deliver genuinely appreciated results, without in any sense implying logical necessity. Indeed, it is then possible to argue, as did Hume, that science is indistinguishable from common sense and owes its success not to its internal truth content, but to the psychology and cultural practices of its adherents. Perhaps there is internal truth content in science, but that needs to be established and cannot be assumed from the windfall of scientific production. Most histories of science unselfconsciously stress the persistent hard work and stubbornness of scientists, rather than their logical insights. But merely to say this does not deal with the issue of the truth content of science. It merely questions the right that science and theory have appropriated for themselves, to be true. It similarly questions the right of formalism to make comparative claims.

But even in the case of abstraction described, our argument by no means insists that formal thought is either worthless or does not lead to progress. Indeed, the evidence clearly suggests the opposite in almost all human cultural activities. Formalism in science, mathematics and logic has led to many wonderful technological developments. The usage of logic as an Aristotelian 'organon' increased our theoretical precision in science. While

> the concepts, methods, and conclusions of mathematics are the substratum of physical sciences . . . [Mathematics] brought life to the dry bones of disconnected facts and, acting as connective tissue, has bound series of detached observations into bodies of science.
>
> (Kline 1954: 5)

Mathematical formalism spilled over into philosophical, religious and cultural thought. It

> supplied substance to economic and political theories, has fashioned major painting, musical, architectural, and literary styles, has fathered our logic, and . . . invaded domains ruled by authority, custom, and habit, and supplanted them as arbiter of thought and action.
>
> (Kline 1954: 15)

If there is an exaggeration of an enthusiast which reduces human history to the achievements of mathematical formulas, it is by no means an entirely empty exaggeration. Mathematical formulas, even entirely on ideological grounds, have had an incomparable and profound effect on Western culture, and, through it, on the international culture. As a formal science *par excellence*, its applied effect is even more lasting when practitioners in art or students of sociology produce models, unaware that their parentage is influenced by mathematics.

The formalization of music, art, dance, linguistics, anthropology, literary criticisms, too, have brought about exciting developments in the form of classical music, modernism, ballet, structuralism and so on. Furthermore, these developments are to be found in most cultures in all recorded history. There is little doubt, for example, that the work of Russian formalists from the 1920s has had a lasting and fruitful impact on literary and cultural production. They saw the form as a communicative 'organon' which is 'autonomous, self-expressive, able by extra-verbal rhythmic, associative and connotative means to "stretch" language beyond its normal "everyday" range of meaning' (Hawkes 1977: 60). They upgraded cultural forms from both bourgeois reification and Marxist reductionism. They shifted the debates from the ontological nature of humans and their cultural products to the process of human and cultural productions. By this process, they helped to recognize more readily the mediating nature of language, art and other cultural forms in our search for knowledge.

However, in spite of these contributions, formalism is still full of difficulties. For example, when Kant constructs his synthetic *a priori*, he does so to redeem empiricism and rationalism. But when Kant does that, he not only salvages theory from its obscurantism and its unconnectedness to experience, but he also *causally* links theory to experience. Theory, then, becomes not only the necessary component for existence – if we cannot know the world it probably does not exist, but it truthfully represents experience. In this belief in theoretical science, Kant does not differ from positivists. When sociological formalists invest similar confidence in their theory by seeking, say, the internal link between theory and practice, or construct analytic scientific models for studying reality and for action, they also make similar assumptions. They then suppose that theory is not a form of reflection but an aid to experiential truth and a programme for action. Then existential matters and human agency are confused with science. Precision is confused with truth and valuable aesthetic ordering is mistaken for the discovery of truthful natural ordering. What we know or would like to know becomes what must be known. A lot of sociologists, including Habermas, are fully aware of these difficulties in their thought. Nevertheless, they seem unable to resist the formalist promise: they succumb to the pleasing aesthetic and cultural ordering and abandon the tiresome, illusive and confusing irregularities of the social and physical world. The problem, however, is that they then insist that what is distinctively cultural and aesthetic ordering to be transcendental. It is this unsubstantiated escalation that we object to.

CONCLUSION

Thus our disquiet about formalism is not just eccentric, but is based on similar concerns to those Habermas outlines with respect to Comtean positivism. We feel that in the same way that positivism defines all the possible routes to knowledge through scientific assumptions, and insists that knowledge acquired by other methods is either false or unreliable, so in the end formalism defines knowledge. Now it is true that within the Kantian-cum-rationalist framework, the limits of rationality are not directly linked to a practical scientific method or image, in the way that it is in positivism. Kantianism supposes only that rationality has to be assumed in a scientific method. Then standards are only supposed to be rational in the broader sense, that no other possible plausible, non-contradictory, empirically falsifiable explanation can be given for them. Nevertheless, as we have seen, what is assumed rational *indirectly* links to the standards of liberal epistemology, which, as far as we are concerned, have been proved to be by no means unequivocal. If what we say about formalism is true, then this has profound consequences on research. If what sociologists are searching for is 'truthful' knowledge using a methodological reduction, the chances are what they will find in history is evidence to support their theory and less about what happens in history. Theory, then, according to formalists, is not reflective but constructs reality.

NOTES

1 For example, Kant's *Critique of Pure Reason, passim.* But these themes appear in various ways in most of the eighteenth-century writings. See Gay 1967; Cassirer 1944; Eliot and Stern (eds) 1979; and Berlin (ed.) 1979.

2 'The philosopher's problem is to unravel the confusions that result when men talk about such matters as freedom and justice without having thought through what they are' (Faurot 1970: 3).

3 The individualism of Kant's *a priori* of the transcendental knowing subject has been criticized by Habermas (1971b), and, in greater detail, by Karl-Otto Apel (1980). Both Habermas and Apel replace the 'monological' subject with the *a priori* of a transcendental 'community' of enquiring subjects. While in one sense more social (i.e. in assuming a linguistic and rule-following community of interacting subjects), this move is no less ahistorical than the Kantian vision it seeks to replace. Apel and Habermas have in mind the contextless context of subjects whose interactions are governed only by a concern for truth, and who thus exist outside tradition, power or affective inter-dependencies.

4 As exemplified by comments by Tom Bottomore 1962: 32–3; or Raymond Aron 1968: 14.

5 For example, Olive Banks (1971) talks about the application of sociological perspectives to various social institutions.

Part II

Formalism in contemporary sociology

Chapter 3

Claude Lévi-Strauss
Universal categories and the end of racism

The fact that man can have the idea 'I' raises him infinitely above all other beings living on earth. By this he is a *person* and by virtue of his unity of consciousness through all the changes he may undergo, he is one and the same person . . . This holds even if he cannot yet say 'I'.

(Immanuel Kant, *Anthropology from a Pragmatic Point of View*, 1974 [1798])

INTRODUCTION

It is not often that we encounter Lévi-Strauss in the literature as a champion of racial equality, and yet racism clearly occupied his thoughts. But when he debates with abstract liberal universals, he means not only to criticize Western racism, but he also hopes to reassert a sociological orientation. Most commentators, however, are merely satisfied to outline and debate with his considerable original contribution to structuralist analysis.[1] By this they neglect his racial equality themes and sociological orientation. In doing so they not only depoliticise his work, but they also remove the ambiguities in it. They concentrate on his technical solutions to linguistic, anthropological and epistemological problems[2] and therefore remove the dynamic motivation of his thought and erase what is sociological in it. They present his formal theoretical procedure, without its overall sociological intention. His overall intention, like that of most sociologists, is to make sense of empirical reality. But this formalist interpretation of Lévi-Strauss cannot entirely be blamed on his commentators, for firmly lodged in his own sociology is the formal theoretical procedure that he follows.

It is an advantage to concentrate on his equality theme not only because it is central to his sociology, but also because it provides a focus in his work and addresses the general theme of our thesis. By it, we hope to outline his sociological re-examination of liberal philosophical assumptions, which he finds to be partial, relativistic and parochial. In the place of abstract notions of human nature, he adduces his idea of the 'savage mind', which he believes is suggestive of a deeper human reality, without carrying rationalistic assumptions.

However, in spite of his considerable achievement in transforming abstract universals into demonstrable ones (rather akin to Cassirer's notions of symbolic forms), Lévi-Strauss in the end fails to break out of liberal abstraction. By starting his project where liberals left off, he partially limits his solution to that framework's rationality. He remains informed by the constraints of the formal needs of liberal philosophy and epistemology. By the same token, then, he fails to confront racism at a sufficiently effective level, at the sociological level. He makes this mistake because of the four following reasons. *First*, in spite of his appreciation of history and context in social analyses, that appreciation remains intellectual. For example, although he recognizes the existence of Eurocentrism and its imperialism of knowledge, he does not consider the practical consequences of such domination on social change. He incorrectly hopes that as soon as people recognize the fact of imperialism and their ignorance of other societies, they will give up their racism. *Second*, in spite of his own criticism of naturalism, his own notion of the unconscious, which he borrows from Freud, has naturalistic and intuitionist implications. *Third*, the Durkheimian notion of system, whose sociocultural manifestation he transforms and claims to have correlates in the unconscious, is not only naturalistic and deterministic but also contradictory. For Durkheim the system is social structural and non-derivative: the empirical structure is what counts, not its origins. The empirical social structure and culture have meaning which need no metaphysical foundations for their existence or effectiveness. But Lévi-Strauss wishes to link structure and meaning to an underlying unconscious. *Fourth*, in spite of his correctly identifying cultural evolutionism as racist, and vigorously arguing against it, his own theory of science and its relationship to myth is sufficiently ambiguous to imply a form of cultural evolutionism.

Thus, Lévi-Strauss admirably exemplifies the theoretical dilemma of contemporary sociology: the dilemma between theory and history and between epistemology and emotive human action. He resolves this problem in quite a familiar fashion. He either contradictorily maintains that the formal theoretical procedure and history are more or less compatible, or more honestly but yet more problematically, he starts with theory and applies it to historical content at the latter's cost. Regardless of this, Lévi-Strauss does recognize the ethnocentrism of liberal thought, and goes further than Marx in recognizing and challenging Eurocentrism.

Thus, he contributes towards sociology and racial equality in at least three ways. He substitutes Eurocentric (and racist) liberal universals with demonstrable and substantive universals. He constructs a collectivist structuralist model which he hopes will provide us with a procedure for studying other societies, without making philosophical or racist assumptions. And he contributes towards a framework which *may* be used to study ideology in general and racism in particular, by examining the social construction of knowledge.

In the following section we outline Lévi-Strauss's equality theme and criticisms of liberal philosophy. He argues that the latter has little to say about empirical entities and leads to racist assumptions. We shall then discuss how he tries to construct different kinds of universals, which are substantive and sociological. Finally we lament that in spite of his extraordinary and original contribution to sociology, his solutions fail to resolve the issue of the relationship between theory and history. His theoretical system still adheres too closely to aspects of liberal philosophy, and consequently remains too formal to be able to deal with social problems such as racism.

LÉVI-STRAUSS'S RACIAL EQUALITY THEME

In contrast to many Lévi-Strauss commentators, we identify his *aim* as clearly sociological and seeking racial equality. Not only does he say this, but otherwise his work would make no sense. He makes his most explicit equality arguments in the 1952 UNESCO pamphlet, *Race and History* and also in *The Savage Mind* (1966) and *Structural Anthropology: 1* (1968) but references can be found throughout his work.

In *Race and History*, he makes clear his disquiet about Western racism in the way he lectures academic racists. Striking at the very heart of Western liberalism, he argues for cultural diversity and cultural collaboration. Similarly he strikes out in *The Savage Mind*:

> a good deal of egocentricity and naïvety is necessary to believe that man [*sic*] has taken refuge in a single one of the historical or geographical modes of his existence, when the truth about man resides in the system of their differences and common properties.
>
> (Lévi-Strauss 1966: 249)

From the beginning, then, Lévi-Strauss dissociates himself from an explicit or implicit racist view which presents non-Europeans (he calls them people without writing) as stupid, irrational, unscientific, uninquiring, unable to cope with nature because they are too superstitious to classify it, or are too illogical to control it. He sociologically insists that understanding other societies would involve an intimate comprehension of their social context, ethical evaluations, social structure and political system, etc., before any comparison in morality or judgement can be made. To do otherwise is to conduct an abstract *philosophical* and not sociological analysis. Lévi-Strauss was completely attuned to this way of thinking. He breaks down his arguments in the following way.

Biological determinism

The 'original sin of anthropology', for Lévi-Strauss, is to confuse race and biology and to forget the 'sociological and psychological productions of human civilisations' (1952: 8). For him, racial contribution to civilization should be accounted for by the historical, social and geographical environment and not by 'special aptitudes inherent in the anatomical or physiological make up of the black, yellow or white man' (1952: 8. See also 1969: 100). For Lévi-Strauss, races too are defined by the historical and cultural factors and the differences in their biological make-up are very slight.

Historical change and progress

Lévi-Strauss also distrusts cultural evolutionism because of its stealthy racism. He prefers different notions of progress and history. The 'so-called primitive societies', he argues, have a history which spans as long as does European history. They too experience 'wars, migration and adventure. But their social arrangements are specialised in ways different from those which we have chosen' and in some cases have 'remained closer to the very ancient conditions' but 'in other respects they are farther from those conditions than we are' (1967: 46). Therefore, progress is not the same as historicism, it is:

> neither continuous nor inevitable; its course consists in a series of leaps and bounds or, as the biologist would say, mutations. These leaps and bounds are not always in the same direction; the general trend may change too, rather like the progress of a knight in chess, who always has several moves open to him but never in the same direction . . . [I]t is only occasionally that history is 'cumulative', that is to say, the scores add up to a lucky combination.
>
> (Lévi-Strauss 1952: 21)

Thus, the assumption that other societies are 'stationary' or less developed than our own, which is progressive and advanced, indicates an understandable ethnocentric psychology which appears in any assessment of the value of a different culture. After all, 'the line of their development has no meaning for us, and cannot be measured in terms of the criteria we employ' (1952: 24). But though understandable, such psychology must not be taken to be apodictic fact.

Having thus set up the scene, Lévi-Strauss makes his next crucial argument. Given that people develop in different directions for divergent motives, and given that history is only occasionally 'cumulative', then the last such obvious accumulation of human endeavour was in the neolithic revolution. It was marked by advances in agriculture, stock-rearing, pottery and weaving; all of which have significantly helped us to increase our per capita supply of energy and have prolonged human life. In spite of the tendency to regard the most recent discoveries as the most significant and previous ones to be due to chance, 'in the last eight or ten thousand years all we have done is to improve all these "arts of civilisation".' Early achievements and those of other cultures tend to be ignored by contemporary Western people, in order to deny them their rightful claim to have contributed to human progress. Such indefinable assumptions persist because past technological changes are treated as accidents, where the knowledge of fire is connected with lightning or a bush fire, and cooking is said to have arisen from an accidental roasting of an animal, and the invention of pottery as a result 'of someone's leaving a lump of clay near a fire'. People are thought to have begun their 'career in a sort of technological golden age, when inventions could, as it were, be picked off the trees as easily as fruit or flowers' (1952: 34).

Lévi-Strauss believes that these naïve people fail to recognize that each process involves complicated technological and scientific knowledge, gathered over thousands of years. In contradistinction to both classical liberalism and Marxism, he believes that no society is intrinsically cumulative:

> Cumulative history is not the prerogative of certain races or certain cultures. It is the result of their *conduct* rather than their *nature*. It represents a certain 'way of life' of cultures which depends on their capacity to 'go-along-together' ... [It is] characteristic of grouped societies . . . while stationary history (supposing it to exist) would be the distinguishing feature of an inferior form of social life, the isolated societies.
>
> (Lévi-Strauss 1952: 43)

This very last point about isolation brings us to his next argument about cultural diversity. But before we turn to it we should note that for Lévi-Strauss *technological* advancement on its own does not unambiguously denote historical accumulation of the 'arts of civilisation'. Thus by allowing other societies to share in the glory of our contemporary achievements, at least by implication he suggests that 'civilisation' is not found only in technologically advanced countries.

Here Lévi-Strauss is arguing against a Western historicist assumption, woven into our common-sense and philosophical thinking, that not only is Western thought progressive, truthful and superior, but that it must be so. He suggests that it is possible to make such assumptions *only* by ignoring historical and sociological evidence, by depending too much on historicist theory. What is needed is to go back and examine empirical evidence. He makes his argument more explicit with his notion of cultural diversity.

Cultural diversity

Lévi-Strauss is convinced that progress cannot and has not appeared in cultural isolation. Various cultures have collaborated in

order to make progress.[3] They voluntarily or involuntarily inter-
relate by migration, cultural borrowing, trade coalitions and
warfare. But collaboration is not the same as imperialism. Each
culture contributes not by providing a 'list of inventions which it
has personally produced, but in its difference from others'. Then,
other cultures feel gratitude for the different contributions, even
if they do not fully understand them. Therefore, world civilization
is an abstract limiting concept, marking 'the coexistence' of cultures of various kinds in a worldwide coalition, each reserving 'its
own originality'. For people to make progress, they must collabor-
ate, when the 'differences in their contributions will gradually be
evened out' (1952: 54).

In that case, historical progress is not only multidimensional in
its accumulation, but all cultures, technologically advanced or not,
contribute towards periodic advances. He partly believes this
because he thinks that the modern age made its greatest advances
in the neolithic revolution and partly from his conception of
science.

Science and rationality

Lévi-Strauss recognizes that science and myth parted company in
the seventeenth and eighteenth centuries, so that science may
'build itself up against the generations' mythical and mystical
thought'. It did that by 'turning its back upon the world of the
senses . . . a delusive world'. Scientists then preferred the
intellectual certitude of mathematical formulas (1978: 6). By this
rationalistic schism, 'scientific thought was able to constitute
itself'.

However, even if the process was once necessary for the
development of knowledge, Lévi-Strauss regrets its radical continuation. He regrets the contemporary discontinuity between science,
which is seen as responsible for knowledge, and mythology or
belief which is thought to be false, because of its consequences on
scientific thought and on the study of other cultures. He finds
some of these distinctions unacceptable. While there is a difference in the types of knowledge acquired by different systems
and cultures, that is only because their goals are also different. The
similarity of myths and totems from all over the world have convinced him of a deeper biological and cognitive similarity between
people, the distillation of which must characterize human nature.

Humans use this equipment to classify and gather knowledge. He makes this point by criticizing both Malinowski and Levy-Bruhl.

He rejects Malinowski's presumption that the thought of the people 'without writing . . . was entirely . . . determined by the basic needs of life . . . finding substances, satisfying the sexual drives', through which they are said to 'explain their social institutions, their beliefs, their mythology . . . functionalism' (1978: 15–16). Lévi-Strauss is quite simply not persuaded that such people are incapable of abstract and scientific thought. He says nothing about regress but all cultures must also be assumed, from time to time, to contribute towards that too. The inference is that they are savages and are like animals and that they exist intuitively but not intellectually.

He also rejects the radical separation between science and belief, as it was inferred by Levy-Bruhl. Levy-Bruhl suggested that non-Europeans are pre-logical and are 'entirely determined by emotion and mystic representations'; they are incapable of intellectual labour. Lévi-Strauss is on the contrary 'convinced that non-Europeans can also be moved by a need or a desire to understand the world around them, its nature and its society . . . proceed by intellectual means, exactly as philosophers, or even to some extent a scientist can and would do' (1978: 16). Clearly, Lévi-Strauss does not entirely submit himself to a conventional view of science by suggesting that there is no *qualitative* difference between modern science and mythology, but he sometimes comes close to this view. The difference is not in any case *ad hominen,* for all humans are capable of logical and abstract thinking. Indeed, he often suggests that mythical thought is more intellectual than practical. In fact, for Lévi-Strauss, its main purpose is that 'it meets intellectual requirements rather than or instead of satisfying needs' (1966: 9). Lévi-Strauss *does* believe that distinctions exist between different types of knowledge, not because different cultures or races have different *types* of logic by which they acquire knowledge, but because they use the same logic for different purposes. He sums it up thus:

> delimitation of concepts is different in every language, the use of more or less abstract terms is a function not of greater or lesser intellectual capacity, but of differences in the interests – in their intensity and attention to detail.
>
> Even if [mythical thought] is rarely directed towards facts of

the same level as those with which modern science is concerned, it implies comparable intellectual application and
methods of observation. In both cases the universe is object of
thought at least as much as it is a means of satisfying needs.

(Lévi-Strauss 1966: 2–3)

Lévi-Strauss insists that examples exist from all over the world
which show that animals and plants 'are not known as a result of
their usefulness; they are deemed to be useful and interesting
because they are first of all known' (1966: 9).

We shall return to this issue of science, to show that there are
difficulties in his view that mythical thought is largely intellectual
but not very practical. For the moment it is sufficient to indicate
that Lévi-Strauss is unhappy with the idea that thought in other
societies is mystical, ideological or mere belief, in the sense of
being false; or at least not more so than Western thought. He
agrees that thought over there is mythical, but only in the sense
that it is foundational or primary. For Lévi-Strauss, then, mythological thinking is not something to be ashamed of, but it is a
characteristic which distinguishes people from brutes. It is a characteristic which not only unites different races and cultures: it is
what makes them all rational and human. The fact that people feel
opposed to this view points to the predominance of abstract
Western ideology.

The universality of ethnocentrism

Finally, Lévi-Strauss pins down his egalitarian project by a problematic but very interesting argument. He suggests that the existence of
universal prejudice itself proves, or at least hints at, human equality.
Universal prejudice is characterized by the psychological tendency,
all over the world, to 'reject out of hand the cultural institutions –
ethical, religious, social or aesthetic – which are furthest removed
from those which we identify ourselves' (1952: 11). That tendency
leads Westerners to talk of others' behaviour as barbarian. For
Lévi-Strauss, such 'crude reactions' connote ignorance and show
'instinctive antipathy' and a general repugnance for others' ways. But
'there is no need to dwell on this naïve attitude which is nevertheless
deeply rooted in most men' (1952: 11), except when it hinders the
appreciation of cultural diversity as exemplified by the abstract and
historicist cultural evolutionism.

But in spite of these disadvantages, Lévi-Strauss wishes to dwell on such ignorance just long enough to indicate some of its advantages. In the first place, this tendency being universal itself signals that in human ignorance at least, people are inseparable. The exclusion of 'savages' from humanity is 'precisely the attitude most strikingly characteristic of those same savages' (1952: 12).

> Humanity is confined to the borders of the tribe, the linguistic group . . . the village, so that many so-called primitive peoples describe themselves as 'the men' (. . . 'the good', 'the excellent', the 'well-achieved') thus implying that other tribes, groups or villages have no part in the human virtues or even in human nature, but that their members are at best 'bad', 'wicked', 'ground monkeys' or 'lousy eggs'.
>
> (Lévi-Strauss 1952: 12)

In this resounding prejudice, Lévi-Strauss discovers universality. But he also discovers in it an anti-imperialist attitude which helps some cultures remain distinctive, and as such, increases their contribution to the universal culture. He professes that this prejudice safeguards us all from the contemporary tendency to over-communicate, where we are threatened 'with the prospect of our being only consumers, able to consume anything from any point in the world and from every culture, but losing all originality'. However, for a culture to 'be really itself and to produce something, the culture and its members must be convinced of their originality' and even their superiority (1978: 20).

In sum, Lévi-Strauss's project is centrally sociological and against racism, especially in the ways it contradicts various historicist liberal assumptions of progress, evolution, science and rationality. In their place, he exalts cultural diversity and collaboration, in the belief that even ethnocentric attitudes, if so recognized, can play a positive role in achieving an international rational coalition. Thus, unlike so many other Marxists, Lévi-Strauss's critique of liberal categories is not just negative. In their place he proposes alternative universal categories, which do not just brush aside, but aim to include the intellectual contribution on non-Westerners. Thus, his political ideas also promise us a framework for analysing non-Western societies without racist assumptions.

LÉVI-STRAUSS'S CONTRIBUTION: EMPIRICAL UNIVERSALS

Lévi-Strauss contributes further to sociology by replacing Eurocentric and racist liberal universals with formal but substantive empirical ones. What remains characteristic of liberal thought is its identification of irreducible universals in the physical, human and societal natures. In all three, the universals are governed by (or at least should be governed by) identifiable and incontrovertible laws. The laws of nature are discovered via science to form the laws of physics; the laws of human nature are made possible by a philosophical discourse to culminate in an epistemology; and the laws of societal nature are elicited by political economy to climax into liberal/capitalist economics.

Lévi-Strauss rejects liberal formalism. But, while rejecting it, he is quite convinced that some new kind of universals *are* necessary, both in order to explain human communication with nature and with other humans, but also in order to reassert human equality. Liberals too have constructed their universals at least partly for that purpose. But as Marx has argued, and Lévi-Strauss concurs, their universals are abstract, and take no account of social inequalities. Universality depends entirely on their omniscient timelessness. Thus, for Lévi-Strauss, as it was for Marx and Durkheim, who have influenced him, nature, human nature and societal nature are empirical. And it was in an attempt to reconstruct these views that Lévi-Strauss developed new empirical notions of human nature by his discussion of the savage mind, culture and nature, communication, classification myths and totems. He did this in the belief that formal categories were necessary to ensure understanding.

Human nature and its characteristics

For Lévi-Strauss human nature is both biological and cultural. In both cases, it is empirical. It is from that perspective that his critique of liberalism takes a fairly familiar turn:

> the strength and the weakness of the great declarations of human rights has always been that, in proclaiming an ideal, they too often forget that man grows to man's estate surrounded, not by humanity in abstract, but by a traditional culture.
>
> (Lévi-Strauss 1952: 13)

But when this traditional culture proves indifferent to abstract notions of progress, many turn back to cultural evolutionism. Lévi-Strauss thought this was a mistake. For in spite of cultural differences, which are necessary for world civilization, 'the human mind is everywhere one and the same . . . has the same capacities' (1978: 19). He tries to avoid these errors, not by constructing yet more abstract universals, but on the one hand by grouping empirical manifestations of people's mental and institutional constructs of the social life, and on the other by generalizing from their biological make-up. From such a source, he hopes to identify real human nature from its historical and sociological attributes and not simply by constructing abstract and idealized notions of human nature.

As previously suggested, even if Lévi-Strauss is not impressed by liberal universals because they are abstract, racist, and have no relevance for practice, he is clear that some notion of human nature is crucial in order to avoid racist assumptions. He finds such a notion firstly in the idea of the 'savage mind'.

The Savage Mind

In the first place, the mind is a biological universal. For example, mathematical thought 'reflects the free functioning of the mind' where 'the activity of the cells of the cerebral cortex . . . [are] obeying only its own laws' (1966: 248, footnote). But the functions of the mind are not merely biological, they also have cognitive capacity. What is exceptional about this mind is the 'ends it assigns itself', to analyse, synthesize and mediate (1966: 219). This mind aids a 'reciprocity of perspectives' in which 'man and the world mirror each other', and enable us:

> to understand how it is that attentive, meticulous observations turned entirely on the concrete finds both its principle and its results in symbolism. Savage thought does not distinguish the moment of observation and that of interpretation any more than, on observing them, one first registers an interlocutor's signs and then tries to understand them: when he speaks, the signs expressed carry with them their meaning.
>
> (Lévi-Strauss 1966: 222–3)

The classificatory system is thus viewed as a 'system of meaning' (1966: 223).

The savage mind expresses 'the real principle of dialectical reason' in its 'intransigent refusal to allow human (or even living) to remain alien to it' (1966: 245). It functions to make nature available to us, to internalize the cosmos. 'It illustrates the structure of what lies outside the symbolic form' (1966: 245). But what is most characteristic of this mind is not only its cognitive capacity, but also its timeless quality to 'grasp the world as both a synchronic and a diachronic totality'. Thus, this mind shows its ability to tackle both history and structure. Lévi-Strauss's striving empiricalism appears to be transforming itself into a Kantian idealism. This mind is now said to work like a set of mirrors, placed opposite each other, reflecting a 'multiple of images' which form simultaneously, but 'none exactly like any other'. It is the *constellation of images* which has the property of 'expressing a truth'.'The savage mind deepens its knowledge with the help of *imagines mundi*. It builds mental structures which facilitate an understanding of the world in as much as they resemble it. In this sense savage thought can be defined as analogical thought' (1966: 263).

The significance of this idealistic intrusion into Lévi-Strauss's thought is that he wants to emphasize that people everywhere have the same mental capacities, the same biological make-up and similar cognitive abilities: they have the savage mind. Except, as Leach suggests, non-Western societies illustrate a '"reduced model" of what is essential in all mankind' (Leach 1974: 18). For in them, adds Lévi-Strauss, we discover 'those "facts of general functioning" . . . which stand a chance of being "more universal" and "more real"' (1967: 45–6).

This idealistic account of the mind is further confused when Lévi-Strauss discusses the relationship between culture and nature, between the savage mind and its classificatory capacity, the savage mind and the communicative capacity of the mind, and when he attempts to identify empirical universals. In this context it becomes obvious that as he envisages it, the savage mind is empirical in its symbolic signification.

Culture and nature

Lévi-Strauss outlines the characteristics of human nature in the ways that nature and culture countersign each other in a symbolic chiaroscuro (see Hawkes 1977: 38–9; Lévi-Strauss 1968: 50–1). While not wishing to reduce nature to culture, 'what we witness at the level of culture are phenomena of the same kind from a formal point of view' (1978: 10). And there lies the key to the symbolic relationship between culture and nature. As Leach observes, the point is 'to discover how relations which exist in Nature (and are apprehended as such by human brains) are used to generate cultural products which incorporate these same relations' (1974: 25). But the process also works the other way. Thus, Lévi-Strauss avoids both Kantian notions of mind construction of nature, but he also avoids crude materialist notions of the natural construction of human culture. Since brains are biologically the same all over the world, then, according to Leach, Lévi-Strauss suggests that when cultural products are generated:

> the process must impart to them certain universal (natural) characteristics of the brain itself. Thus, in investigating elementary structures of cultural phenomena, we are also making discoveries about the nature of man.
>
> (Lévi-Strauss 1974: 26)

Thus, for Lévi-Strauss both culture and biology in different but formally compatible ways, are universal in the symbolic characterization of humans of nature. He maintains this view without reducing one into the other, as so many commentators seem so keen to suggest.[4] Neither does Lévi-Strauss suggest that culture is natural, nor that nature is cultural, that is, no more than he suggests that music is language or the kinship system is music. But these levels are translatable into each other. But while he resists such reduction, he does make his case more ambiguous by introducing the Freudian notion of the unconscious (e.g. *Structural Anthropology: 1*: 22–5). But, as Leach rightly observes, since 'all cultures are the products of human brains', people must have common characteristics. Therefore, 'the universals of human culture exist only at the level of structure never at the manifest fact' (Leach 1974: 27). While such a notion creates difficulties for philosophers, for reasons discussed previously, it is reasonably comprehensible to sociologists: that is, if this is what Lévi-Strauss *is* saying. Thus, culture and nature have their own manifest independent existence. The point is they communicate. They are linked by the savage mind, to the advantage of human cognition. For, in the final analysis, both are *formally* universal and are therefore comparable.

The savage mind, classificatory capacity and taxonomic ordering:
aesthetics

For Lévi-Strauss a remarkable characteristic of human existence is
that human minds classify both the natural and human worlds. But
since 'the most basic postulate of science is that nature itself is
orderly', then when 'a native thinker makes the penetrating comment that "All sacred things must have their place" . . . their place
is what makes them sacred'. If we disrupt this systematic harmony
by removing sacred objects from their place, 'the entire order of
the universe would be destroyed' (1966: 10).

Consistently with Durkheim's ideas, he insists that classification
must be systematic. Science needs order, and order must meet two
conditions: it must be internally coherent, which though not obvious, must be 'revealed in the study of transformations, through
which similar properties in apparently different systems are
brought to light' (1967: 31). What is important about a system is
the way in which different 'yet connected planes' are 'foliated' (see
1967: 11–12). Furthermore, 'privileged instances' of social totality
are 'manifested in experience', through observation. He concludes that sacred objects 'contribute to maintenance of order in
the universe by occupying the places allocated to them' (1966: 10),
because detailed observation and systematic categorizing of
relations and connections can sometimes lead to scientifically valid
results.

Therefore, aesthetic ordering gives valid results, not because it
signals truth, but because it can 'open the way to taxonomy and
even anticipate some of its results'. To be sure, 'taxonomy, which
is ordering par excellence, has eminent aesthetic value' (Simpson
quoted in Lévi-Strauss 1966: 13). Then, in spite of the lack of a
causal link between 'sensible qualities and property' in taxonomy,
'any classification is superior to chaos':

> Not all poisonous juices are burning or bitter nor is everything
> which is burning and bitter poisonous. Nevertheless, nature is
> so constituted that it is more advantageous if thought and
> action proceed as though this aesthetically satisfying equiva-
> lence also corresponded to objective reality.
>
> (Lévi-Strauss 1966: 15–16)

For Lévi-Strauss what is crucial is that *some* classification should
exist, with the ability to '"focus" on planes, from the most abstract

to the most concrete, the most cultural to the most natural, without changing its intellectual instrument'(1966: 136). Unlike Hegel, he is not convinced that the method or the tool changes with usage. For Lévi-Strauss, as for Kant, knowledge acquisition needs a rational epistemology. Therefore, a system has a 'preconceived grid' which can be compared to cross metal blades used to cut potatoes. It orders reality with 'sufficient affinities for the elements obtained to preserve certain general properties' (1966: 149). Now Lévi-Strauss collects the fruits of his analysis:

> even the simplest techniques of any primitive society have hidden in them the character of a system, analysable in terms of a more general system. The manner in which some elements have been retained and others excluded permit us to conceive of the local system as a totality of significant choices, compatible or incompatible with other choices, which each society, or each period within its development, has been led to make.
>
> (Lévi-Strauss 1967: 19)

Furthermore, quite in keeping with Durkheim, in the same way as the system is a source of meaning, it also ensures personal identity and individuation: 'individuals are not only ranged in classes; their common membership of the class does not exclude but rather implies that each has a distinct position in it and there is homology between the system of individuals within the class and the system of classes within the superior categories' (1966: 172).

But, when humans classify reality in their 'heterogeneous and arbitrary classification', they also create a 'memory bank', by which to 'assail nature' using the 'science of the concrete'. A science which 'we prefer to call "prior" rather than "primitive"' (1966: 16) – i.e. 'bricolage'. He quotes Bergson with approval and adds that myths and rites are not falsely ideological, but that they preserve the methods of the science of the concrete. Mythical thought is the means by which the bricoleur, 'someone who works with his hands and uses devious means compared to those of a craftsman', reaches 'brilliant unforeseen results on the intellectual plane'. Unlike the engineer, the bricoleur is not limited by the scarcity of appropriate material. 'His universe of instruments is closed and the rules of his game are always to make do with "whatever is at hand"' (1966: 16–17).

Thus, for Lévi-Strauss 'non-scientific' forms of knowledge acquisition are not false attempts by which non-Westerners try to understand reality or a successful opiate to dupe themselves with or a rationale behind which they hide to protect themselves from a demanding reality. Rather, mythical thought is a parallel mode of acquiring knowledge of our own. If we take magic, for example, it is not a stage in the technical evolutions of science. It has 'a well articulated system, and is in this respect independent of existence'(1966: 13). They are parallel modes of knowledge acquisition. Thus, mythical classification, like aesthetic taxonomy, is not primitive, but perhaps 'prior' to science, 'mythical thought for its part is imprisoned in the events and experiences which it never tires of ordering and reordering in its search to find them meaning. But it also acts as liberator by its protest against the idea that anything can be meaningless with which science at first resigned itself to a compromise' (1966: 22).

Thus, the savage mind which constructs myths and invents totems, does so to classify nature, not in a way inferior to science, or with less logic than science, but in a fashion which is comparable and parallel to science, but desiring different ends. Lévi-Strauss does not share the positivist's view that myths and totems are rude efforts of prescientific communities, yet to learn the proper procedure for scientific enquiry, their efforts being merely the first stage to a longer learning process. Instead of which, he eloquently observes that 'the "bricoleur" may not ever complete his purpose but he always puts something of himself into it' (1966: 21). But what does 'prior' mean? Does it mean anything like what Comte meant by metaphysical? If not, in what sense is mythology prior to science? What consequence does it have on the relationship between science and belief that the bricoleur 'may not ever complete his purpose'? Most importantly, Lévi-Strauss does not adhere to a naïve correspondence theory which implies not only the possibility of corresponding laws of science and nature, but their necessity for knowledge to be possible.

In the end, Lévi-Strauss shows a profound ambiguity in his views about the relationship between science and mythology. In the first place he is determined to show that mythology is equally effective as science in the process of knowledge acquisition. At the same time, quite rightly, he is deeply haunted by his own profound respect for the technological consummation of contemporary society. It does not appear that Lévi-Strauss deals with that ambiguity to his own satisfaction. We shall return to this issue towards the end of the chapter.

The savage mind and the communicative capacity

If the savage mind depicts the central characteristic of human nature, making it possible for people to classify themselves, their social organization and nature, then communicative capacity is intrinsic to that mind. In his discussion, Lévi-Strauss seems to have at least three different notions of communication: idealist, biological and conventional. The idealist characteristic is instinctual and is illustrated in the way people use symbols and signs, 'which is a conversation of man with man, everything is symbol and sign, when it acts as intermediary between two subjects' (1967: 20). The system of signs, as shown by Mauss, connotes an 'unconscious system of communication . . . the implicit logic of the principle of reciprocity' (Badcock 1975: 49). Thus, for Lévi-Strauss, taxonomy is in fact more than mere description: it is a process of identifying, classifying analytically constituent parts, 'to establish correlations between them' (1967: 21). 'Classificatory systems belong to the levels of language: they are codes which, however well or badly made, aim always to make sense' (1966: 228). Since we do not have any special explanation for this communicative capacity, it must be intuitive mind construction, which is very reminiscent of Kant. But Lévi-Strauss also believes that our communicative capacity is complemented by our biological make-up (see below). And given his comments about cultural diversity and collaboration, Lévi-Strauss also clearly believes that conventional modes aid communication.

But, as we have previously seen, signs and symbols only have meaning in a system. The system has its own laws of involvement and exclusion. While it functions according to a formal logic, its main characteristic is its translatability into another system: 'analogous logical structures can be contrasted by means of different lexical resources' (1966: 53), in spite of great geographical and cultural distances of the people who are communicating. The symbolic terms in any system have significance only in terms of their structural, historical and cultural context (1966: 55). 'The operative value of the systems of naming and classifying called totemic derives from their formal character: they are codes suitable for conveying messages . . . received by means of different codes in terms of their own system' (1966: 75–6).

Therefore, classical ethnologists mistakenly reified this form and tied it to 'a determinate content when in fact what it provides is a method for assimilating any kind of content'. In fact, none of the systems have their own intrinsic value, separate from others:

> totemism . . . corresponds to certain modalities arbitrarily isolated from a formal system, the function of which is to guarantee the convertibility of ideas between different levels of social reality. As Durkheim seems sometimes to have realized, the basis of sociology is what may be called 'socio-logic'.
>
> (Lévi-Strauss 1966: 76)

Thus the mythical system establishes structural similarities between 'natural and social conditions . . . it makes it possible to equate significant contrasts found in different planes: the geographical, meteorological, zoological, botanical, technical, economic, social, ritual, religious and philosophical' (1966: 93). In other words, mythical systems operate to achieve communication not only between cultures, but at different levels within the same culture. In mythological systems, totemic system, like the kinship system, Lévi-Strauss takes the view that these systems are languages for making sense of the structural and historical elements of a culture, for the benefit of both outsiders and members of that culture. This ties in well with Lévi-Strauss's ideas about cultural diversity being both projective and protective. Badcock sums up that view thus: 'any "language" like totemism or caste must perform two social functions: it must integrate society and consolidate it, but it must also discriminate and subdivide it into the necessary sub-groupings which everyday life makes desirable' (1975:48). In short, living in a moving world is also communicating on manifold levels.

Whereby the communicative capacity of the mind now works to increase social integration and intercultural communication. Though ethnocentrism aids cultural diversity, as we saw it is also capable of increasing those communities' isolation. To think that, however, is to overlook that 'one of the essential functions of totemic classifications is to break down this closing in of the group into itself and to promote an idea something like that of humanity without frontiers' (1966: 166). But the totemic universalism:

> not only breaks down tribal frontiers and creates the rudiments of an international society. It also sometimes goes beyond the limits

of humanity in a biological, and no longer merely sociological, sense, when totemic names are applicable to totemic animals.

(Lévi-Strauss 1966: 167)

To summarize: Lévi-Strauss pursues his intended equality project in the theory of human nature, not by imposing European standards of comprehension on world civilization, but by attempting to understand other people from their comprehension of their own civilizations. Like his contemporary Cassirer, Lévi-Strauss wishes to develop a notion of symbolic universals, which are empirical in the sense that they derive their characteristics *from cultural production*; but, at the same time, are essential in the sense that the uniformities and analogies between different cultural products of our own and other societies signal a deeper representation of what is irreducibly human. To some extent, people's irreducibility is linked to their vital and biological characteristics. But, more importantly, it can be associated with the existence and the persistent functioning of a dexterous, mediating, synthesizing, communicating and problem-solving human mind. The mind, then, is a tireless and timeless agent for familiarizing us with and decoding for us physical nature and social life. What is most attractive about Lévi-Strauss's social epistemology is not just that it depends on the actual sociological raw material to construct it, but that he also does it using *international* sociological raw material.

The technique of universal communication: binary opposition

If Lévi-Straussian structuralism constitutes an ingenious way of bypassing sterile debates between rationalists and empiricists, then binary opposition provides an interesting technique of the mind for abolishing the polarity between particulars and universals. These oppositions function as a formal language at different levels of space and time. They exemplify a simple system, which 'proceeds by the aggregation, at each of the two poles, of new terms, chosen because they stand in relations of opposition, correlation, or analogy to it' (1966: 161). But these relations are not necessarily homologous. Hawkes clarifies the point thus: '"analogical thought" works by imposing on the world a series of structural "contrasts" or "oppositions" to which all the members of culture tacitly assent and then proposing that these oppositions are analogically related in that their differences are felt to resemble each other. As a result an analysis of the analogical relationship between the opposition of "up" and "down", "hot" and "cold", "raw" and "cooked" will offer insights into the nature of the particular "reality" that each culture perceives' (Hawkes 1977: 52).

Lévi-Strauss's example of the distinction between what is 'edible' and 'inedible' makes the point, as ways of distinguishing 'us' from 'them' – 'natives' from 'foreigners'. They become analogically related. Frogs' legs, for example, help distinguish and codify the relationship between the French and the British (Hawkes 1977: 52). For Lévi-Strauss, the symbolic representations provide an abstract formal language which makes similar 'systems of differences' (1964: 150); and, through binary opposition, link up various aspects of reality:

> This modelling of the appearance according to specific, elemental, or categorical schemes has psychological as well as physical consequences. A society which defines its segments in terms of high and low, sky and land, day and night, can incorporate social or moral attitudes, such as conciliation and aggression, peace and war, justice and policing, good and bad, order and disorder, etc., into the same structure of opposition. In consequence, it does not confine itself to abstract contemplation of a system of correspondence but rather furnishes the individual members of these segments with a pretext and sometimes even provocation to distinguish themselves by their behaviour.
>
> (Lévi-Strauss 1966: 170)

This is an extremely clever turn in his argument for in it he not only indicates how the formal structuration of our distinguishing mind functions to specify in us how to conduct ourselves socially and morally, but also bridges universal considerations with subjective ones. Thus, while each system has its own particular interests and rationale, its 'logic', it receives its meaning only in relation to other 'logics' (1966: 161). So, in spite of their differences, indeed, *because* of their differences, that communication takes place. The logic:

> is then definable by the number and nature of the axes employed, by the rules of transformation making it possible to pass from one to another, and finally by the relative inertia of the system.
>
> (Lévi-Strauss 1966: 162)

The advantage of this technique is that it is entirely formal and does not depend on any particular content for its operations: that makes it universal. By its trans-cultural, trans-historical status, according to Lévi-Strauss, it has the formidable task of linking through the myths, totems, kinship systems, different histories and spirits from different regions of the world. Thus, the operations of binary opposition are not bound by any particular race, cultural system or period. Their raw material is sociological, which finds meaning in their *placement*. These social and physical entities do not, then, need to link up to metaphysical ontologies. The logic of binary opposites makes communication possible between seemingly unrelated social and physical entities. It opens up the various logical systems and salvages them from a static functionalism. Then the various cultural products in each system become translatable, transferable and arbitrary sub-systems of meaning, which transcend their relativistic tendencies of their particularity. Particulars, then, by their placement, are able to communicate universally. 'Like phonemes, kinship terms are elements of meaning; like phonemes, they acquire meaning only if they are integrated into system' (1968: 34). Hawkes puts it this way:

> Each system, that is, kinship, food, political ideology, marriage ritual, cooking, etc., constitutes a *partial* expression of the total culture, conceived ultimately as a single gigantic *language*.
>
> (Hawkes 1977: 34)

For Lévi-Strauss, the identification of that language brings us nearer to 'unconscious attitudes of the society or societies' (1968: 81).

What Lévi-Strauss seems to suggest, then, is that the epistemological principles of opposition are aesthetic rather than correspondent. Meaning is achieved because of the sociological and psychological *ordering* of cultural products and does not accrue from their *nature*. Nature may resemble and thus further help identify the placing of these entities and sometimes may even provide the biological limits for it, but it does not constitute meaning (1966: 263). The mechanism by which this ordering is done is by binary opposition.

Cultural production and empirical universals

Thus, Lévi-Strauss's materialism is as crucial for understanding his racial equality project as it is central in constructing his structuralist system. It forms the starting point for his empirical or symbolic universals. Furthermore, this materialism is neither tainted with Hume's scepticism nor by rationalist accusations of relativism. He tries to avoid this polarity by his social epistemology:

> In spite of the fact there is no necessary connection between sensible qualities and properties, there is very often at least an empirical connection between them, and the generalization of this relation may be rewarding from the theoretical and practical point of view for a very long time even if it has no foundation in reason.
>
> (Lévi-Strauss 1966: 15)

Thus Lévi-Strauss, by his own admission, wants to end the false opposition introduced by, for example, Dilthey and Spengler, between physical and social sciences. He rejects the neo-Kantian polarization between explanation and understanding. The anthropologist brings 'to light an object which may be at the same time objectively very remote and subjectively very concrete'.

The process by which the 'bricoleur' works leads to the creation of empirical universals. For even though concrete daily concerns and historical memories suppress these human universals, including myths, totems, kinship systems, linguistic forms and incest taboos, they all give us the clue about the possibility of the stable forms beyond historical time. In the final analysis, they signal the way that the natural and social worlds are rationally classified. Thus both music and mythology are highly efficient 'machines for the suppression of time': they function trans-historically as entities whose non-discursive *forms* give information above and beyond any discursive *content*.

Indeed music (and perhaps myth) can perhaps be said to consist entirely of form. At the beginning of *The Scope of Anthropology*, Lévi-Strauss asks himself the following rhetorical question, to which he obviously means yes to be the answer:

> Is it not the character of myths . . . to evoke a suppressed past and to apply it, like a grid, upon the present in the hope of discovering a sense in which the two aspects of his own reality man is confronted with – the historic and the structural – coincide?
>
> (Lévi-Strauss 1967: 7)

Myth characterizes the 'primitive universal logic, in uncontaminated form', and reveals to us its message which can be read like an orchestra score (see Leach 1974: 56–60). The elders as people responsible for guarding and perpetuating religious and social institutions pass on this score down to the younger members (Leach 1974: 59–60). The score (myth) tells the whole story without being fragmented or losing meaning. And like linguistics it aims at what is under the surface, at the 'unconscious foundations' (Lévi-Strauss 1968: 18). Hawkes observes:

> Lévi-Strauss's concern is ultimately with the extent to which the structures of myths prove actually formative as well as reflective of men's minds: the degree to which they dissolve the distinction between nature and culture. And his aim . . . is not to show how men [sic] think in myths, but 'how myths think in men, unbeknown to them'.
>
> (Hawkes 1977: 41)

Much the same can be said about all Lévi-Strauss's empirical universals – symbolic universals.

SOME CRITICAL COMMENTS AND CONCLUSIONS

If it is true that Lévi-Strauss's project is egalitarian, then the most obvious underlying weakness of his analysis is the claim that the enlightened perception of universal categories will bring about the end of racism. But his impatient reply to the charge of political naïveté may indicate that he is aware of these criticisms, but does not find them threatening. Be it as it may, as stated in the introduction there are still other serious difficulties in his work.

Firstly, in spite of his full appreciation of historical and social context, the former remains intellectual because it does not structure his theoretical conception and the latter is of a secondary order because it only participates in analysis to provide illustrations for his symbolic universals. Thus, historical and sociological context is drained of its lifeblood to serve the construction of his elegant universals. In spite of his spirited critique of liberal philosophy, his attachment to formalism, in the end, smuggles back into his work important aspects of abstract philosophy.

How that happens is shown by our second criticism. In spite of his own rejection of naturalism, his notion of the 'unconscious' seems to have naturalistic and intuitionist connotations. As we have seen, naturalism is used both as the foundation and validation of liberal philosophy, in empiricism and rationalism.

Lévi-Strauss uses the unconscious in the same way. By his suggestion that the formal unconscious of the mind directs us to organize our sociological context (1968: 20–5) in a certain way, he comes close to Kantian idealism. But as we have claimed in our third objection, he also holds that although the social system has a 'logic', it is an empirical, sociocultural logic (1968: 51). In his polemic against Sartre, he suggests that his apparent opposition between formal (analytic) and historical (dialectic) realms 'is relative, not absolute'. It corresponds 'to a tension within human thought which may persist indefinitely *de facto* but which has no basis *de jure* . . . The term dialectical reason thus covers the perpetual efforts analytical reason must make to reform itself if it aspires to account for language, society and thought; and the distinction between the two forms of reason in my view rests only on the temporary gap separating analytical reason from the understanding of life' (1966: 246).

This would be true and within our terms legitimate, if the relationship between theory and history in Lévi-Strauss's thought was not itself, in the end, at least partially analytic and fixed. Whatever else he may claim, by finding justification for his empirical, demonstrable, substantive, symbolic universals in the unconscious workings of the mind, he renders history merely an *illustration* of the working of the mind. Sartre called him a transcendental materialist and an aesthete (see Lévi-Strauss 1966: 246), and that is what makes him contradictory. Sartre would wish him to give up both these characteristics and embrace phenomenological existentialism. In our view, that will only signal another form of metaphysics. Our argument is that he should give up the transcendental materialism of his social epistemology and remain an aesthete – that will dissolve the contradiction and sustain his sociologism. But by retaining a notion of the unconscious, Lévi-Strauss moves away from his aesthetic theory of science to a correspondent and idealist one. Like Kant, then, he recognizes a necessary and truthful relationship between the mind and the *noumena* – precisely what he set out to criticize in liberalism. By doing that, Lévi-Strauss undermines his own structuralist construction which shifts meaning away from abstract human nature to human relationships. Once again, he assumes that knowledge is founded on intuition and formal categories of the mind and is not due to historical experience. The mind, then, consistently suppresses time and context to achieve that index of rationality which is cross-cultural and trans-historical. Meaning accrued from cultural products once again appears to be an automaton of intuited individuals. Thus, because Lévi-Strauss's objection to liberalism is not against the notion of *a priori*, but against an *abstract* priority, this distinction does eventually seem to dissolve: transcendental materialism, in the end, metamorphoses into transcendental idealism.

Lévi-Strauss's ambiguities about the relationship between theory and history become most evident when he slips back into the cultural evolutionism he had set out to abolish. That happens when he gives three conflicting definitions of the relationships between myth and science. In the first place, he suggests that the two are unconnected forms of knowledge acquisition: the mythical form is intellectual and the scientific one is practical.[5] Science is efficient, purposeful and dull, while myths are brilliant, slapdash and responsive. Secondly, he insists that mythical thought is a 'prior' intellectual form, which clearly signalled the demand for practical, problem-solving scientific form. Then the brilliant 'bricoleur' or Heath Robinson gives way to an experimental scientist. This second view of the relationship accepts the positivist identification of science, on the move from the theological to the positive stage; it implies cultural evolutionism. Finally, he quite rightly observes that non-Western, non-industrial societies were in the past as they are now: no less scientific than ourselves. After all, techniques of pottery, cooking, etc., imply highly developed scientific knowledge. In short, Lévi-Strauss does not seem to be clear whether mythological thought is unconnected to science, or whether it is prior to science or is just the same as science. At the same time he wants to keep them separate, or connect them up in an evolutionary schema, either qualitatively in the case of the priority of myth, or conventionally by insisting they are the same.

Lévi-Strauss's theory of science is in conflict with his aesthetic social epistemology because of his formalism. The distinction between intellectual and practical intent does not solve this problem. He often claims that the difference is not in their 'logic' but in what they try to accomplish. But do they try to accomplish different things, or are they based on different theoretical assumptions? It would appear that myth as much as the sciences sets out to explain and control and relate to nature. This much we agree with Lévi-Strauss. What he does not seem to realize is that interpretation one and two imply a qualitatively different *interpretation* of myth and science from the third one. They imply that myth is aesthetic ordering and science is correspondent to nature.

Thus, in spite of his deliberate and ingenious attempt to avoid Eurocentric and racist assumptions, Lévi-Strauss's adherence to formalism delivers him back there. Had he not been concerned about certitude of knowledge, he would not have been at such pains to fight racism by redefining human nature so that it must appear that humans are anthropologically the same. That is a problem for a rational society, not for philosophy. For if people were not anthropologically equal, racism would still be morally indefensible; not because nature says so and science agrees, but because *we* say so. Rationality has little to do with validating metaphysics, but with human behaviour and the way we define it: and that is the work of sociology.

To conclude, we would argue that Lévi-Strauss is acutely aware of the dangers of allowing abstract theory to *construct* sociological analysis. But in spite of his valiant attempt to avoid this trajectory by adopting sociological formalism, he ends up re-admitting the logic of abstract liberal philosophy in his work, which recreates most of the difficulties he sets out to criticize. Had he not wished to ground his perfectly acceptable theory of symbolic universals in the unconscious, he would not have opened his whole theoretical system to a metaphysical ambiguity which suppresses time and context. Since we do not have reliable historical and sociological explanations for why people all over the world turn out comparable cultural products (in thought, technology and art, etc.), except in terms of cultural diversity and collaboration, rather than turn to metaphysics, we should draw a research programme to find out. It is true that metaphysical research programmes in the past have helped us to develop contemporary sociology, but the confusion between theory and history that we have pointed to is one good reason why that must now be avoided.

If Lévi-Strauss is drawn into using such a programme, Habermas is determined sociologically to reconstruct and defend it. We believe to no avail.

NOTES

1 With the emergence of 'post-structuralism', critical interest in Lévi-Strauss has waned somewhat over the last few years. For recent accounts see Tilley (1990) and Honneth (1990). In the context of the

present discussion, it is interesting to note that Honneth interprets Lévi-Strauss as a critic of modernity. In his view Lévi-Strauss's structuralist anthropology is grounded in a Romantic and humanist critique of modern society which contrasts its imbalances with the naturalism of primitive thought, and is motivated by the desire to use anthropology to redress this balance: 'Through its choice of theoretical means, ethnology must to some extent turn itself into that natural world-view the progressive destruction of which has led modern society into a state of painful turmoil. Therefore, not only that which ethnology examines, but also the methodological form in which that examination is conducted must be determined by a consistent solidary attention to the wider inter-connectedness of natural life' (Honneth 1990: 100).

2 See, for example, Edmund Leach's surprising comment about Lévi-Strauss's disagreement with Sartre on the nature of Marxism (1974: 14–15); or Roger Poole's introduction to *Totemism* (1964: 10 and 12); or C.R. Badcock (1975: 14–19).

3 Mythological universalism appears to be at least partially conventional.

4 For examples of this interpretation, see Leach (1974: 37, 52 and 112–14); or Badcock (1975: 35–7 and 51–2).

5 Lévi-Strauss does not use this term to mean 'moral' in the sense of German idealism; he simply means 'technological'.

Chapter 4

Jürgen Habermas

Universal categories and the primacy of the Occident

What Habermas has in mind is the following idea: the *ideal society* would be that in which everything proceeded with the same rationality which is founded in unrestricted rational science . . . My doubts are . . . whether the ideal rational practice, without any regard to the possibility or impossibility of realizing it, is as rational as it appears.

(Bubner 1981: 127–8)

The theorist has to be aware that in constructing a world he or she expresses his or her own needs and interests; the desire to universalise them does not allow them to be imputed on others.

(Heller 1982: 32)

INTRODUCTION

In a throw-away remark, Habermas laments that the theory of language and action has still not found its Kant (1979: 23); someone who can complete the process by which the foundation of rationality moves from philosophy to the linguistic community. He clearly sees his work as contributing to this transformation. His project is a classical one: he wants to transform critical theory into a theory of the civilizing process in which freedom is ensured. To achieve this he constructs a social epistemology in the form of a theory of communicative action which rejects at one and the same time liberal abstraction *and* sociological reductionism. The universality of his 'reconstruction' of the human language community is intended to eliminate dogma and parochialism without sacrificing a correct representation of actually existing groups, cultures and individuals.

And yet, for all Habermas's technical success, his theory of communicative action remains highly ambiguous. His odyssey through theories of science, linguistics and rationality, as well as his scholarship in analytic philosophy, epistemology and hermeneutics, fails to resolve the ambiguities in his notions of *freedom*, *theory* and *capitalism*. He is ambiguous in his notion of 'theory' because, though opposed to abstract liberal universality, his universal-pragmatic categories have the same function. Instead of rejecting abstract universality, therefore, he corrects it by juxtaposing a sociological interest in it. But the consequence of this juxtaposition is that this theory which is meant for everyone, in the end represents no real concerns and applies to nobody in particular.

His theory of freedom reveals similar difficulties. It is said to be dependent on satisfying universal needs, but only as they are defined by Western rationalism. At times he implies that one or all three of his cognitive interests are either absent or can be found only in a reduced form in 'traditional societies'. Thus, though he makes much of autonomy and responsibility in his analysis, he tends to identify as 'irrational' most positions which are at variance with his position, including Western ones. We are not sure, then, what is the source and the status of his interest in emancipation; whether it is anthropological, capitalist, utopian, or merely Habermasian.

Finally, he is also ambiguous about the nature of capitalism. For while he recognizes an intimate link between capitalist exploitation and technocratic ideology, he chides Marcuse for presenting technology and its ideology historically. Having insisted that there is a link between technocratic ideology and capitalism, then, Habermas also suggests that it is motivated by purposive-rational action: we are then not sure whether capitalism is an historical or an anthropological development.

We believe the source of his ambiguities lies in his juxtaposition of a rationalistic perspective with a sociological orientation. He synthesizes conflicting 'world views' in the hope of constructing a social epistemology. But this sociological formalism betrays a partial commitment to liberal formalism. Thus, his formalistic reconstructive voyage around Western ideas not only signals analytical difficulties, but it also raises moral questions about the wisdom of reintroducing many of the racist assumptions of nineteenth-century thinkers into sociology.

Contrary to his intentions, by grounding knowledge and action in language-theoretics, Habermas drives a wedge between analysis and history. Truth, consensus, morality, interest, emancipation and production, etc., are no longer entirely due to historical sensual activities of subjects, but are the requirement of language-compulsive rationality. His linguistic formalism is also morally indefensible, because it outlines the limits of rationality and civilization in terms relative to the history of Western philosophy.

Habermas intends to accomplish three related tasks: theoretical, political, and utopian. *First,* he wants to fuse previously contradictory philosophies into a systematic sociology by reconstructing 'species competence' into deep structural rules for generating 'meaningful symbolic configurations' (McCarthy 1982: 60).[1] Even if such a reconstruction initially polarizes theory and practice, it would also break the instrumental link between enlightenment and action. In breaking this link we shall, he believes, also expose the discrepancy between the *actual* and the *ideal* bourgeois conceptions of reality, through the process of a self-reflective science. The distortions result when the technological mastery of nature takes precedence over and dominates moral and political concerns. *Secondly,* Habermas politically sets out to advertise, criticize and overcome technocratic anti-humanist tendencies in contemporary societies. *Thirdly,* his rational reconstruction has a utopian end of stimulating the starting point for the process of human emancipation from oppressive ideologies and social structures.

Thus, theoretically, politically and counterfactually, Habermas, no less than Plato, Kant, or Lévi-Strauss, means to construct a method of reaching understanding upon which he can build a stable, rational and technically purposeful, free, moral society. As a Marxist sociologist he nevertheless tries to avoid liberal fundamentalism. However, unlike Lévi-Strauss who makes the understanding and incorporation of other cultures the starting point of his anti-racist social epistemology, Habermas treats other societies as mere idealized records of earlier stages of social evolution. *Human* freedom is thought to be aided by the reconstruction of *Western* beliefs.

Next we shall discuss Habermas's objection to abstract liberal philosophy and bourgeois technocratic politics, in order to indicate his theoretical and political adjustments and his sociological and Marxist orientation. There follows an attempt to point out his ambiguities in both his conception of emancipation and of capitalist relations. Finally, we give a detailed account of the nature of his theory of communicative action and show that the ambiguities at the heart of the project have moral and analytical implications.

THE CRITIQUE OF TECHNOCRATIC RATIONALITY IN LATE CAPITALISM

Habermas is clearly conducting a sociological critique of liberal capitalism, because: (i) he objects to abstraction and idealism; (ii) he objects to the imperialism of technocratic ideology which seeks to abolish the ethics of the good life; and (iii) he argues for the historical and contextual rootedness of knowledge.

Critique of philosophical liberalism

Like Marx, Habermas criticizes liberal capitalism by attacking the pivotal characteristics of its epistemology: namely, abstraction, ahistorical theory and individualism.

Habermas counters modern abstract thought by comparing it to the classical view of Aristotle and by criticizing formalism. In the classical period, Habermas finds that politics was: (i) conceived as the 'doctrine of the good and just life' which is a 'continuation of ethics' and part of custom and law (1974: 42); (ii) a process of learning to cultivate character; (iii) a 'contingent praxis' grounded in a necessary logic: it constitutes a prudent understanding of the social environment and not a universal knowledge.

In contrast, modern politics is Hobbesian. Science provides the correct universal standards and general rules for institutional relationships, regardless of 'place, time, and circumstances'. The final manifestation is in social engineering where ethical and technical questions are 'positivistically bisected'. Science distances itself from humanistic culture, disregarding the insights of German idealism, which portrays theory not only as a technique, but as a practical/moral force (1971a: 65).

Turning his attention to liberalism, Habermas objects to the tendency to identify universal 'world views', with respect to nature, history and society. These ahistorical views have already been theoretically and empirically discredited (1984: 1). Scientific analysis cannot provide a model for social life; atomic physics cannot interpret the lifeworld. Knowledge cannot be abstract in the scientific or philosophical sense. Theory encompasses a dual relationship between theory and practice. It is a social praxis, 'which as societal synthesis, makes insight possible'. It is also a political praxis, 'which consciously aims at overthrowing the existing system of institutions' (1974: 2). Critical theory is different from science because it is conscious of its history and is not objectivistic. But it is also unlike philosophy which is 'too conscious of its origins as something that had ontological primacy'. Abstract rules for conducting the good life, then, are non-reflective and only undermine human will and freedom.

Habermas continues his critique of philosophy and liberal capitalism by showing that knowledge is historically rooted and interest bound. To do this, he refutes Kantian transcendental subjectivism, rejects instrumentalism and insists on consensus and reflection as presuppositions of knowing. Rejecting the traditions of the 'philosophy of consciousness', he agrees with Marx that knowledge is the product of people solving their historical problems (Held 1980: 255). As Bernstein observes, 'theory can never be used directly to justify political action' (1979: 216). To assume that theory 'can provide an absolute authority in deciding what is to be done' mutilates both theory and praxis (Bernstein 1979: 216).

Theory cannot be a mere organon, for that would imply that no reflection is necessary for political action but only the execution of past procedures. Judgement would then remain entirely technical and lose its moral and political basis. In rejecting a mechanical notion of the application of ahistorical theory to practice, Habermas is aware that theory 'cannot have the same function for the organization of action of the political struggle, as it has for the organization of enlightenment' (1974: 39). Theory helps enlightenment and the reconstruction of distorted notions: it helps reclaim the night from the 'nightmares' that Marx was so eloquent about. It gives insights 'into causalities of the past'. Theory is retrospective; it aims to make obvious and liberate us from the 'historical compulsions of the past'. Thus, though this theoretical liberation cannot solve the problem of action, its astute interpretation and its ability to increase self-knowledge contribute a material force.

But apart from increasing enlightenment it increases consensus among those involved in strategic action. Theory cannot guarantee from the outset 'a world-historical mission in return for the practical sacrifices' (Habermas 1974: 33).

As a child of the Enlightenment Habermas, like Marx, wants to link self-knowledge to social knowledge and intimate a symmetry between enlightenment and progress. But at the same time, he rejects the Enlightenment fundamentalism which insists on subjectivism, instrumentalism and scientific, economic, political/ moral formalism. These are in fact describing the historical truth of liberal capitalism and are not laying down the fundamental rules for human action. According to Habermas, Marxists too have this ahistorical tendency. For when they reduce political action to technical control, they are not just 'vulgar' and positivistic, they become 'bourgeois' engineers who want:

> a theory or science so secure and well grounded that it provides, once and for all, authoritative decision procedures for what is to be done . . . They fail to grasp that this makes science itself into ideology.
>
> (Bernstein 1979: 217–18)

Habermas's critics, like Bubner and Heller, have accused him of doing just that himself.

Habermas's theory of communicative rationality aims to counter philosophical subjectivism. He objects to liberal individualism at a number of levels. First, he objects to Kant's notion of transcendental ego because it exists outside historical experience and is isolated from other consciousnesses – i.e. it is 'monological'. Secondly, individualism is incapable of explaining a communicative competence. Thirdly, because the scientific practice is communal and the structure of its knowledge is consensual, subjectivism is incapable of showing how science is possible. 'Through its structure, autonomy and responsibility are posited for us. Our first sentence expresses unequivocally the intention of universal and unconstrained consensus' (Habermas quoted in Held 1980: 247).

The workings of language assert sociality and deny subjectivism. Communicative competence implies *a priori* intersubjectivity and consensus. Communication makes science possible and valid. Language makes us communal and distinguishes us from animals. It extends knowledge and action from the limits of instrumental reason, because it 'arises from symbolic interaction between societal subjects who reciprocally know and recognize each other as unmistakable individuals' (Habermas quoted in Held 1980: 303).[2]

Thus Habermas objects to liberal abstraction, ahistorical theory and individualism. He conceives theory historically, individuals sociologically and science communally. He therefore reasserts the sociological and historical rootedness of human life, knowledge and interest, and refuses to accept the philosophical view put forward by liberals and capitalists.

The critique of technocratic politics

Habermas objects to liberalism because it encourages instrumental rationality. The latter, he thinks, is an inadequate route by which to satisfy human interests. While purposive-rational action is able to fulfil a technical interest, it cannot satisfy: indeed, in excess it often suppresses communicative and emancipatory ones. As it tightens its grip on our affairs, it also progressively abolishes our critical will. Then, 'science, technology, industry and administration interlock in a circular process' (Habermas 1974: 254), where the relationship of theory to practice 'only asserts itself as purposive-rational application of techniques assured by empirical science' (1974: 255). The scientific potential is reduced to a technical control; enlightenment gives way to instruction. In technocratic ideology Habermas not only perceives a greater danger than bourgeois class-domination, but in its transcendence he also detects a greater freedom than the one from capitalist oppression.

Habermas objects to the predominance of instrumental reason on philosophical and political grounds. On philosophical grounds, as we have seen, he believes it plays down moral and political judgement in science and social life. Politically, he thinks it depoliticizes the masses and encourages the 'decline of the public realm as a political institution' (1971a: 75). Technological rationality, then, permeates the whole of society, and technology appears as an autonomous value system which usurps 'the domain of praxis' (1974: 270), because a 'theory which confuses control with action is no longer capable of such perspective' (1974: 255). Scientific techniques, now rational *and* moral, are employed to realize specific ends. Choices are thereby made in accordance with the efficiency criteria and the 'rationality' of the decision-making process, and not in order to satisfy objective needs (1974: 270–1).

Political agreements are not reached through enlightened discussion, they are achieved via compromise (1974: 271). The stability and adaptability of these quasi-biological systems dictate the system's requirements in reproducing life. Decision-making is reduced to ideological domination (1974: 273–4). Habermas who is not threatened by the *existence* of, but only the domination of a technocratic ideology, prefers only to bind it and limit it within a system which also includes other forms of explanations. His difficulties are less acute than Marcuse's or Nietzsche's, for example, who question the self-presentation, the intention and the integrity of science and technology. Habermas resolves his problems merely by adding the tonic of communicative and emancipatory interests, which he hopes will make science reflective. Though his perspective on technology is non-reductive, he thus leaves its ideology untouched by the romantic critique of science. Similarly, though his position avoids instrumentalism, and purports to avoid naturalistic historicism, by confining instrumental reason to nature and by insisting that nature can only be acted upon by that reason, Habermas does eventually link progress to science and technology. This tendency is strongest when he discusses the rationality of other cultures.

The cognitive interests distance his critique of positivism from the romantic critique of science where science itself, and not merely its illegitimate extension into the lifeworld, is thought to threaten individuality and autonomy. But, while exposing its conservatism, Habermas fails to see any merit in the romantic critique of science. The positivist account of *natural* science therefore goes unchallenged. For Habermas, as his critique of Marcuse demonstrates (see 1971a, ch.6), technologically it is understood in anthropological terms, i.e. it is viewed ahistorically.

He is convinced that this technocratic ideology is evident in Marx's work. The Marx who sociologizes Hegel's theory of history and historicizes political economy, according to Habermas, also reduces his historical project to one of labouring. He reduces 'reflection to the level of instrumental action. By reducing the self-positing of the absolute ego to the more tangible productive activity of the species' he removes the 'motive force of history' (Habermas 1971b: 44).

Nor are the fomal freedoms of liberal capitalist society sufficient to defend the lifeworld against 'inner colonialization' by technocratic rationality. For Habermas, the mere existech of a generalized 'free' mass media does not guarantee democracy. That view assumes that the bourgeoisie is the 'reasoning public' and represents the general interest. Convinced they know what people want, members of the bourgeoisie 'sought to change society into a sphere of private autonomy free of political interference, and to transform the state into an authority restricted to a limited number of functions' supervised by themselves and guided by the constitution (Held 1980: 261).

But the constitutional rights of free speech and freedom of action remain abstract. Journalists are motivated by the cash nexus and exemplify a general lack of conviction. With the aid of instrumental reason, the state and monopoly capitalism can enhance the process of depoliticization. The commercialization of the media works to exclude political and moral issues from discussion. General needs are mediated through state corporatism, where 'large organizations strive for a kind of political compromise with the state and with one another, excluding the public whenever possible'. The public is involved only to give plebiscitary support, which destroys the original notion of public opinion. Public opinion is created through 'publicity', 'public relations work' and replaces 'discursive will formation' (Held 1980: 262). The state then regulates, and hopes to abolish, class conflict from the political process. Instead of the mass media using the technical potential to aid the popular will, it uses it to control people. Politics becomes administration (Habermas 1974: 4–5), where the society has 'immunized' itself from the public will through the mass media.

Habermas objects to technocratic politics because it is undemocratic. Instrumentalism replaces decisions about ends. Instead of informing the democratic process here, the mass media manipulates the public will. Both processes aid capitalist exploitation.

Habermas's historicity

For Habermas the critique of positivism and instrumental reason is only the first phase of his reconstruction of historical materialism. In this phase, by fusing Marx's sociological notion of humans constituting themselves to the Frankfurt School criticism of positivism, he hopes to recover that aspect of knowledge which he believes positivism had 'effaced' and allow knowing subjects 'an active role in constituting the world they know' (Held 1980: 300). For him, historical materialism gives a comprehensive explanation of social evolution while it accounts for the theory's own origins and application (Habermas 1974: 1). Since liberal social philosophy assumes a monological contemplative stance, it is incapable of relating to praxis and remains instrumentalist. Historical materialism, he insists, has a practical intent, which avoiding the weaknesses of traditional politics and modern social philosophy 'unites the claim to scientific character with a theoretical structure referring to praxis' (1974: 3). In *Knowledge and Human Interest,* Habermas grounds knowledge in history and epistemology, and converts the latter to a social theory.

So while the first phase of his argument constitutes a critique of liberal abstraction and instrumental reason informed by a Marxist sociology, the second phase reintroduces a Kantian epistemology to 'rescue' sociology from relativism. The need for such a rescue is, for him, made obvious by Marcuse's and Marx's desire to historicize technology. But as well as such relativism, Marxists are also often reductionist.

EMANCIPATION IN CAPITALIST SOCIETY OR FROM CAPITALIST RELATIONS

An epistemological stance which has been converted to a social theory will recover the reflective orientation sufficiently to avoid both relativism and reductionism. Habermas starts this recovery by reconstructing liberal epistemology and sociology. Like Lévi-Strauss, believing that representations 'are never independent of standards', he constructs symbolic universals which are both logical and empirical (1971b: 197–8). However, this puts his systematic sociology in an empty void, somewhere *between* theory and history. It is doubtful that in this ambiguous placing between Kant and sociology, he succeeds in fusing deep structures to empirical acts. His ambiguities are most obvious when considering his views of *emancipation* and *technology.*

In the first place, Habermas fails convincingly and theoretically to combine anthropological to historical compulsions, and seems to be unsure exactly which one of the two motivates freedom. He seems equally unsure about technology. In both cases, he is unclear about whether freedom is possible under capitalism, or whether we have to wait for it until capitalism is transcended.

If the source of our freedom and social production is anthropological – due to emancipatory and purposive-rational interests – then there is no reason to envisage only the possibility of freedom after capitalist transcendence, which he does. On the other hand, if emancipatory and instrumental interests are historically created, there is every reason to believe that freedom and technical progress is possible only after capitalism is transcended. Habermas refuses the invitation to choose between the two or to clarify their relationship.

Put differently, Habermas's freedom is not due to intuition, existential ontology or violence. It results from a rational, free communication that serves as a precondition for science, knowledge and social life. What is now unclear, then, is whether it results from an inherent logic of communication, or is it, as some Marxists say, due to the reaction against the tyranny of social and historical conditioning? He insists that interest in emancipation is neither *a priori*, in Kant's sense of transcendental logic, nor naturalistic and empirical (Habermas 1971b: 196). What we still need to know, however, is how he resolves the conflict of this juxtaposition. For if he conceives the source of freedom to be sociological, à la Marx – which he partially does – that makes action immanent not to cognitive interests or universal pragmatics, but to each community, nation, society, working class or race, etc. If, alternatively, he demands that freedom is made possible by our universal/anthropological interests, which he also partially does, then he is delivering his framework to liberal fundamentalism, with the possibility (as he very well knows) of making its findings irrelevant to other societies. But instead of clarifying these difficulties, his commitment to some kind of fusion between the two leads him to notions such as quasi-transcendental and universal pragmatics (we shall return to this later).

But it is difficult to understand Habermas's concept of quasi-transcendentalism. In Kant, transcendental logic structures knowledge through the mind. Experience is the necessary data for the workings of the mind. In sociology, knowledge results from the interaction between individuals/groups with each other and with the social institutions they have created. It is construed by their understanding *and* misunderstandings of these present and past relationships. Habermas seeks to reside somewhere between the two, but where? Similar difficulties appear in his notion of technology. Let us examine these issues in greater detail.

Quasi-transcendental interest in emancipation

Ottmann (1982) presents Habermas's notion of interest in Kantian terms of 'invariant' and 'objective' and constitutive of 'the object

domain of possible experience'. But Habermas actually follows
Fichte in linking and perhaps even in subsuming theoretical
reason to practical reason. Without dissociating itself from science
as a process of self-reflection, the interest in emancipation over-
rides the former. Identity and will of reason arise when reflection
articulates itself in experience; then, to reflect is to pursue emancipation. But reason is also 'subject to the interest in reason' and
aims at the pursuit of reflection: 'the category of the cognitive
interest is authenticated only by the interest innate in reason'
(Habermas 1971b: 198).

The confusion is particularly accute when he characterizes
these interests as neither empirical nor transcendental, factual nor
symbolic, motivational nor cognitive. 'For knowledge is neither a
mere instrument of an organism's adaptation to a changing environment nor the act of a pure rational being removed from the
context of life in contemplation.' He adds to our confusion by
insisting that interest 'aims at existence, because it expresses a
relation of the object of interest to our faculty of desire. Either the
interest presupposes a need or it produces one.' Furthermore:

> Our interest in obeying moral laws is produced by reason and is
> yet a contingent fact that cannot be comprehended *a priori*. To
> this extent, an interest based on reason also implies the thought
> of something that determines reason.
>
> (Habermas 1971b: 201)

and:

> The *basis of reason* is attested by the interests of reason, but it
> eludes human knowledge, which, to attain it, would have to be
> not either empirical or pure but both at once.
>
> (Habermas 1971b: 202)

Habermas links thought to freedom, because logic presupposes
emancipation, autonomy and responsibility. Reason, then, compels truthfulness in knowledge. As Bubner suggests, interest in
emancipation for Habermas implies that 'knowledge does not
serve as an interest different from itself'. But, by not following
Marx in linking freedom to class struggles, his solution sometimes
confuses 'is' with 'ought'. Rational choice, then, replaces practice
'so that practice and rationality become the same thing' (Bubner
1981: 128). Bubner adds:

It would be a fallacy to think that what ideally *ought* to be, simply on the grounds that it is constantly taken for granted as a starting-point, is what in some way or other *exists*.

(Bubner 1981: 200)

and:

unity between theory and practice suffers . . . from the fact that a theoretical method has been vaguely extended beyond the limits of theory.

(Bubner 1981: 202)

While Marx links natural consciousness of everyday life and its subsequent oppression and alienation to the search for emancipation, Habermas counterpoises natural consciousness to emancipation. Freedom is then not due to the pressure of everyday life: it is the result of a 'counterfactual' rational utopia. For Habermas, it is not social tyranny which brings about its transcendence, but the transcendence of natural consciousness by rational thought which leads to emancipation. But unless utopias arise from the demand for natural rights, as expressed in natural consciousness, they will evaporate into fantasies.

Bubner cannot see how a systematic separation of ideal and actuality can be mediated in the way that Habermas suggests. He observes:

Since, however, the ideal condition of society, like the Kantian 'Kingdom of Ends', is not of this world, indeed, since it is defined through negation of reality in general, even the dialogue as a model of social communication under conditions of pure reason remains a *utopian* postulate, which continues in permanent opposition to the actual forms in which human beings deal with each other.

(Bubner 1981: 187)

For Habermas, as for the Young Hegelians, criticism replaces political action.

Agnes Heller makes a similar point in a different way. When reason takes over from natural consciousness, 'the lack of the sensuous experience of hope and despair, of venture and humiliation . . . the creature-like aspects of human beings are missing' from his theory. The Habermasian person has 'no body, no feelings'; the 'structure of personality' is identified with cognition, language and interaction'. The good life, in spite of his Aristotelianism, amounts to rational communication, and the 'needs can be argued without being felt' (Heller 1982: 21–2).

Emancipation, then, has no subject, and the proletariat is replaced by practical reason. Class struggle is substituted for by 'rational argumentation', and emancipation is not explained in terms of social needs, but 'by the transcendental theoreticism' (Heller 1982: 26–8). As rational beings, rational choices are not a value: 'if we choose at all, we cannot choose anything but rationality'.

By arguing for the idealized freedom to defeat capitalism, Habermas's analysis lacks the precision of a political programme and remains intellectual and abstract. By severing the symmetry between natural consciousness and natural rights – which does not imply instrumentalism – he introduces damaging rationalistic standards from outside the social equation. The Fichtian preference for practical over theoretical reason without a political programme renders this ethical dominance purely formal, and carries no real value in social struggles. Finally, history and theory being interwoven, the interest of reason expresses itself in history from which it finds its substance. But unless Habermas is presenting a conventional view of theory, he is either reproducing Kant's idealism or is being poetic. If theory is poetic, its significance is not certain and universal, but exultant, creative and stimulating. Poetry has no substance, just meaning; its analysis is not scientific, but evocative. Evocations are powerful, but they cannot be represented as rational and incontestable grounds for truth and freedom. Thus, Habermas's juxtaposition, rather than fuse 'is' to 'ought', confuses them. He confuses normative claims for freedom, which are the product of social oppression expressed in natural consciousness, with an abstract theorem. He has consistently resisted probes[3] to explicate a necessary political counterpart for achieving such freedom, and which would close the gap between utopian and social life. His notion of emancipation, like Lévi-Strauss's anti-racism, remains intellectual in spite of efforts to construct a social epistemology which presupposes a lifeworld.

Dehistoricizing purposive-rational interest

Habermas objects to abstraction almost as much as he opposes technocratic ideology. It is therefore curious that in his debate with Marcuse and Marx, he should appear to defend a view which dehistoricizes technology. Thus, Marcuse's criticism of Weber's pessimism about humanistic science and technology may serve just as well against Habermas.

Marcuse tries to show that in Weber's work, there is an historical link between 'capitalism, rationality and domination'; a similar link is evident in Habermas. The Western idea of reason, writes Marcuse:

> realizes itself in a system of material and intellectual culture (economy, technology, 'conduct of life' science, art) that develops to the full in industrial capitalism, and that this system tends towards a specific type of domination which becomes the fate of the contemporary period: total bureaucracy.
>
> (Marcuse 1968: 203)

The full weight of Marx's criticism of liberal fundamentalism and Husserl's humanist critique of science can be felt in this statement. Marcuse sustains an historical sense of Western culture, while he objects to Weber's historicist idea of the self-motivating, amoral, domineering bureaucracy. In fact, capitalist rationality is irrational, even in its own terms. Asceticism becomes a fetter and a danger to the affluent society. 'In the unfolding of capitalist rationality, *irrationality* becomes reason', tied to the bourgeois technical reason. Thus capitalism, imperialism, industrialism and technical reason are historically linked.

Habermas responds both to this scientific humanism and the attempt to historicize technology with some irritation. He accuses Marx and Marcuse of confusing labour with interaction and purposive-rational with communicative interest. Technology can only be a human project '*as a whole*, and not one that could be historically surpassed'. The notion of New Science is an impossible 'sobering consideration'.

Habermas thus subscribes to the view that past and foreign contributions in technology ascend an incremental scale towards modern Western technology. Technology logically corresponds to purposive-rational action 'regulated by its own results, which is in fact the structure of work'. Being dependent on social labour for our self-preservation, it is impossible to envisage how 'we could renounce technology, more particularly *our* technology, in favour of a qualitatively different one' (Habermas 1971a: 87).

He thus not only insists that causality in nature is instrumental, but also seems to misunderstand Marx's and Marcuse's objections. Rather than renounce anybody's technology, they condemn an historicist conception of it, which tolerates class ideology. They are extending their ideology critique from economics and politics to science. Habermas makes these criticisms at all, because he reduces Marx's production to work, and Marcuse's humanization of science to fantasy.

Habermas rightly identifies a strong romantic theme in Marcuse's notion of interaction between humans and nature, which wrongly allows the latter a subjective status. Habermas is correct to oppose the romantic rhetoric which substitutes technological progress 'by an awakened nature'. Particularly, for Habermas, to present nature as a partner in and not an object of human action, implies that this relationship is symbolic interaction and not purposive rational action (1971a: 88). Nevertheless, by retaining a Weber category of purposive rationality, Habermas, though he would like to add ethics and self-reflection to science, cannot. A self-reflective science cannot have limits set by instrumental reason: it must determine its own limits in accordance with the demands of its project.

Habermas's difficulties arise because he separates the means of production and its technical rules from the social relations of production. By analytically polarizing labour and interaction, he creates a theoretical dichotomy twice over. He separates the capacity to produce from the human need to interact; and then he abolishes interaction altogether from the process of production. The interactive domain is in communication, which is unconnected with production.

Habermas, who objects to philosophical formalism, scientism and rationalism, easily succumbs to their lure by following the logic of his own sociological formalism. His eclectic reconstruction of a social epistemology juxtaposes Marx's historical materialism with Kantian formalism, which Marx had deliberately cast off.

As happens with Lévi-Strauss, then, Habermas's *political* intention to give a sociologically valid and philosophically grounded account of contemporary society, in order to achieve freedom, is subverted by methodological rationalism. The rationalistic standards he imposes on social context and history appear to lay down the rules for their conduct. Human action and sociology is de-radicalized and strangulated by formal rules. In the end, even his ethical formalism fails to insulate him from the accusation of using theory instrumentally, as an organon, and not as an aid to research. His counterfactual theory of communicative action appears abstract, without a political programme. The abstract nature of that project becomes most explicit when he presents science and technology as *enabling* entities of cultural formation and not as aspects of social production. Since when acting on nature purposive-rational organizes its function to the exclusion of communicative and emancipatory interests, its rules are beyond human intervention. Scientific and technological concepts become historicist, with an internal, autonomous logic, which determinately directs social production.

Thus, by placing theory somewhere between transcendental philosophy and sociology, and by wishing to transcend natural consciousness, Habermas renders theory abstract and ambiguous. He also makes the object of his theory – achieve emancipation – and the method of achieving it (science) ambiguous and abstract too. In an uncommonly frank statement, Habermas ruefully admits:

> The deeper I penetrated into the theories of action, meaning, speech acts, and other similar domains of analytic philosophy, the more I lost sight in the details of the aim of the whole endeavour. The more I sought to satisfy the explicative claims of the philosopher, the further I moved from the interests of the sociologist who has to ask what purpose such conceptual analysis should serve.
>
> (Habermas 1984: xxxix)

Regrettably, his sociological corrective does not resolve the ambiguities of his juxtaposition of sociology and philosophy.

COMMUNICATIVE ACTION AND THE ROAD TO FREEDOM

The theory of communicative action is meant to identify the features of communication which are unfolded in the process of social evolution, and which are thus universal and rational. The theory of communicative action not only depicts the *process* of rationalization, it also lays down the *rules* for civilization. As such, it constitutes the third phase of Habermas's reconstruction of historical materialism. As we saw, the first phase sociologized abstract thought, while the second made sociological thought rational. In this phase, Habermas attempts to construct a viable universal pragmatics which would avoid abstraction, relativism and reductionism.

For him, rationalization implies more than modernity. It is construed on the basis of legitimate, just, consensual, free and rational progression. To achieve freedom, therefore, is to enter the process of rationalization as specified by his theory of communicative action. In that world he constructs, his theory identifies a rational, empirical, progressive, unrepressed and non-repressive *social contract*, made possible by the rational learning process in structural and personality systems. It is a social theory which becomes a 'continuation of theory of knowledge'. This theory is said to be able to identify rational rules and to specify those who are capable of following them, in order to reveal the evolutionary plan people follow (acquired through the learning process), upon which the theory itself is based. To avoid the implied historicism of these views, Habermas links necessity and progress to the learning process and language.

But he denies that he is merely a linguistic formalist. In response to a criticism from Bubner, he retorts:

> I am far from wanting to renew the dialectic self-movement of the concept in language-theoretic terms. The rationalisation of life-world structures and corresponding alteration in the forms of the intersubjectivity of possible understanding, which I *describe* in structural terms, can be *explained* only in connection with evolutionary dynamics of the social system.
>
> (Habermas quoted in Bubner 1982: 236)

For him, then, neither is communication equated to action, nor is language reducible to communication. Language is a 'medium of communication that serves understanding' (1984: 101). People reproduce themselves by rational social action and communication, and set out to reach agreement (1984: 397). His rational social theory has a developmental logic, which is tied to language as the most substantive and basic human characteristic.

For Habermas, the rational search for freedom has always transcended particular cultural quirks and indicated universal interest. Therefore, into his theory of communicative action Habermas packs all the traditional Western universal claims to reaching understanding and autonomy. Their source includes Greek thought, German idealism, linguistic philosophy, psychoanalysis, logic, Marxism and so on. He grounds universal characteristics in language, because he believes that they can then be fused to a modern sociological orientation there.

Universal pragmatics

Universal pragmatics indicate a species *competence to communicate* and to reach *consensus*. Both communicative competence and consensus have universal as well as sociological characteristics, though we are not quite sure how they relate. Universal pragmatics are meant to restructure 'universal validity of speech . . . (and) universal conditions of possible understanding . . . (as) presuppositions of communicative action'. This orientation towards understanding also dogs other forms of action, including conflict, competitive and strategic action (1979: 5). Communicative competence and consensus ensure universality and truth. It is not surprising, then, that Michael Schmid should call his sociology a fundamental anthropology, which identifies labour and language as presuppositions of all societies. Language ensures intersubjectivity and labour material reproduction (Schmid 1982: 162), thus adding to Marx's alleged instrumentalist project the required dose of communicative interest and action.

Communicative competence

Communicative acts make explicit the processes of emancipation. Bubner observes:

> Language reveals itself to be an interest of reason . . . Dialogue as true realisation of linguistic ability of human beings, represents the concretion of partners' mutual recognition of each other as subjects with equal rights.
>
> (Bubner 1982: 48)

To communicate is to 'raise universal validity claims and suppose they can be validated'. For both the speaker's and the listener's sakes, such communication must be in good faith. Language, as a medium of distortion and exercise of power, is also a medium of criticism. The reconstruction of communicative competence brings forth what is universal in speech:

> In being uttered, a sentence is placed in relation to (1) the external reality of what is supposed to be an existing state of

affairs, (2) the internal reality of what the speaker would like to express before a public as his intention, and, finally, (3) the normative reality of what is intersubjectively recognized as legitimate interpersonal relationship.

(Habermas 1979: 27–8)

Regardless of distortion, every competent speaker can create a milieu based on realizable assumptions which are free of conflict. Speech anticipates consensus.

What is still unclear, however, is if language is capable of distortion, what makes it an example of rationality *par excellence*? If universality is grounded in language, why is human knowledge and freedom not already certain? Why must we assume that only Habermas's reconstruction makes that possible? Is it not possible to learn the truth and take our freedom through rhetoric, propaganda or deception? Propaganda depends on simplification, misrepresentations and distortion, not always to manipulate people, but also to exalt them into emancipatory action. Why should either the oppressor or the oppressed *ever* choose to 'play fair'? To do so would not indicate their 'rationality' but their naïvety. No good reasons are given for why oppressors and oppressed should seek a consensus. Besides, rational theory is not the only kind of enabling fiction; propaganda is such, too, it is a prelude to political action. In fact, McCarthy suspects that Habermas's 'pure' communicative action is an exception rather than a rule. The normal structures of deception, insincerity, inauthenticity, and so on, upon which everyday life is based and symbols are formed, have no place in Habermas's theory (McCarthy 1982: 63). So, if counterfactual theory is more than propaganda, what is its real status?

Consensus

According to Habermas, truth content and intersubjectivity, which through argumentation ultimately leads to a rational consensus, are 'always and already' implicit in language. Consensus makes social contracts of Hobbes, Locke and Rawls and transcendental philosophy of Kant and Apel rational. Thus, social contracts and transcendental philosophies provide him with the 'formal grounds, which possess legitimating force' whose power is 'to produce consensus and shape motives' (Habermas 1979: 184).

These two influences, of the sociophilosophical social contracts and transcendental philosophy, leave a conflicting mark on Habermas's theory of consensus. Habermas sometimes seems to suggest both that consensus is something we *achieve*, and that it is something that we have already *presupposed* in discourse:

> The goal of coming to understanding is to bring about an agreement of reciprocal understanding, shared knowledge, mutual trust, and accord with one another. Agreement is based on recognition of corresponding validity claims of comprehensibility, truth, truthfulness, and rightness.
>
> (Habermas 1979: 3)

The sociological fact of consensus provides evidence of validity claims redemption in reason. But this is an idealist solution which Habermas also explicitly rejects. For Habermas, morally relevant conflict 'excludes the manifest employment of force as well as "cheap" compromises'; for it is open to consensual resolution (1979: 78). Independently of 'accidental commonalities of social origins, tradition, basic attitude', people can fundamentally agree on matters, due to the 'structures of possible interaction' (1979: 88). Equally, it must be said, however, regardless of any such structures that Habermas puts so much trust in, people fundamentally disagree *because* of their cultural differences.

Apart from this objection about the ambiguity of its status, another objection has been raised against Habermas's notion of consensus, in two different ways. First, Bubner is not convinced that mere intersubjective discourse over private interests needs to imply universality of interests. 'What the parties to the dialogue approve in the light of present interests does not from then on create any obligations for all agents.' Agreements which result from such a dialogue do not indicate 'the necessary interests of everyone' (Bubner 1981: 197–8).

> The dialogue is thus no longer merely a method of critical testing for interests or principles of action which originate in a pre-communicative sphere of real practice. The dialogue is the place in which the setting of norms and the discovery of interests themselves take place.
>
> (Bubner 1981: 199)

Secondly, Heller insists that to prove a theory does not mean scientists agree, but simply that they are not dogmatic and have

considered opposing arguments and are ready to defend and
amend their theory; 'ascribing arguments to different interests is
no argument in itself'.

> The theorist's pretension to know the interests of *others* better
> than they do themselves, and the claim that others can recog-
> nize their *real* interests only through the interpretation of *the*
> theory (indeed through *one* single theory) – these claims must
> be renounced.
>
> (Heller 1982: 30)

Idealized notions of consensus presuppose these assumptions. In
any case, Habermas does not specify *how* consensus can be
achieved, given that it is often absent. He is unclear about how
linguistic rules and utterances homologize their levels and is
unsure about the status of consensus. He clearly wants it to be
sociological and to be presupposed in language. But other than
indicate the wisdom or the inevitability of such a juxtaposition, he
fails to establish the links. Furthermore, both notions of communicative competence and consensus are incapable of coping with the
dissidence of the everyday world. Language use which is other than
rationalistic is considered bad faith, even if it can programmati-
cally improve the user's chance for freedom. But the real world of
everyday language is of prejudiced, common people and not that
of philosophers; Habermas's ideal dialogue anticipates 'a completely different *Praxis*' (Bubner 1982: 49). There, disapproval is
liable when decisions are taken and conflict is resolved by other
than complete mutual and rational agreement. It is not only
unrealistic to burden human action with these abstractions, but as
counterfactual standards they measure up to a fictional world
which will never come alongside the one we live in. By using these
arguments, Habermas appeals to the liberal traditions of the social
contract and transcendental traditions.

Evolutionary theory and rationality

Whether he means to or not, Habermas's theory of communicative
action with its built-in theories of change and rationality, takes
over from political action. The struggles for democracy, freedom
and equality are transferred from the unpredictable social,
political and industrial arenas to the struggles for communicative
rationality and strategic action. He resolves the problem of politics

by giving social and personality change an internal development logic. In one of his clearest statements about his general views, he presents his preference for theory over history in these fatalistic terms:

> Every general theory of justification remains peculiarly abstract in relation to the historical forms of legitimate domination. If one brings standards of discursive justification to bear on traditional societies, one behaves in an historically 'unjust' manner. Is there an alternative to this historical injustice of general theories, on the one hand, and the standardless of mere historical understanding, on the other?
>
> (Habermas 1979: 205)

His answer to this self-imposed liberal dilemma is to construct a developmental account of historical sequences, through which the psychology and moral consciousness of all societies are said to run.

But if this decreases the problem of political action, it increases his ethnocentrism and that of nineteenth-century sociologists. Heller turns a good phrase:

> Like Marx, he envisages the future as the outcome of our history, which is at the same time the outcome of History. It is a teleological reconstruction of history, where teleology is not identical with the concept of tending towards a hidden goal, but with the logic of evolution . . . Habermas offers us not a theory of history but a new philosophy of history.
>
> (Heller 1982: 36)

Having given up the hope of cross-cultural rationality, and believing that universality must transcend history, Habermas now builds his theoretical-pragmatic theory in Western terms. Other cultures merely provide the raw material for his 'prehistory' of this theory of modernity.

Evolutionary theory

Habermas identifies three developmental processes in his theory of evolution: personal, social structural and technological. Each of these processes has a different object and has its own developmental logic. The first one depicts the 'ontogenesis of the individual' so that s/he can develop the capacity for formal and moral thought, and the ability to interact with others:

society on its own, separated from the personality system, cannot bear the burden of evolution. The two (social system and personality system) are complementary and only when *taken together* do they produce a system capable of evolution.

(Habermas quoted in Schmid 1982: 164)

The second process is the logical development of normative structures of society. The third one is technological development 'as a whole . . . which can be converted into instrumental action, increasing by accumulation', following a developmental logic too. This Spencerian model can be seen, according to Schmid, as 'factual development of specific *stages, phases* or steps'. They are logically independent of each other and have their own structures.

The process of the logical development of the social system looks familiar enough: it is a fusion of Parsons's to the nineteenth-century sociologies of Marx, Spencer and Weber. In *Towards a Rational Society*, Habermas nominates 'traditional societies' as civilized at all, only because they enter the evolutionary scheme, which is moving towards mature capitalism. What guarantees them a place in that scheme is 'centralized ruling power', 'division of labour into subeconomic classes' and a legitimizing ideology.

The superiority of the capitalist mode of production to its predecessors has two roots: the establishment of an economic mechanism that renders permanent the expansion of subsystems of purposive-rational action, and the creation of an economic legitimation by means of which the political system can be adapted to the new requisites of rationality brought about by these developing subsystems.

(Habermas 1971a: 97-8)

Agricultural workers and craft producers can tolerate very limited technical innovation and organizational improvements. Their cultural sub-systems and technical knowledge have not developed sufficiently or their 'rationality would have become an open threat to authority of cultural tradition that legitimize political power' (Habermas 1971a: 94-5). Modern societies are superior because their principles of rationality are universally valid and are not constrained by traditional ideologies. They are freed from the 'cultural validity of intersubjectively shared traditions'. In capitalist societies instrumental processes are not restrained by normative ones, which guarantees 'permanent expansion of subsystems of purposive-rational action and thereby overturns the traditionalist "superiority"' (Habermas 1971a: 96). In this discussion about rationality, there is more than a hint of technological determinism in Habermas's subordination of the normative to instrumental processes:

> Traditional structures are increasingly subordinated to conditions of instrumental or strategic rationality: the organization of labour and of trade, the network of transportation, information, communication, the institutions of private law, and, starting with financial administration, the state bureaucracy ... [i]t generates substructures that train the individual to be able to 'switch over' at any moment from interaction context to purposive-rational action.
>
> (Habermas 1971a: 98)

Habermas makes three assumptions in this analysis. First, he suggests that traditional societies are fundamentally 'controlled' by their communicative interest to the exclusion of purposive-rational and emancipatory interests. Secondly, he is making a categorical distinction between the rationality of 'traditional' and capitalist people. Finally, he implies that the motive force of capitalist expansion is not normative (or emancipatory) developmental logic, but instrumental reason. For, though in 'traditional' societies the former restricts the latter, under capitalism the purposive-rational action 'overturns' traditionalism.

Thus capitalism is motivated by technological reason; and, according to this discussion, that also makes it the most advanced social system.

Habermas has consistently adhered to these three evolutionary positions throughout his work, without ever giving conclusive evidence or arguments for them. He appears to be quite uninformed about contemporary social history. He both underestimates the elements of feudalism retained by many 'advanced' capitalist societies, Britain and Japan for example, and overestimates the element of 'traditionalism' found in Third World countries. An example for this is that of the Third World capitalist development, which has consistently proved the above Durkheimian–Parsonian moral determinism wrong. The capitalist development of Japan, South Africa, Latin America and the Middle East (including Iran and Saudi Arabia), proves precisely that capitalism uses traditional hierarchies of instrumental and normative structures to reap enormous profits and to create (especially in the cases of Japan, Hong Kong, Korea and Taiwan, etc.) some of the most dynamic of all the international capitalist structures. Furthermore, the relatively easy uptake of some of the Western ideas, lifestyles and modes of thought in these societies, challenges the assertion that they are *fundamentally* constituted by a different rationality, which is incapable of coping with technical progress. Besides, he cannot have it both ways: that rationality is linked to formal aspects of language and communication and therefore universal and that some people don't have it as good. But if rationality is understood conventionally (which Habermas refuses to accept completely) then differences in perception can exist without there being any need to place them in a hierarchy. Besides, it is too reductive to argue that technology is responsible for capitalist social transformation. In numerous instances, Third World transformations were due to colonial demand for agricultural and administrative local labour-power. The colonial administration, then, introduced a legal and educational framework, not for 'rational' reasons of running these societies more humanely and more efficiently, but to aid 'irrational' exploitation and state coercion.

But apart from these empirical factors, it is still incumbent upon those who argue that capitalism is the most advanced, civilized or rationalized form of social (not just technological) organization to prove that *and* avoid technological determinism.

Habermas's theory of evolution is also concerned with the logical development of the personality system. For him, interactive competence is an indicator of the stability of moral consciousness of that person and his or her ability to communicate with another or his or her community. If a person is not hindered by the 'motivational structure . . . from maintaining even under stress, the structures of everyday action in consensual regulation of action conflicts', such interactive competence is thus possible. But moral consciousness is also indicative 'of the degree of stability of general interactive competence', and people are morally good when they master this competence.

The fusion of ego development and moral consciousness is a crucial part of Habermas's theory of evolution. It allows him to emphasize the connection between ego and universality. As a symbolic organization, ego identity is universal because 'it is found in the structures of formative process in general and makes possible optional solutions to culturally invariant, recurring problems of action'.

Following Piaget, Furth and Kohlberg, Habermas identifies stages, phases and steps in the acquisition of interactive competence of a child, and the ability to 'move about in the structures' of reality. There are three logical stages in the mastery of communicative competence and context independence: (i) reflectivity; (ii) abstraction and differentiation; and (iii) generalization.

The actor must be able to understand and to follow the individual behaviourial expectations of another (level I); he must be able to understand and to follow (or to deviate from) reflective behaviourial expectations – roles and norms (level II); finally, he must be able to understand and apply reflective norms (level III).

At the first level, nature is not distinguished from freedom; 'imperatives are in nature as well as in society as the expression of the concrete wishes'. The second level is where the subject learns to distinguish duty from will. At the final level, the subject distinguishes tradition from autonomy. The developmental direction moves from the concrete to the abstract, from duty to autonomy, from homogeneity to differentiation and justice. The development of moral consciousness is parallel and is linked to the levels of role competence. Regardless of their social or cultural background, as competent agents, individuals will be in fundamental agreement.

Schmid quotes the following passage to demonstrate the sequence of moral development:

> At a preconventional stage, when actions, when motives and acting subjects are still perceived on the level of reality, only the consequences of action are evaluated in cases of action conflict. At the conventional stage, motives can be assessed independently of concrete action consequences . . . At the post-conventional stage, the systems of norms lose their naturalistic validity: they require justification from universalistic points of view.
>
> (Habermas quoted in Schmid 1982: 165)[4]

This schema has factual and theoretical difficulties. It is doubtful that 'primitive' and 'traditional' societies are accurately described by 'preconventional' and 'conventional' stages, with capitalism as the 'post-conventional'. Lévi-Strauss and some British anthropologists have questioned this characterization; and Lévi-Strauss in particular argues for the opposite view. He shows that rather than being naturalistic, as Habermas suggests, 'primitive' societies are too 'intellectual'. But even if Habermas's characterization is essentially correct, it is still up to him theoretically to justify the *necessity* and the *direction* of his evolutionary hierarchy. Schmid suggests that Habermas provides no clear theoretical grounds for the assertion of such a necessity direct.

It does not do to point to the achievement of the West, for that is not in question. But Habermas does not change his assumptions and instead translates his psychological schema on to a societal level.

He attributes to neolithic societies the conventional structure of action for solving moral conflicts, but only a preconventional legal system. Early civilized societies have a conventional system, but a postconventional world-view; while the legal system is under-developed. But 'in modern societies the action system has at last acquired post-conventional features, the world-views propagate a universalism, and the law is based on a separation of private morality and legality'. The aim of this 'sequence' is to discover a method for uncovering universal rules for all action (especially action guided by norms) and for discovering 'the developmental logic internal to the rules'. As Giddens observes, then, 'the "child-hood of society" is like the childhood of the individual, the one a more rudimentary version of the other'. But this discredited view from the nineteenth century has strong racist implications.

The identification of moral and instrumental development with the personality systems raises various interesting issues. Given that these developments apply equally to every child, incremental according to age, then all children should in principle achieve the same moral development. By sociologizing the distinctions between preconventional, conventional and postconventional structures of action, he is also implying that the processes of development are not universal. That would mean that children from different cultures experience different sequences and internal logic, which will not do. Habermas has to choose: either this psychological developmental scheme is not universal but culturally bound, or it is universal but unconnected to an hierarchical notion of moral development. Either way, Habermas is in difficulties.

There is a third, pragmatic alternative which does not suit his systematic sociology. The Piagetian thesis of child development, as adapted by Habermas, does not signify a transcendental account of human development, but it is just a thesis, a starting point for some empirical research. Psychological and moral developments are not formal, but are totally mediated in culture, class, race and language. What the general theory provides is a research project and nothing else.

In sum, by identifying components of social evolution in terms of the history of Western thought, Habermas's rationalistic account of the internal logic of personality and social and technological developments becomes relativistic. Leaving aside the difficulties of Spencerianism, the translation of personality into structural developments and technological determinism in his views, his position can be construed to be racist. This last difficulty is most acute in his theory of rationality.

Rationality

Near the start of *The Theory of Communicative Action* (vol.1), Habermas makes the following manifesto:

> I would like to defend the thesis that there were compelling reasons for Weber to treat the historically contingent question of Occidental rationalism, as well as the question of meaning of modernity and the question of the causes and side effects of the capitalist modernization of society, from the perspective of rational action, rational conduct of life, and rationalized worldviews.
>
> (Habermas 1984: 7)

But apart from defending Western thought, Habermas wishes to indicate a close intimacy that exists between rationality and knowledge. To know is not to possess knowledge, but, like Weber, is to realize ways of acquiring and using it. An expression is rational if it corresponds to the objective world and 'is open to objective judgement'. Judgement is objective when it meets conditions of trans-subjective validity claims, in accordance with a consensus theory of truth. Thus, Habermas's theory of rationality juxtaposes both correspondence (instrumental reason) and consensus (communicative reason) theories of truth. There is no reason to believe that Habermas is *mistaken* in this juxtaposition, but to avoid ambiguity he needs to specify how the physical and communicative causalities relate; but alas, he does not do that. What he does specify, however, is that his theory of rationality has a communicative and an evolutionary aspect to it.

For Habermas, it is the theory of argumentation which makes

communication rational. Argumentation is the thematic context for validity claims. In an argument reasons are given, their soundness is checked out and contested, in the hope of persuading others. In a discourse, the speaker raises validity claims with the aim of reaching understanding. Consensus has to be achieved, because the 'rationality inherent' in the process of reaching agreement is 'based *in the end* on reasons'. The rationality of those involved can be determined by whether they can give such reasons. Rational practice, then, depends on argumentation as a 'court of appeal', which also ensures that force is avoided. Rational people base their demands using established cultural standards, but also reflect upon them. Cultural values can only be the starting point of rationality; reflection frees people from illusion.

Habermas's theory of argumentation seems to imply a rationalistic circularity. When people are involved in rational discourse, they are bound to reach rational ends. But rational ends can only be reached by rational argumentation. Bubner shows no sympathy for this view:

> The mere demand that one should enter into arguments and reciprocal exchange of speech between equal partners is never in itself a guarantee of genuinely rational intersubjectivity . . . One should not therefore allow oneself to be deceived by such declarations of readiness for argumentation into thinking that in the act itself ideal conditions are produced.
>
> (Bubner 1981: 83)

In any case, not every dialogue expresses consensus 'so that we need only to take refuge in speech in order to find that freedom which we lack amid the violence of historical *Praxis*' (Bubner 1982: 48). A naïve belief in free discourse is also ideological; therefore freedom can only be anticipated. In fact, rational discourse sometimes leads to bad and oppressive decisions and relations – examples of that are to be found in numerous broken relationships and marriages. While quarrelsome, unfair and competitive arguments, aiming at *not* reaching understanding, have been known to lead to genuine solutions. Besides, asks Bubner, if people are already rational, 'why do they have to enter into dialogue and ideal conditions at all?' (Bubner 1981: 82). Dialogue is meant to produce rationality 'under conditions which still *fall short of* rationality' (Bubner 1981: 82).

The point is, if reflection is to be based on cultural values of each society, how then can Habermas externally determine universal standards for reflection from the consideration of the philosophical history of one society? Should that not be, as Winch would insist, an internal task for each culture? McCarthy makes this point:

> The claimed universality of the structures Habermas singles out cannot be established inductively; for it is quite clear that they are no characteristic of communication in all cultures and in all historical epochs, nor even of all communication in advanced industrial societies. The abilities to differentiate the 'worlds' of external nature, internal nature and society, to distinguish the 'validity claims' of propositional truth, moral-practical rightness and sincerity/authenticity, to deploy these distinctions reflectively in communicative action and, at another level, in argumentative discourse, are not – as a matter of fact – to be met with universally.
>
> (McCarthy 1982: 65)

Without wishing to get into comparative ethnocentrism, as Lévi-Strauss points out, it is possible to envisage that different cultures might have specialized in some areas Western societies have not, and in those areas are more informed.

But Habermas still wishes to sustain universal value and sociological comprehensiveness. Perhaps, in the end, the answer lies in cross-cultural discourse and comparative analysis and not in the Western reconstruction.

If we now turn to his idea of rational change, he believes that this depends both on instrumental and normative action. In both forms of action, archaic societies exhibit reduced models of Western ones and cannot therefore be rational to the same extent. Though their formal 'operations' are the same, 'higher-level competence appears less frequently and more selectively with them' (Habermas 1984). Thus, rationality of world-views depends on a formal-pragmatic basis, and though he agrees with Lévi-Strauss about the 'Savage Mind', non-Western minds exhibit four confusions. First, they confuse culture and nature; then, they confuse people with things; then they mix up language with the world; and finally they confuse tradition with empirical validation. This description begs a lot of questions that Habermas never answers. It is a representative compilation of Western ideas about other cultures, but no convincing evidence is presented by Habermas to prove his assertions about those societies, nor is there evidence to prove that what happens there (if it does) is qualita- tively different from what is happening here. Indeed, some of these characteristics can be just as easily used to represent important aspects of Western societies.

However, Habermas argues that in confusing culture with nature, archaic societies muddle domains of physical nature with sociocultural environment. Myths and magic 'systematically impede the separation of an objectivating attitude to a world of existing states of affairs from a conformist or non-conformist attitude to a world of legitimately regulated interpersonal relations' (Habermas 1984: 49). But his interpretation of these societies is too literal. He confuses understanding with a mode of representation. If people were unable to distinguish cultural from natural factors, it is highly unlikely they would have been as adept as they are in surviving their own world and the imperialism of the modern capitalist world. What is remarkable is not their confusion, but their theoretical and technical dexterity. His remarks certainly do not show agreement with Lévi-Strauss, or take these factors on. But as well as their inability to distinguish nature from culture, continues Habermas, they cannot tell apart things from people. This is connected to the alleged previous confusion, and the objection to it also refers to that. Finally, myth confuses language and things. Believers in myth do not properly differentiate between 'language and world'. But this would imply that people don't understand their symbols, which they have inaccurately constructed. This is a most extraordinary claim: since symbols have always been understood in terms of the *meaning* they convey, how can their users misunderstand them?

The source of these difficulties, for Habermas, is that mythical world-views reify the linguistic world-view and do not allow a categorical uncoupling of nature from culture. The result is that the world is 'dogmatically invested with a specific content that is withdrawn from rational discussion and thus from criticism'. In this world, personal autonomy appears occasionally and subjectively, which makes traditional norms unjust, since there is no way of formally distinguishing between natural and social reality. Their world-views are closed: reflection gives way to natural consciousness:

> Mythical worldviews are not understood by members as interpretive systems that are attached to cultural traditions, con-

stituted by internal interpretations of meaning, symbolically related to reality, and connected with validity claims – and thus exposed to criticism and open to revision.

(Habermas 1984: 52–3)

If those societies do not understand their mythical world-views thus, it is difficult to envisage another justifiable way of understanding them.

Habermas justifies his opinion that they have a reduced capacity for rationality in his final assertion that they confuse tradition with validation. The first pointer is they must distinguish 'causes from motives, happenings from action'; they must differentiate 'is' from 'ought', something he himself fails to do. However, as discussed previously, the evidence generally points to the contrary view about 'primitive' societies. They have not only endured history, they have also endured Western imperialism. Such imperialism is evident in Habermas's own views. For, though he states that validity depends on culture context, this does not mean that 'ideas of truth, of normative rightness, of sincerity, and of authenticity that underlie . . . the choice of criteria are context dependent in the same degree' (1984: 55). But if internal judgement is unreliable, what makes external judgement more reliable? He believes his criteria are universal because they are linked to the internal learning process of Western history, but that still means they are external for Third World societies. He knows nothing about any Third World societies; and even if he did, he most certainly does not conduct an external or internal dialogue with them. Instead, he presents a four-point plan for civilization, which reflects the rationalistic history of Western philosophy.

Cultural traditions have to display the following characteristics if rational action is to be possible within the lifeworld. First, there must be formal concepts for objective and social worlds, which permit differentiated validity claims (propositional truth, normative rightness, subjective truthfulness); which stimulates objectivity, norm-conformity and expressiveness. Second, traditions must be undogmatic, meanings can be elaborated, alternatives suggested and analysed; where the learning process and argumentation become explicit and moral/practical insights and aesthetic perceptions are used. Third, cultural evaluation should be institutionalized in the learning process to encourage the formation of cultural sub-systems in science, law, morality, music, art and literature. Finally, instrumental reason should be freed from cultural traditions, to allow it to be socialized into economic and social life.

The process of modernity or of civilization or of progress then merely conventionally coincides with the rationalistic intellectual and social history of Western capitalist societies, with the proviso that it is counterfactually projected into an even more formal rationalistic freer future. According to Habermas, people ignore this schema because they are either irrational or, being lower down the evolutionary hierarchy, misunderstand themselves.

CONCLUSION

Habermas develops his systematic sociology against the backcloth of a critique of liberal fundamentalism, sociologism and reductionism. In his view, to give way to any of these perennial problems of social knowledge is to give way to dogmatism and parochialism and therefore to undermine freedom. He hopes that his theory of communicative action will have the universalism of formal philosophy, without giving way to abstraction; that it is pragmatic without being sociologistic; and it retains Marx's notions of physical and social causality, without accepting historicism and economism.

But his sincere aims are doomed from the start. It is our contention that he can achieve none of these objectives as long as he is seeking formal, watertight criteria for judgement. For that without fail polarizes him from sociology towards philosophical formalism. We object to his sociological formalism not only because it reduces complex social issues to simple problems of language and consciousness rationality, but also because it creates many *analytical* and *moral* difficulties. Analytically, we have discussed many ambiguities in his work, including those in his central concepts of emancipation, theory, capitalism, rationality, progress and technology. His formalistic orientation demands that he satisfies validity claims of philosophy *and* sociology. But when he presents these concepts philosophically, he appears rationalistic, abstract and ethnocentric. When he views them sociologically, he worries about relativism.

As well as analytical difficulties, Habermas's sociological formalism, quite unlike Lévi-Strauss's, is from the beginning making standard racist assumptions, based on the belief that all humanity and its cultures can be understood exclusively in terms of the history of Western philosophical debates. Consequently, while he is completely unfamiliar with any Third World societies, he is prepared to use the success of Western technology – which worries him in the context of the West – as a yardstick for measuring civilization. He also uncritically accepts all the standard racist nineteenth-century descriptions – and a few from structural functionalism – as accurate descriptions of those societies. Then, all the Western psychological, social, and moral structures of action are arbitrarily presented as the apex of an evolutionary schema, while he outlines others as being at various stages of achieving such maturity. We are completely convinced that the formalistic requirement for a general-universal theory encourages such practices.

NOTES

1 This move prompted left-wing critics like Göran Therborn to note and reject Habermas's 'eclecticism'. See Therborn 1971.
2 The original is Habermas 1971b: 137.
3 From, among others, Heller, Bubner, Giddens and McCarthy.
4 The original is Habermas 1979: 156.

Part III

Some consequences of formalism for sociological analysis

Chapter 5

Modernization, modernity and beyond
Recent trends in social theory

INTRODUCTION

This chapter considers two debates within sociology in the light of our critique of sociological formalism. The first is that around 'modernization theory' and goes back to the early 1960s. The more recent concerns notions of 'modernity' and 'postmodernity'. Our purpose is to show that the apparently new 'debate' reproduces many of the features of the old. Even the notion of 'postmodernity', which is critical of foundationalism, remains formalist in so far as it becomes a sociological doctrine, as it does when the talk is of a 'postmodern condition'. Postmodernism shares with modernism and modernization theory an *a priori* sociological method and a tendency to assume that the social can be read off underlying structural or intellectual changes. Our concern in this part of the discussion is primarily with the sociological *reception* of postmodernist arguments.

The argument will proceed as follows: (i) we first offer a critical discussion of the assumptions of modernization theory; (ii) there follows a general outline of the notion of modernity; (iii) we examine the postmodernist critique of the second's universalism and foundationalism; (iv) we then outline the main characteristics ascribed to society by a would-be sociology of postmodernity before considering Habermas's critique of the relativist and 'young' conservative assumptions of the postmodernist position; (v) finally, we shall argue that as *sociological* accounts, modernizationist, modernist and postmodernist approaches are not as far apart as is assumed. Our concern is with these concepts as they are used in *sociological* not *philosophical* discourse, in that they both presume

a formalist foundation, despite all efforts made – particularly by
postmodernists – to avoid it.

We thus raise the question: 'is the theory of postmodernity and
the more familiar theory of modernity really as distinct as is
assumed by the main protagonists?', or 'is there a distinctive sociology of postmodernity?' Our answer is no in so far as they share a
common *logic of explanation.*

MODERNIZATION THEORY: THE STUDY OF THE THIRD WORLD

> The speed and above all the radical nature of change, in-
> toxicated many of the eighteenth and nineteenth centuries,
> leading them to extrapolate . . . from the direction of current
> change as they understood it in a way such as to anticipate some
> secular millennium, some total consummation.
>
> (Gellner 1964: 144)

If the pace of change promotes teleology, this era's Western
scientific, technical and economic successes at home, and military,
cultural and religious ones abroad, would appear to some to constitute the proof of its ethical legitimacy. Teleological and ethical
legitimacy have thus made alternative or parallel views of social
organization and thought unviable, and have helped to constitute
a Western domination of the world theatre. As exemplified by
Habermas, formalism endorses Western categories to the extent
that even *human* freedom is linked to them, as the Rushdie case
illustrates. Habermas's 'rational' theory of the evolution of science
and techniques, psychological and cultural, reflects this bias.

The implications and motives of tying Western ethics and
rationality to human progress are most evident in the study of
Third World people or black people in Western capitalist societies.
Thus modernization theory and theories of racism provide excel-
lent examples of formalistic analysis in practice. Formalism is
historically motivated too. Among other things, it perpetuates this
domination through the stereotyping of Third World and black
peoples, their social organization and thought. If policies are
based on formalist studies, formalists must also accept the political
and moral responsibility for further oppressing these people.
Instead, however, formalists assume the responsibility lies with

black people who are accused of ignorance, backwardness, diffidence and stubbornness.

Modernization theory is formalist on a grand scale: it self-consciously universalizes ahistorical Western concepts. Analytical, moral and political motives and consequences of using formalism are nowhere more evident than in modernization theory. Through it the Third World societies are experienced as extensions of the interests and anxieties of industrial capitalist problems. By exorcizing the 'irrationalism' of others, it is thought we can ensure our own rationality. Their example of barbarianism out there serves as a warning to Western 'irrationalists'. Against the negative stereotypes of other societies, modernization theorists present idealized notions of Western scientific, cultural, economic, political and psychological rationality and progress. They construct a binary opposition, not to aid the understanding of Third World societies, but to support their domination and help other formalists win ideological contests at home. If the analysis of these societies does not explicitly use the language of 'before' and 'after' rational Western intervention, it suggests it.

Western cultural successes are nowhere more overtly celebrated than in modernization theory. The characteristics of the Western way of life, especially capitalist relations, are thought to be indispensable for the Third World development. Western knowledge and methods are here elevated to the status of law-like imperatives with self-evident 'natural' authority. Third World people may share in this privilege if they adopt Western ideas and ways of life. Since the history of Western philosophy, on this view, identifies the limits of *any possible* experience, Third World people too are obliged to go through the same stages that Western capitalist societies had followed.

Modernization theory is held together by three constitutive themes, all of which are meant to stress the vertical polarization between capitalist and peasant societies: (i) the idea of progress; (ii) the distinction between tradition and modernity; and (iii) the modernization programme. These themes amount to more than analytical tools for studying other societies. In their unison they are systematic programmes for action: they are a normative theory of history which would transform traditional societies into modern ones. Modernization theory, by this account, is a transcendental theory or formal science providing a legitimate basis for rational understanding and action. As Finkle and Gable suggest, the process of modernization is 'the multiple and interrelated transformations in all of the systems by which man organizes his life and society' (1966: v). But the analytical and moral difficulties of formalism are also to be found in this analytical breakdown.

The idea of progress

Like Habermas's theory of evolution, modernization theorists' notion of progress is historicist, technological determinist and shares Spencer's notion of cultural evolution. Their assumption that Western capitalist societies are logically the most advanced provides them with the criterion by which to assess other societies. For them, a society's progress is identified by (i) how much it resembles a capitalist economic system; (ii) by the extent to which it has accepted the Western technical, cultural and psychological lead.

'Progress' is equated with capitalist economic progress, and the transition towards it is one-directional. There is no relativism here. Progress is, to use Gellner's metaphor, like a cogged mountain railway in which one moves forward without slipping back. Marxism and communism contribute to this process, not because their political theory is sound, but because they weaken the moral consensus of traditional societies and place them on a ladder towards modernity:

> Marxism is embraced by the impatient, in backward societies, in order to break out of vicious circles of stagnation.
>
> (Gellner 1964: 135)

and:

> They are interested in [Marxism] as an ideology which might best steel them and their countries and their elites for the arduous road to industrialization. Marxism is not intended for the over-coming of the ills of industrialism: its role is to bring them about. Marxist revolutions precede, and do not follow, industrial development.
>
> (Gellner 1964: 137)

The collapse of East European communist regimes may seem to vindicate that interpretation, but it does not vindicate the historicist assumptions which underpin it. Capitalist economic rationality is a precondition for all progress and must not be resisted, improved upon or overcome, but should be fully embraced. As George A. Theodorson (1966) observes, all industrialization inevitably changes social patterns to resemble those in the West. Therefore, industrial patterns come to those 'who accept the machines of the West'. Capitalist development is formalized into progress which other societies must experience to become modern.

In the 1960s modernization theorists self-consciously adopted modern America as the final destination for humanity. It is true that various societies can choose how they get there, but their final arrival is inescapable. Unlike the misplaced aspiration to an idealized communist society, modern societies are already here to imitate.

As a sub-text of modernization, therefore, Third World societies would be irrational not to adopt the capitalist road and subsequently entertain capitalist domination and exploitation. The formalism of modernization theory is not innocent. It is formalism as an ideology of domination.

Progress is measured in concrete technical, cultural, psychological terms. It is the transformation (i) '*from* simple and traditional techniques *towards* the application of knowledge'; (ii) 'from subsistence farming *towards* commercial production', 'specialization in cash crops' and 'agricultural wage labour'; (iii) '*from* the use of human and animal power *towards* industrialization proper'; (iv) '*from* farm and village *towards* urban centres' (Smelser 1966: 28-9). Modernization can only take place when significant linguistic and cultural, technical, scientific and economic changes are achieved. When anti-colonialist and democrats resist these changes, they also delay the education of a Third World élite, on whose shoulders the task of modernizing their societies must fall. To be sure, Third World languages and cultures are inappropriate modernizing tools: 'oriental languages generally do not contain the scientific and technical vocabulary of Western civilization' (Hauser 1966: 57-8). By using them, orientals make bad judgements. 'Advanced industrial nations are the fashion makers and pace setters in most phases of social and economic life' (Pye 1966: 84). In order to become modernized, traditional people must in every sense be Westernized.

The process of modernization is thus all-embracing and historicist. 'Non-machine societies' cannot pick and choose those 'aspects of western culture' they prefer, they must accept them *in toto*. Technological advancement is coupled with 'an increase in universalism, achievement, suppression of immediate emotional release . . . [to achieve] affective neutrality' (Theodorson 1966: 297–301).

André Gunder Frank counters the characterization of the Third World contained in modernization theory generally, and Rostow's theory of the stages of 'take off' and 'modernization' in particular, by showing that since the capitalist exploitation of the Third World is several hundred years old, it is inaccurate to identify those societies as 'traditional'. But since the category of 'exploitation' is not one accepted by modernization theorists, Frank's criticisms have had little impact upon them. They accept that 'strains' may arise, but these are exceptions which are part of change, with a relationship of 'mutual benefit':

> Both – breakdown and growth – are inherent in the process of modernity. They indicate the pitfalls, problems, and challenges of modernity – and the fact that modernity constitutes perhaps the greatest challenge that mankind has posed for itself in the course of its history.
>
> (Eisenstadt 1966: 161)

Within this perspective, we cannot question capitalist rationality and organization. In Spencerian fashion, modernization theory identifies Western capitalist social arrangements, technology and rationality as the exemplary destination for humanity. This theory formalizes Western experience of science, culture and personality developments for the world to imitate. The analytical and moral implications of that are most evident in the theorists' polarization of tradition from modernity.

Tradition versus modernity

The notion of progress enabled modernization theorists to polarize the concepts of 'tradition' and 'modernity'. It is this distinction, rather than differences of class, gender, race or wealth, which is crucial for social analysis. The movement from the former to the latter, the 'before' and 'after', amounts to a normative process of history (cf. Eisenstadt 1966: 1); it also implies an ethical transition from less moral to more moral status:

> Transitional societies . . . have ceased to be viable, subjectively
> or objectively: their norms can no longer be effectively inter-
> nalized, and their external arrangements can no longer be
> sustained – either through the direct impact of modernization
> institutions, or through the sheer 'demonstration effect' of a
> measureless richer and more powerful alien world.
>
> (Gellner 1964: 170)

Tradition *has* to give way to modernity, but while it exists, the two
are distinct.

For modernization theory traditional people are economically
and technically less-developed, are inefficient and lack creativity.
Their economic activities are ritualistic and tend to become
confused with political ends. Rituals inhibit change because they
confuse production (e.g. planting, harvesting and exchange) with
the maintenance of social stability. In short, traditional people are
incapable of conducting rational means–ends oriented actions.
Philip Hauser believes that traditional people are intolerant of new
ideas, inflexible about familial roles, live in villages and have
parochial social orders of 'diverse racial, ethnic, linguistic, and
territorial groups' (just like the USA!) (Hauser 1966: 58–9). They
invest non-productively in jewels and waste too much time on
'traditional cultural and religious rituals, ceremonies and festi-
vals'. Their dependence on agriculture, kinship and communal
ownership renders their techniques and economic organizations
conservative; their horizons are 'limited by their locale'. They are
conservative because they are immobile and have relatively simple
occupational differentiation.

Traditional peoples' political system too is conservative because
it is integrated into kinship and land. Stability here is not assured
by democratic elections of political leaders but ascribed by class,
gender and occupation. Colonialism has disturbed this stagnation
and increased people's chances of escaping from 'ignorance and
superstition to knowledge and control, from poverty and tyranny
to wealth and at least the possibility of freedom' (Gellner 1964:
218).

Part of the conservatism and 'backwardness' of traditional societies lies in their pre-scientific cognitive structures. Not only is
their knowledge 'pre-Newtonian' (Rostow 1963: 4), but they remain hostile to innovation and experiment. They would rather
rely on the wisdom of elders, the family, the village leaders, land-

lords and others in position of authority. There is no evidence of this; everything points to the contrary.

The cognitive conservatism of traditional societies is echoed in their impoverished moral and cultural resources: 'they have similar ideas about good and bad, what is beautiful and ugly, or what is familiar and strange; and they bring up children expecting them to behave in similar ways' (Finkle and Gable 1966: 120). Morality and culture are constricted by an unquestioning adherence to 'sacred texts'.

Finally, traditional peoples' psychology and personality is exemplified by their repugnance for 'getting their hands dirty' and for low-level creativity. Due to their socialization, traditional peoples are not autonomous, coherent or orderly, and therefore understandably lack an achievement orientation (see Hagen 1966). Their parents overprotect and suffocate their childhood activities: 'The use of initiative comes to alarm him (the child), because it alarms her (the mother)' (Hagen 1966: 135).

The account of traditional societies found in modernization theory is little more than a projection of European stereotypes. This can be seen not merely as crude characterization, but also as failure to appreciate the social *and* cognitive function of ritual and 'primitive' classification. Binary totemic classification, for example, is both a way of understanding *and* controlling nature. What is taken by modernization theory as conservatism is often a highly flexible adaptation to, and means of resisting some of the effects of colonialism. Similar points can be made with respect to the Western view of the cultural and political systems of Third World societies as conservative and undemocratic. British anthropologists have shown that problems of legitimacy and representation must be faced by 'traditional' societies just as they are by 'modern' ones. This is a precondition of social stability in both cases. The confusion arises through the conceptual reduction of democracy and legitimation to the acquisition of Western institutions. A reduction to which formalists are tempted precisely because those institutions and constitutions are themselves formalized (e.g. based upon written constitutions, laws, etc.). It is thus easy to recognize formalist conceptual systems.

The empirical misdescriptions are, we would maintain, traceable directly to the formalist nature of modernization theory. Its formalism acts precisely to disguise, not least of all to itself, the relativism and particularism of its own assumptions. Armed with a set of putative universals, modernization theorists are able to universalize their own specific prejudices and orientations. It exports its own brand of particularism wrapped in such universalistic slogans as freedom, democracy, justice and the common good. The orientation of modernization theorists towards their own values ironically parallels their characterization of traditional society: unquestioned, closed, static and suspicious of alternatives. This is not to say that the Third World has nothing to learn from Western societies. Quite the contrary. But the reverse is also true.

To modernity is ascribed the opposite characteristics imputed to tradition. Modern society is said to be universalistic and innovative. It encourages individual autonomy, is open to change and social mobility, and has its cognitive system grounded in experience, experiment and critical reflection. Modernizers do not develop their categories within historical time; they construct precise models which they believe will provide the policy-maker with the correct tools for change:

> concepts that are part of the system model are 'boundary', 'stress or tension', or 'equilibrium', and 'feedback' . . . we shall define these concepts, illustrate their meaning, and then point out how they can be used by the change-agent as aids in observing, analyzing in diagnosing – and perhaps intervening in – concrete situations.
>
> (Chin 1966: 8)

Although there are different *routes* and more than one *method* of achieving it, depending upon the starting point, there is only one *end*; one 'core of "modernization"' (Chin 1966: 2).

For Gellner, unlike the belief systems which make the world 'morally palatable' and 'underwrite the social arrangements of the believers', the cognitive models of modernization are grounded in non-relativist modern science. Science has 'guarantees of stability, it is morally meaningless, and it respects no hierarchies' (Gellner 1964: 179). Western science separates knowledge from common-sense and rescues the former from the relativism and particularism of the latter.

The contrast between tradition and modernity can be summed up as shown in Table 5.1.

Table 5.1 Traditional v. modern society

	Traditional society	Modern society
Status	Ascribed	Achieved
Cognitive structure	Pre-Newtonian/knowledge as wisdom (particularistic)	Scientific/experimental (universalistic)
Moral codes	Closed: based upon authority of texts or word of respected individuals (particularistic)	Open: rationally reconstructible (universalistic)
Economic activity	Ritualistic, not means/ends orientated	Governed by purposive-rational orientation
Innovation/change	Resisted (conservative)	Welcomed (innovative)
Personality structures	Conservative, non-individualist, passive	Innovative, individualistic, active

The route to modernity

Having established the formal disadvantages of tradition, modernization theorists are now in a position to suggest the formal programme for action: they do so with a Messianic zeal.

Within the modernizing society, power is increasingly concentrated in the hands of 'those possessing diplomas from the schools of industrialized societies' (Gellner 1964: 39). Embracing modernity consists not merely in such cultural developments as giving up a 'victim complex' towards the West (Hauser 1966: 30), but also entails fundamental structural changes.

Peasant relationships must give way to capitalist ones. Peasant–landlord class relationships are transformed into labour–capital relations, and there is a shift from 'ascribed' to 'achieved' status. The new modernizing élite, which is the vanguard of modernization, is required to mobilize the nation, communications, business, the military and administration. Within this élite, intellectuals must introduce 'constitutional liberalism, and politicized nationalism' (Finkle and Gable 1966: 321–2). Similarly, the binary opposition between tradition and modernity must be rigorously defended: belief must be distinguished from knowledge, superstition from science, etc. The modernizing élite are radical. They do not merely tinker with the system, as Frank (1972: 341) supposes, they transform its very nature.

Modernization theory and formalism

What is most striking about modernization theory's formalism is its total utilitarianism towards theory, politics and morality. The pleasurable end that it seeks to achieve is the extension of capitalist interest. In the pursuit of that end, it disregards any contrary evidence. That makes modernizers' analysis superficial and abstract and takes little notice of historical and contextual evidence, which does not support its formal assumptions. Descriptions are then mistaken for explanations and classifications as evidence. Apart from creating many policy difficulties, such a perspective does not actually lead to 'modernization': instead it creates greater hardship and dependence for Third World people. Such formalism deradicalizes the investigative stance of sociological analysis. The peoples and cultures of the Third World are presumed to bear the full burden of responsibility for their failure to modernize. Multinationals, the international division of labour and the policies of colonial and ex-colonial powers are consequently not just exonerated, but resistance to their institutions is equated with hostility to modernization. Formalism reduces practical reason to instrumental reason: nationalism and the struggles for socialism and communism are not attempts to create alternatives, but mere precursors of modernity. Finally, to reject any of the foregoing is tantamount to irrationality:

> Virtue, salvation, the good life, consent, the general will, and the rest . . . are merely near vacuous labels attached to quite different criteria and questions . . . [about] how to become industrialized, and just what to do with an industrial society when one has it.
>
> (Gellner 1964: 36)

As an example of formalism, modernization theory is both analytically questionable and morally and politically suspect.

THE CONCEPT OF 'MODERNITY'

How are the formalist assumptions of modernization carried over into the analysis of *modernity* which has been so central to socio-logical debate? The present twist in this debate is the dispute between 'modernity' and 'postmodernity'. Excluding those who comment from the sidelines, the participants fall into two broad categories: the postmodernists, and those who wish to defend aspects of the project of modernity (e.g. Habermas 1981 and 1987b) and/or the claims of some modernist 'grand narrative' (e.g. Callinicos 1990 in the case of Marxism). But it is again in the work of Habermas that modernity receives its most systematic exposition, critique and defence.

The Theory of Communicative Action, particularly the second volume, contains a theory of modernity which rivals Weber's. Habermas adds a novel twist to the theory of modernity by departing from the Weberian/Critical Theory formulation that modernity is characterized and constituted by the extension of instrumental reason. Instrumental reason is merely a precondition for establishing a far more profound transformative process: namely, the 'internal colonialization' of the lifeworld by systems logic. The whole of *The Theory of Communicative Action* can be understood as an attempt to develop and secure this, by no means transparent, claim. In defending this position Habermas once again attempts a rational reconstruction of social evolution re-miniscent of modernization theory.

In Habermas's more recent discussion in which not the ex-tension of instrumentalism *per se*, but the expansion of 'systems logic' into the cultural sphere ('lifeworld') characterizes modern-ity, the nightmare is no longer that of the totally administered society governed by instrumental reason, but a situation in which social interaction is mediated solely through the objective relations of power and money. There is in here a return to Marx. Habermas's 'concluding reflections' are entitled 'from Parsons via Weber to Marx', and we can see the reason for this quite clearly. Critical Theory has taken a wrong turn in interpreting modernity through the Weberian concept of 'rationalization'. In contrast, power/money reinstate commodity fetishism and reification as modernity's central characteristic. Habermas is essentially asser-ting the validity of the Marxian claim that modernity is to be characterized by the domination of the material over the social world (relations between men take on the character of relations between things – Lukács) against Weber's argument that modernity is to be equated with rationalization. Where Habermas still departs from Marx is in his insistence that this process cannot be understood in economistic terms, but must be understood as the subordination of communication to efficiency:

> The process of reification can manifest itself just as well in public as in private domains, and in the latter areas it can attach to consumer as well as to occupational roles.
>
> (Habermas 1987a: 342)

While agreeing with neo-conservatives, such as Daniel Bell, that modernity destroys traditional values, for Habermas there is no turning back: one cannot defend the lifeworld by reconstituting traditional values on the basis of reason, its opposite. The challenge of modernity is to reintegrate the lifeworld on the basis of 'post-traditional' values and to defend it from its fragmentation along several lines of cleavage: fragmentation of society into expert and laity, the fragmentation of personality in which we are faced with a simple choice between specialization and hedonism; and the fragmentation of social spheres into public and private, and into scientific, aesthetic, ethical and political domains. It is in this argument about post-traditional values that the association between the older theories of 'modernization' and Habermas's evolutionary defence of modernity again becomes apparent:

> the differentiation of science, morality, and art, which is characteristic of occidental rationalism, results not only in a growing autonomy of sectors dealt with by specialists, but also in the splitting off of these sectors from a stream of tradition continuing on in everyday practice in a quasi-natural fashion . . . Everyday consciousness sees itself thrown back on traditions whose claims to validity have already been suspended; where it does escape the spell of traditionalism, it is hopelessly splintered. In place of 'false consciousness' we have a 'fragmented consciousness' that blocks enlightenment by the mechanism of reification. It is only with this that the conditions for a *colonialization of the lifeworld* are met.
>
> (Habermas 1987a: 355)

While breaking with Weber in certain key areas, Habermas's recent work remains a variation on the theme of modernity. It retains the following characteristics:

1 The polarization of modernity and tradition, and an essentially evolutionary view of their relationship in which there is 'no turning back'.
2 The assumption that technical change will feed through into society and culture, such that the latter, in the last analysis, reflect the former.

A more radical break with the modernist tradition is articulated by so-called 'postmodernists' who reject the linear analysis still present in the works of Habermas; and it is to these arguments that we now turn.

THE CRITIQUE OF FOUNDATIONALISM AND THE NOTION OF A 'POSTMODERN SOCIETY'

In the following sections we shall examine the *sociological* reception of postmodernist arguments and ask whether they have in fact managed to shake off modernist assumptions. Before this we should examine what is meant by, or more precisely what sociologists take to be, postmodernism.

Postmodernism and the critique of foundationalism

What do sociologists typically understand by the terms 'postmodernity' and 'postmodernism'? Risking a definition of postmodernism is problematic not merely because it is a rather unpostmodern thing to do, but also because it is likely that terms which have been adopted from literary and art criticism and architecture, etc., into philosophy, history and sociology have been transformed in the process.[1] It is by no means clear that even within the social sciences there is more than an elective affinity in usage. Nevertheless, we would suggest the following as a list of features of postmodernism as it has come, or is coming, to be understood by sociologists:

1 *The rejection of 'grand narratives'* – i.e. of 'single-order' theories or discourses which attempt to be comprehensive and inclusive of a wide range of human cognitive and cultural practices. Scepticism towards the claims of grand narratives is closely associated with scepticism towards their totalizing pretensions.

As we shall see, this tendency may be identified within both Marxist and non-Marxist sociology, though it has become particularly influential in the former.

2 *Anti-foundationalism:* world-views which attempt to ground or justify single-order theories in some absolute – e.g. in sense data, transcendental categories of an isolated knowing subject (Kant), or human communicative communities (Habermas) – are spurned. Postmodernism displays what one of its critics has calls 'an aversion against the universal' (Honneth 1985).[2]

3 *The critique of attempts to adjudicate between competing cognitive claims from a position of assumed, or usurped, privilege.* Within the English-speaking world the best-known expression of points (1) to (3) is Richard Rorty's *Philosophy and the Mirror of Nature* (1979) though Rorty has distanced himself from the post- modernist position.[3] Rorty's polemic is aimed at the claim of epistemology, and by extension Western philosophy generally, to be able to adjudicate between rival cognitive claims or to play the role of cultural arbitrator. Rorty attacks the pretensions of the theory of knowledge to act as cultural arbiter, and recasts philosophy as 'conversation'.

4 *Anti-Eurocentrism:* The postmodernist critique of grand narratives has also become associated with an intellectual critique of Western 'rationality' in general, and of its cognitive imperialism and its excessive self-assurance, and a social critique of the 'Enlightenment project' on the grounds of its cultural parochialism. Thus Heller and Fehér identify the notion of the 'end of the European project' as one of the central assumptions of postmodernists:

> At some point the time had to come when Europeans were bound to question the project 'Europe' as a whole; when they had to expose the false claim of universalism inherent in the 'European particular'. The cultural and political campaign against ethnocentrism has in fact been a major campaign *for* postmodernity.
>
> (Heller and Fehér 1990: 2)[4]

In a similar spirit, Bauman notes: 'there is hardly a power left in the world which can blithely entertain an ecumenically universalistic ambition' (Bauman 1989: 57).

5 *In place of grounded positions, postmodernism embraces what its critics would consider 'relativism', and in particular a relativism of*

'discourses'. There are two central aspects here: (a) its radical anti-essentialism (scepticism towards notions of *noumena* or 'real structures'), particularly anti-humanist essentialism; (b) its anti-materialism – the tendency to prefer explanations of social practices couched in the language of 'discourses' rather than in more conventional sociological, and particularly Marxist materialist, terms (see the discussion of Keane, below). Foucault's analysis of repressive and 'humane' punishment as incommensurable forms of 'penal discourse', and his consequent refusal to side himself with 'humane' penal practices, illustrates both this and the scepticism towards 'Western' notions of progress and improvement (Foucault 1977).[5]

In our critique we shall not take issue with each of these points (with which we have in any case some sympathy), but will argue that they are inconsistent with what has become a postmodernist *sociology*: i.e. a general diagnosis of the 'postmodern condition'.

The idea of a 'postmodern social condition'

In the process of its absorption into sociological discourse, postmodernist arguments have been transformed from a *critique* of 'logocentrism', etc., into a set of positive sociological *propositions* about postmodernist *society*.

1 *The declining significance of production and the corresponding increasing significance of consumption.* This argument is in fact not so new. It is foreshadowed in the work of neo-Marxists in the 1970s, notably in Manuel Castells's influential analysis of urban form and collective consumption. Likewise, theories of postindustrial society, whether of left (Touraine) or right (Bell), have tended to characterize modern capitalism primarily as a means of consumption. But the postmodernist implications of this argument have more recently been brought out by Bauman who considers the following proposition:

> in the present-day society, consumer conduct (consumer freedom geared to the consumer market) moves steadily into the position of, simultaneously, the cognitive and moral focus of life, integrative bond of the society, and the focus of systemic management. In other words, it moves into the selfsame position which in the past – during the 'modern'

phase of capitalist society – was occupied by work in the form of wage labour. This means that in our time the individuals are engaged (morally by society, functionally by the social system) first and foremost as consumers rather than as producers.

(Bauman 1989: 46)

2 *The increasing domination of the symbolic, the sign, over meaning and function.* This view is associated above all with the French sociologist Jean Baudrillard for whom 'today the scene and the mirror no longer exist; instead, there is a screen and a network' (1983: 126). What is now sold and bought is the sign. The commodity is the image, and the image is increasingly one of the fantasy integration of the subject into a perfectly ordered and controlled world; the world of the computer and the 'simulation':

> All these changes – the decisive mutations of objects and of the environment in the modern era – have come from an irreversible tendency towards three things: an ever greater formal and operational abstraction of elements and functions and their homogenization in a single virtual process of functionalization; the displacement of bodily movements and effort into electrical or electronic commands, and the miniaturization, in time and space, of processes whose real scene (though it is no longer a scene) is that of infinitesimal memory and the scene with which they are equipped.
>
> (Baudrillard 1983: 128–9)

Such assertions have been taken up in more mainstream sociological analysis by Lash and Urry, for example, in their influential *The End of Organized Capitalism* (1987). Using, somewhat uncritically, Baudrillard's arguments, they assert that postmodernity 'refuses the distinction between art and life, the cultural and the real' and that contemporary mass audiences are increasingly exposed to cultural objects in which 'the boundary between the cultural and life, between the image and the real, is more than ever transgressed' (1987: 287).[6]

3 *The decline of class and class struggle and their replacement by diverse lines of tension (e.g. generational, gender, ethnic, linguistics, etc.).* A key component of this argument is that there are no 'privileged' points of social cleavage, and no prospects of a unification of

diverse oppositional forces into a coherent challenge to the existing social order. For Heller and Fehér '*post-histoire*' consists largely in living after the age of class, class struggle and 'class culture':

> The modern division of labour, with its capacity to stratify society along functional lines, began to break down the strict segregation of class cultures as early as the end of the nineteenth century.
>
> (Heller and Fehér 1990: 134)

Like Bauman, they draw the connection with consumerism: 'The demise of class-related cultures can be explained in terms of the increase in consumerism' (Heller and Fehér 1990: 141).

The decentring of class is illustrated with particular clarity in the careers of ex-Althusserian, now 'post-Marxist', sociologists like Hindess and Hirst who have each come to reject the single-order models that they themselves defended and developed in the 1970s (see, for example, Hindess 1987). The result has been the rather unpostmodernist adoption of social democratic politics and institutional analysis. Nevertheless, there are affinities between their critique of Marxism, particularly in its Althusserian form, and the postmodernist critique of single-order systems in general.

4 *Finally, the intellectual pluralism of postmodernist arguments is imputed to postmodern society.* Such societies are themselves held to be increasingly unintelligible, a babble of more-or-less mutually uncomprehending discourses, lacking a coherent ideology or central authority which maintains order and consensus, or in terms of which society can hope to understand itself. The demise of the possibility of a unifying discourse, demonstrated by the crisis of scientific confidence and of likely social bearers of a coherent alternative, characterizes postmodernity. The pluralism of postmodernist analysis will be considered later in the discussion of John Keane's arguments of a postmodernist politics.

Our argument with this sociological reception of postmodernism is that *it paradoxically replaces the grand narrative of modernity with a grand narrative of postmodernity. It thus reproduces precisely those totalizing characteristics of which at the level of intellectual critique it is most critical.* In other words, the notions of a 'postmodern condition' is itself paradoxical and self-contradictory. If our argument is valid, we would expect that 'postmodern' socio-logy would reproduce some of the features of more conventional 'modernist' sociology at the level of substantive analysis. We can illustrate that this is indeed the case by comparing John Keane's proposals for a post- modernist and relativist conception of democracy (1988) with that of Karl Mannheim in the 1930s.

Keane's starting point is a critique of the Marxist theory of ideology from a perspective informed by the relativism of post-modernist arguments:

> Perhaps the most serious objection to the latent positivism of Marx's theory of ideology is that it falls victim to the assump-tions, common to all scientism, that it is true knowledge capable of technical implementation.
>
> (Keane 1988: 200)

His objections to the theory of ideology are twofold. First, it rests upon a materialism which fails to recognize the linguistic/symbolic nature of *all* social relations; secondly, it is dogmatically unreflective in its failure to recognize that the position from which it makes its judgements is itself open to ideology critique.

The grounds for the first argument are familiar. Keane argues that 'all social life – including the forces and relations of pro-duction in both their objective and subjective dimensions – is structured through codes of signification'(1988: 223). The rela-tivism of this first objection links it to the second:

> During the past decades, the epistemological self-confidence of the Marxist theory of ideology has dissolved. In its place there has developed a strong revival of the tradition of cognitive and ethical relativism . . .
>
> (Keane 1988: 229)

This intellectual critique of the theory of ideology is echoed in Keane's postmodernist diagnosis of contemporary society. Not only is the theory of ideology incoherent in its own terms, it is also inappropriate to a society in which there are no certainties, no fixed points. Here Keane emphasizes the theoretical and political implications of cognitive pluralism:

> To defend relativism requires a social and political stance which is thoroughly modern. It implies the need for establishing or

strengthening a democratic state and a civil society consisting of a plurality of public spheres, within which individuals and groups can openly express their solidarity with (or opposition to) others' ideas.

(Keane 1988: 238)

In his reconstruction of the theory of ideology, its task is restricted to the critique of master discourses. Anything goes so long as it allows that anything goes.

But there are problems in characterizing Keane's arguments as 'postmodernist' in inspiration which we shall later argue apply to the debate as a whole. His argument in fact bears a strong resemblance to Mannheim's analysis of *modernity* in *Ideology and Utopia* (1936). The main strands of Keane's critique of the Marxist theory of ideology are also the main strands of Mannheim's critique of 'total ideologies': they are only partially reflective; were they more reflective they would be forced to recognize the relativity of the position from which they launch their critique. The unfolding of the intellectual realization of the time-bound (*Zeitgebunden*) nature of belief echoes increasing cognitive heterogeneity and social pluralism.

Keane's analysis departs from Mannheim's not in its diagnosis, nor in the structure of its argument, but in its normative conclusions. For Mannheim, relativism is the problem posed by modernity, by the historical decline of the single-order belief systems associated with religion. Its solution lies in the hands of the historical investigator who, through detailed reconstruction rather than grand synthesis, may hope to put back together what modernity has torn asunder (see Scott 1987). In contrast, for Keane, relativism is not the problem but the solution. Hope of any intellectual synthesis must be abandoned and in its place we must embrace pluralism both intellectually and in our political institutions. Unlike Habermas, who views postmodernist relativism as a variant of conservatism, Keane welcomes its libertarian and democratic potential.

We have discussed Keane and compared him to Mannheim, because it illustrates several key features of postmodernism as a sociological diagnosis of our times. First, Keane's argument illustrates the tendency to ascribe exactly those characteristics to *postmodernity* which were previously ascribed to *modernity* and for essentially the same reasons. Sociological theories of postmodernity, like theories of modernity before them, contrast the pluralism, cognitive and institutional, of contemporary society with the homogeneity of tradition (or, in the case of postmodernity, modernity). As Gillian Rose bluntly observes: 'in social theory the notions of the "modern" and the "postmodern" are, in the first place, fundamentally the same, and, in the second place, are not "modern" or "new" – for want of a neutral term' (1988: 362). Postmodernist analysis is just as trapped in simplifying historical dualism as sociological usage of more familiar notions such as tradition and modernity, mechanical and organic solidarity, or *Gemeinschaft* and *Gesellschaft*. Postmodernism as a sociological doctrine is in the structure of its analysis if not in its explicit values, the theory of modernity in disguise. The disguise is the reidentification of the great historical divide with the break from modernity rather than tradition. In either case we have radically discontinuous theories of history, and the tendency to treat both premodernity and modernity as homogeneous.[7]

The difficulty arises with the very idea of a *sociology* of postmodernity. The sociological move must be to project the characteristics postmodernism ascribes to discourses, whether 'artistic', or 'intellectual', on to social relations; to speak of a postmodern *society*. But how can such a grand diagnosis be made other than on the basis of a new grand narrative? The paradox is noted by one of the most influential advocates of postmodernism, Lyotard: 'the great narratives are now barely credible. And it is therefore tempting to lend credence to the great narrative of the decline of great narratives' (1989: 318).[8]

Bauman has noticed this paradox, but is willing to embrace it:

Proper analysis of the postmodern condition brings us . . . back into the orthodox area of sociological investigation (though an area now structured in an unorthodox way). This means that rather than seeking a new form of a postmodernist sociology (a sociology attuned in its style, as 'an intellectual genre', to the cultural climate of postmodernity), sociologists should be engaged in developing a sociology of postmodernity (i.e. deploying the strategy of systematic, rational discourse to the task of constructing a theoretical model of postmodern society as a system in its own right, rather than a distorted form, or an aberration from another system).

(Bauman 1989: 61)

But how? If, as Bauman argues, the postmodern diagnosis of culture is correct, the conditions for a 'systematic rational discourse' no longer exist. Indeed, how could we even begin to assess a postmodern sociological diagnosis? There is a fatal equivocation in Bauman's honest recognition of the problem which typifies much of the sociological appropriation of postmodernist arguments. Sociologists have not decided whether or not to take postmodernism seriously, but remain suspended in an untenable position in the middle. Either the arguments must be taken seriously, in which case the 'unorthodox structure' Bauman refers to would have to be considerably more unorthodox still, or the postmodernist position has to be abandoned. In either case the challenge of postmodernists has been missed by sociologists who view it as just one more postulate to be fed in to sociological discourse. The grand narrative of a sociology of postmodernism vitiates that which is challenging in postmodernist writings for the sociologist: namely, the deconstructivist critique of the pretensions to which sociological foundationalism may be just as prone as the theory of knowledge. Here again, the *sociological* discussion of postmodernity appears to support Habermas's view of the inherently contradictory character of these arguments.

Before going on to suggest a way in which sociology can examine 'postmodernism' as a sociological phenomenon without slipping into the new formalist terminology of a postmodern 'society' or postmodern 'condition', we shall consider the most influential critique of the arguments of the postmodernists: namely, Habermas's assimilation of postmodernism into forms of 'neo' and 'young' conservatism.

THE MODERNIST RESPONSE AND SOME OF ITS LIMITATIONS

Habermas's early response to postmodernism came in his lecture 'Modernity versus postmodernity' (published in 1981).[9] In it he identifies three strands of conservative reaction against modernity: 'old conservative', 'young conservative' and 'neo-conservative'. The last two he associates with aspects of postmodernism. Of the young conservatives (among whom he includes Foucault and Derrida) Habermas writes:

[They] recapitulate the basic experience of aesthetic modernity. They claim as their own the revelations of a decentred

subjectivity, emancipated from the imperative of work and usefulness, and with this experience they step outside the modern
world. *On the basis of modernist attitudes, they justify an irreconcilable
anti-modernism.*

(Habermas 1981: 13. Emphasis added)

In other words, this strand of postmodernist thinking is premised
upon Habermas's conception of modernity. In contrast, the 'postmodernism' of the neo-conservatives welcomes 'the development
of modern science' (13), has a technocratic conception of politics,
and views aesthetic experience as essentially private and illusory in
its utopian pretensions. Habermas fears an alliance between the
young conservatism of much 'alternative culture' with the neo-
conservatism of the new right. He thus links the postmodernist
critique of modernity to the '*Tendenzwende*' (political and ideological shift to the right in the USA and Western Europe in the
early 1980s). Although the argument is very sketchy at this stage,
largely consisting of unsupported assertions, 'Modernity versus
postmodernity' makes quite explicit the modernist objections to
postmodernist thought: the latter is viewed as an anti-Enlighten-
ment reaction to modernity which can be potentially allied to a
regressive and illiberal politics. Habermas develops the arguments
supporting these assertions in *The Philosophical Discourse of
Modernity* (1987b). The nature of his objections is clear in his
critique of Foucault, and it is on this that we shall focus.

Habermas makes several criticisms of Foucault's 'micro-physics
of power', but most are variations of the old 'genetic fallacy'
argument which was famously made by Popper against Mannheim
and the sociology of knowledge in the 1940s. In its original form,
the criticism is that the central claim of the sociology of knowledge
– that all knowledge/truth is socially situated – is self-contradictory
since this proposition is itself a truth claim and, if true, would only
be situationally true. Similarly for Habermas, Foucault must
address the 'methodological problem of how a history of the
constellations of reason and madness can be written at all, if the
labour of the historian must in turn move about within the horizon
of reason' (1987b: 247). That he fails adequately in the task
Habermas traces to Foucault's conflation of the 'will to truth' with
the 'will to power' (in the notion of 'power/knowledge'), and to
his 'innocent positivism'.[10]

Not without a note of sarcasm, Habermas points up the contrast between this reductionism and his own notion of the disinterested search for truth in which, in his well-known phrase, 'the only force is the force of better argument': 'naturally, Foucault does not allow himself to be influenced by the ostensive lack of coercion of the cogent argument by which truth claims, and the validity claims in general, prevail' (1987b: 247).11 The general criticism is then that Foucault's project – the reasoned historiography of unreason – is incoherent. Such a history can proceed neither on the basis of unreason nor, except at the cost of naïve positivism, reason. But Habermas is not satisfied with this. He also wants to show that the incoherence of the project feeds directly into the concepts Foucault uses. Centrally, these are his conceptions of 'practice' and 'power'.

Both concepts are intended to provide a language for discussing the social which does not start from the subject. But for Habermas, Foucault cannot exclude a subject without, as above, slipping into self-contradiction. Habermas criticizes Foucault for his 'unsociological concept of the social' (1987b: 242) and for his equivocal uses of the concept of practice and, especially, power. The key passage of Habermas's critique appears to us to be the following, and it is worth quoting it in full:

> In his basic concept of power, Foucault has forced together the idealist idea of transcendental synthesis with the presupposition of an empirical ontology. This approach cannot lead to a way out of the philosophy of the subject, because the concept of power that is supposed to provide a common denominator for the contrary semantic components has been taken from the repertoire of the philosophy of the subject. According to this philosophy, the subject can take up basically two, and only two, relationships towards the world of imaginable and manipulable objects: cognitive relationships regulated by the *truth* of judgements; and practical relationships regulated by the *success* of actions. Power is that by which the subject has an effect on the objects in successful actions. In this connection, success in action depends upon the truth of the judgements that enter into the plan of action; via the criterion of success in action, power remains dependent on truth. Foucault abruptly reverses power's truth-dependency into the power-dependency of truth. Then foundationally power no longer needs to be bound to the

competencies of acting and judging subjects – power becomes subjectless.

(Habermas 1987b: 274)

The accusation here is not merely one of incoherence. Habermas is also concerned to show that the result of this subjectless conception of power is, first, that the object of social scientific enquiry becomes disembodied discourse (Foucault is both an empiricist *and* an idealist – a criticism which accords with Kant's argument that 'empirical realism' is compatible with 'transcendental idealism'); and second, that any emancipatory or critical element is lost to such a conception.

The disembodiment of discourse within poststructuralism is directly related to its loss of critical import. Habermas argues that while Foucault 'understands himself as a dissident who offers resistance to modern thought and humanistically disguised disciplinary power' (1987b: 282) there is no basis in his 'genealogy' for such dissidence, and grounds only for pessimism: 'why should we muster any resistance at all against this all-pervasive power circulating in the bloodstream of the body of modern society, instead of just adapting ourselves to it?' (1987b: 283-4).[12] The conception of power as subjectless, and Foucault's treatment of 'humane' punishment as merely the exercise of power in a new discourse of the body, leads him to reject any notion of progress; and with this move he further loses the possibility of a *critique* of modernity:

As soon as he passes from the Classical to the modern age, Foucault pays no attention whatsoever to penal *law* and the *law* governing penal process. Otherwise, he would have to submit the unmistakable gains in liberty and legal security, and the expansion of civil-rights guarantees even in this area, to an exact interpretation in terms of the theory of power.

(Habermas 1987b: 290)

The apparent radicalism of Foucault's position *vis-à-vis* the modern discourse of reform and cure disguises its conservatism and pessimism. For Habermas, critique can only retain its force if we recognize the Janus-faced character of modernity as *both* the expansion of instruments of repression *and* as progress.

It is not merely this refusal of any notion of progress (the 'presentism' of poststructuralism, as Habermas dubs it), but also its disembodied conception of discourse which is the source of its relativism and resignation. Crudely, the conception of a *discourse* of discipline and punishment lacks both a conception of an alternative and a subject who can be liberated, and liberate:

> When, like Foucault, one admits only the model of processes of subjugation, of confrontations mediated by the body, of contexts of more or less consciously strategic action; when one excludes any stabilization of domains of action in terms of values, norms, and processes of mutual understanding and offers for these mechanisms of social integration none of the familiar equivalents from systems or exchange theories; then one is hardly able to explain just how persistent local struggles could get consolidated into institutionalized power.
>
> (Habermas 1987b: 287)

To sum up, Habermas criticizes Foucault, and by extension poststructuralism in general, for (i) its relativism; (ii) its self-contradiction; (iii) its idealism; (iv) its lack of a conception of critique and of emancipatory practice. Furthermore, these characteristics are linked, *and* they all stem from its failure to ground social science in a conception of mutual understanding.

We are interested here in Habermas's arguments not merely as a critique of Foucault, but also as a critique of postmodernist thought in general. In this regard we shall examine the following questions: (i) Are these criticisms justified? (ii) Has Habermas accurately identified the source of poststructuralism's weakness?[13] In the remaining sections of the chapter we shall answer the first question largely affirmatively and the second negatively.

Habermas's critique of postmodernist thought, and his own alternative account of modernity, are open both sociologically and philosophically to the criticism that they are formalist (cf. Chapter 4). With respect to the philosophical issue, Charles Taylor raises a fundamental question (Taylor 1986). Taylor's concern is whether we can rest a theory of communicative action on the narrow base of a purely formal rationality-ethic. For Habermas, it is not an image of the 'good life' with a specific content, but rather a 'procedural rationality' which provides critique with its justification. Taylor argues that such formalist ethics, in which ethical claims are vindicated through appeal to their universalizability rather than their substance, disingenuously rely upon an implicit though hidden substantive ethic. The weakness of this position becomes apparent, Taylor argues, when we pose the question: 'Why should I strive towards rational forms of communication/understanding (*Verständigungsformen*)?' (cf. our critique of Habermas's formalism in Chapter 4). Rational understanding may be only one of my aims: getting my way, for example, may be another. This question for Taylor can only be answered on the basis of a substantive ethical claim: I must be able to show why rationality has such a value for me that all other priorities must be subordinated to it. Habermas's formal argument cannot escape the substantive claim that rational communication is a fundamental value, and this value cannot be secured formally.

The second level on which Habermas's argument is venerable is the sociological one, and this is brought out clearly by Joas (1986), Alexander (1986), and McCarthy (1985). These critics raise the question: 'Can Habermas use system theory neutrally, i.e. without importing some of its substantive assumptions?' The substantive assumptions of systems theory are precisely what Habermas wants to avoid: the assertion that social life *must* obey the logic of a system, and that the internal dynamic of the system is one of perpetual growth and ever greater differentiation. Were Habermas to allow either of these claims, his critical intent, indeed the notion of critique itself, would be lost. Yet reading *The Theory of Communicative Action* raises such doubts. As Joas argues:

> with this mode of expression Habermas confounds the distinction between the theory of action and theory of social order on the one hand, with the questions of the transition to a functionalist/systems–theoretical solution to the problem of order on the other; and with the substantive question of the extent of an intention-independent course of events within societal processes. Action theory as such is not in competition with the theory of order, and does not in any way contain the empirical assumption that all outcomes of action lie within intentions, are under the control, or are within the intuitive knowledge of the actor.
>
> (Joas 1986: 155)

There is an unresolved problem in Habermas's attitude to the views of the previous generation of Critical Theorists. On the one hand, he rejects the relativism and implicit historical fatalism of the formulation of Critical Theory as a 'negative dialectic'. Critical Theory must be grounded if resignation and relativism are to be avoided. But, on the other hand, there is something half-hearted about the conclusion to volume 2 of *The Theory of Communicative Action* when Habermas turns from the critique of modernity to the positive tasks of Critical Theory. His identification of new forms of protest potential in the new social movements not only appears unconvincing in the light of the challenge modernity poses, but it appears not even to have convinced Habermas himself. In a long book exposing the dilemmas of modernity, Habermas leaves little room for explaining why we should not merely give ourselves up to the inevitable. Habermas thus seems himself vulnerable to the criticism he levels against Foucault: resignation.

The suspicion is that there is an implicit fatalism in the formulations of *The Theory of Communicative Action* which is at least as strong as that found in the works of the previous generation of Critical Theorists, or in some poststructuralists and postmodernists. Alexander (1986) polarizes the issue by inviting Habermas to abandon the claims of Critical Theory and throw in his lot with structural functionalism. It is not always clear why Habermas should decline such an invitation.

CONCLUSION

Why has modernization theory and the modernity versus postmodernity debate reached an impasse? What is sociology to make of 'postmodernism'? We suggest that the participants in the debate, whatever their philosophical differences, share a common conception of sociology as totalizing diagnosis, and only by abandoning this notion can we come to terms with the phenomenon of 'postmodernism'.[14]

While sociologists have (unsociologically) tended either to adopt postmodernism or reject it *in toto*, it has been left to the literary critic Andreas Huyssen (1986) to make the basic sociological point that postmodernism in a social and intellectual *movement* which attempts to generalize its self-understanding, and project it on to social relations. An uncritical sociological reception of postmodernism can only assist this process. Huyssen's historical argument that postmodernism is best understood as an oppositional trend or movement, and above all a cultural trend, is more plausible than the notion of a totalizing 'postmodern condition'. Huyssen's interpretation points up the tendency of sociologists to mistake a movement for a society and the parts for the whole, and in so doing reduce social relations to a cultural epiphenomenon. *Society* is not 'postmodern' because it was never simply 'modern'. Both modernism and postmodernism are movements or ideologies attempting to impose themselves. Both are 'incomplete projects', to use Habermas's phrase. But even this term is confusing as it implies that they could potentially be completed. This too would be an 'unsociological conception of the social' (Habermas's accusation against Foucault) because it treats the social as, potentially at least, homogeneous and uncontested.

By placing postmodernist arguments in their historical context and viewing them relationally as a reaction against some aspects of modernism, Huyssen is also able to argue that there are elements of continuity between postmodernism and modernism which the usual 'versus' implied or, as in Habermas 1981, stated suggests:

> the revolt of the 1960s was never a rejection of modernism *per se*, but rather a revolt against that version of modernism which had been domesticated in the 1950s.
>
> (Huyssen 1986: 190)

The continuity, Huyssen implies, stems from a crisis within the modernist movement against which postmodernism is a reaction:

> The situation in the 1970s seemed to be characterized rather by an ever wider dispersal and dissemination of artistic practices all working out of the ruins of the modernist edifice, raiding it for ideas, plundering its vocabulary and supplementing it with randomly chosen images and motifs from pre-modern cultures as well as contemporary mass culture.
>
> (Huyssen 1986: 196)

The modernist versus postmodernist 'debate' is something of an illusion. This is not to deny the very real *philosophical* differences between those who wish to defend and those who wish to question the 'Enlightenment project' (as if there were one such project), but to suggest that *sociologically* the interlockers in the 'dispute' have much in common. They share a monolithic image of society as *either* modernity *or* postmodernity (as though it could not be both). Huyssen picks up on this too when he argues that both Habermas and his postmodernist critics have a onesided view of what modernity is: *either* enlightenment *or* repression:

> Habermas's notion of modernity is purged of modernism's nihilistic and anarchistic strain just as his opponent's . . . notion of an aesthetic (post) modernism is determined to liquidate any trace of the enlightened modernity inherited from the eighteenth century which provides the basis for Habermas's notion of modern culture.
>
> (Huyssen 1986: 200)

Huyssen does not dismiss the importance of postmodernism, as its neo-conservative critics tend to do, but insists upon its relationship to modernism and modernity:

> Postmodernism at its deepest level represents not just another crisis within the perpetual cycle of boom and bust, exhaustion and renewal, which has characterized the trajectory of modernist culture. It rather represents a new type of crisis *of* that modernist culture itself.
>
> (Huyssen 1986: 217)

Huyssen's characterization of postmodernism as a tendency, a reaction against aspects of modernity, strikes us as more historical and, because historical, more sociological than the grand narratives of modernity and postmodernity characteristic of the modernity debate.

Similarly, while Habermas's dispute with the postmodernists focuses essentially on the question of where the great divide comes, and therefore what values to ascribe to it, postmodernists share with Habermas, and with more standard sociological interpretations of modernity such as Mannheim's, a formalist periodization of sociohistorical development.

While accurately locating many of the problems associated with the poststructuralist and postmodernist positions, Habermas has partially misidentified their roots. It is not merely in their equivocal relationship to the philosophy of the subject, but their equivocal relationship to the philosophy of history in which many of the difficulties of the 'postmodernists' lie. But Habermas shares this relationship to the philosophy of history with the writers whom he otherwise opposes. Both seek a single, coherent and unambiguous 'meaning' in social relations and practices. What divided them is their optimism or pessimism about finding it (though the pessimism is itself premised upon some total picture). Neither has broken free from the hold of the philosophy of history which posits two, and only two, possible relations to the world: certainty or anarchy. The task of sociology, as Mannheim inconsistently realized, is to attempt to make sense of the world in the absence of the hope of a grand, new, totalizing and all-encompassing synthesis.

We suggest that in order to understand the phenomena of *either* modernity *or* postmodernity sociologically we must start from the following assumptions: (i) neither conception defines or delineates a social condition in its totality; (ii) both modernity and postmodernity are *ideas* attached to intellectual and social *movements*; (iii) they are social projects aimed at defining social relations, and, crucially, in so doing gaining, at least intellectual, control over those social relations. To talk of a 'postmodern' (or a modern) condition as though this were a social totality is not merely (in the case of postmodernist thought) self-contradictory, it is also to use the language of the philosophy of history to describe societal processes. The substitution of a philosophy of history for sociological analysis is a central characteristic of what we have referred to as 'formalism'. As his own work illustrates, Habermas is wrong when he asserts that the battle between social theory and the philosophy of history is over, and has been won by the former.

The entire modernity versus postmodernity debate has done little to change the relationship between sociology and philosophy. The old subordination remains whether we side with the Habermasians or the postmodernists. In either case highly abstract intellectualistic diagnoses of the (post)modern condition are discussed at a level of abstraction several degrees removed from societal practices. In this mode sociology remains the hedgehog who only knows 'one big thing'.

NOTES

1 For an account of the history of the terms 'postmodern' and 'post-modernism', see Huyssen 1986: 188–99.
2 Honneth too notes the confusions brought about by this conceptual importation: 'In the meantime, the category *postmodern* has reached the social sciences, where it is responsible for confusion, in that it has spawned the most peculiar coalitions' (1985: 147).
3 See, for example, his comparison of Habermas and Lyotard where Rorty appears closer to Habermas despite his criticisms (Rorty 1985).
4 Heller and Fehér are themselves sceptical of this postmodernist claim

precisely because they view the notion of a single 'European project' or European culture as a relatively late (nineteenth-century) invention. If there is such a project, they argue, then it is the idea of modernity itself, and this, though no longer 'European', is not dead. See Heller and Fehér 1990: ch. 11.

5 Postmodernists would reject the accusation of relativism on the grounds that relativism, and anxiety over relativism, presupposes subject/object relations which, since both subject *and* object are constituted, makes no sense. In fact such a defence of 'relativism' has a longish history in the sociology of knowledge, especially in the works of Karl Mannheim.

6 They have also come to influence the work of radical geographers and urban sociologists. See, for example, Harvey 1989; and Cooke 1989.

7 For a detailed critique of the 'historicist' assumptions of modernization theory – though applicable also to a wide range of grand historical theorizing – see Goldthorpe 1971.

8 The point has also turned against postmodernists: 'while Lyotard resists grand narratives, it is impossible to discern how one can have a theory of postmodernism without one. Rejecting grand narratives, I believe, simply covers over the theoretical problem of providing a narrative of the contemporary historical situation and points to the under theorized nature of Lyotard's theory of the postmodern condition – which would require at least some sort of rather large narrative of the transition to postmodernism – a rather big and exciting story one would think' (Kellner 1988: 253).

9 For a lucid account of Habermas's debates with postmodernists, see Jay: 'Habermas and postmodernism' in Jay 1988.

10 'Foucault exposed himself to palpable objections, because his historiography, despite its antiscientific tenor, seeks to proceed both "eruditely" and "positivistically"' (Habermas 1987b: 257).

11 The statement is, if anything, more sarcastic in the original where Habermas uses the word 'impress' (*beeindrucken*) rather than 'influence', as in the translation.

12 Rorty has made a similar point: 'It takes no more than a squint of the inner eye to read Foucault as a stoic, a dispassionate observer of the present social order, rather than a concerned critic' (1985: 172).

13 We are assuming for the sake of this argument that there is no significant difference between the tendencies in poststructuralist and postmodernist thought.

14 Jay, in a sympathetic discussion of Habermas's aesthetic theory, notes that Habermas is aware of the problematic status of 'emancipation' in his work: 'But he has recognized, although many of his critics have been slow to acknowledge it, that [reason's] full realization alone cannot provide us with the substantive visions of the good life which will make discussion worthwhile' (1988: 136).

Chapter 6

Conclusion
Theory and history

'Too many witnesses telling the same thing, Jimmy.'
'Perhaps because it was the truth, Sir.'
'The truth is never exactly the same thing,' said Douglas.

(Len Deighton *SS – GB*: 83)

INTRODUCTION

By neglecting historical and social context we limit our understanding of what we study and invite a philosophical attitude
towards the object of our understanding. A sociology grounded in
philosophy defines its theory of rationality and science formal-
istically. We are opposed to this tendency not out of a preference
for relativism and a dislike of theory, but because we do not believe
that sociological arguments can be secured through transcendental logic, consciousness, or conceptual schemes. It is simply
bad faith to treat sociological 'truths' as immutable and incorrigible. For sociology must be grounded in history and the
concrete, e.g. in a political or ethical engagement. Social knowledge is anchored in our past and present social experiences. Such
knowledge arises from an *attempt* to come to terms with those
experiences and is more akin to individual or group struggles to
understand their lives than it is to a quasi-theological search for a
few fixed reference points to which everything, and therefore
nothing, can be understood.

Philosophy has been used to give sociology such a secure
underpinning. In doing so, a philosophical attitude has also been
absorbed into sociology's substantive analysis. It is the effects of
this absorption that we wish to consider in the first section of this
chapter.

We may think it paradoxical to suggest that sociology exemplifies a philosophical attitude because it has traditionally opposed
philosophy and has focused on substantive issues. Marx's critique
of the 'German ideology', Durkheim's rejection of social analysis
based on social/political philosophy, Habermas's insistence that
epistemology is, or has become, social theory, Mannheim and
Elias's programme for a sociology as opposed to a theory of
knowledge, all exemplify this sociological critique. Our case is, as
we argued in relation to Lévi-Strauss and Habermas, that this is
sociology's ambiguous project. Relativism has been the dizzy
precipice which has driven sociology back from the consequences
of its own arguments and towards the apparent terra firma of
philosophical discourse.

In this chapter we shall conclude by illustrating the remaining
influence in sociology with respect to the following: (i) on an
approach to sociology teaching and research which relies more on
the history of ideas than on substantive analysis; (ii) the kind of
intellectual timidity which stems from this. Finally, we shall make
some proposals for a sociological approach to rationality and
science which moves us away from a view which underpins rationalism and formalism. The view of rationality and scientific knowledge developed here will stress rationality as a *learning process a
posteriori* to experience, rather than necessary and prior to it.

THE PHILOSOPHICAL ATTITUDE IN SOCIOLOGY

The philosophical attitude in sociology manifests itself both in our
self-understanding of the discipline and in our interpretation of
society, particularly of societies with which we are less familiar. In
this section we shall examine the effect of the philosophical attitude in sociology's self-understanding, and on the use to which we
put classical sociological texts.

The past in the present I: sociology's self-understanding

The residual philosophical attitude is nowhere better demonstrated than in sociologists' use of classical texts. It is the followers
of the classical writers, more than those writers themselves, who in
their talmudic/biblical orientation to texts slip into formalism.
There has been a progressive retreat from the object of socio-

logical analysis proportional to the reverence in which the classical texts are held. While Weber was interested in explaining the rise of capitalism, we are interested in the structure of Weber's argument, in the contemporary influences upon it, or in its similarity/ dissimilarity to Marx's interpretation. It is as though *our* understanding of the rise of capitalism is proportional to the adequacy of our grasp of *their* explanations of it. But the situation is more complex than this. In fact, the preoccupation with classical texts may be justified on scholarly grounds, that is to say, in the study of the history of ideas, but it certainly cannot be used to provide explanatory 'models' or secure, once and for all, research techniques or programmes. Otherwise the assumption is that truth is *revealed* to us through classical texts; and more through respectful exegesis than critical dialogue. Here a surface hermeneutic is preferred to a deep hermeneutic, and any kind of hermeneutic is preferred to an independent investigation of the object of the text. This reverence is, paradoxically, a hindrance even to understand the work of the classical sociologists.

The philosophical attitude draws us towards 'analytical reductionism' and 'conceptual parochialism'. The social history of the discipline is understood exclusively through a focus on the theoretical and cultural systems it creates.

In *Philosophy and its Past* (1978), Ree, Ayres and Westoby show how philosophers make bad historians of ideas. Russell's biography of Leibniz is used to illustrate the 'analytical reductionism' consequent upon the carrying-over of philosophical modes of discourse on to the self-understanding of philosophy's past. Russell hoped to discover 'great philosophies' without regard to 'dates or influences'. The actual sociohistorical location of philosophical texts bears no logical relation to their philosophical arguments, and was therefore of no immediate relevance: 'philosophical truth and falsehood, in short, rather than historical fact, are what primarily demands our attention' (Russell quoted in Ree et al. 1978: 29). Biographical detail makes good tittle-tattle but nothing more, and is in any case a good deal less interesting than the ideas those individuals happen to produce.

The single legitimate focus of philosophical analysis of past philosophies is on their logical coherence, as measured and understood against *our* modern standards of adequacy, relevance, coherence, etc. Past thinkers become curiously modernized. For all relevant intents and purposes they are as our contemporaries.

Thus, as Ree et al. observe, Leibniz is treated by Russell as a secular thinker, in fact as an analytical philosopher. His theological justifications for his ontology are ignored, and his religious convictions excluded. Leibniz becomes exclusively a precursor of the kind of analytical approach Russell himself exemplified. In Quentin Skinner's terms, Russell demonstrates 'conceptual parochialism': 'the capacity of the observer to fore-shorten the past by filling it with his own reminiscences' (1969: 27. See also Dunn 1968).

For Ree et al., this approach makes it possible for philosophers to represent philosophy as a 'self-contained, eternal sector of intellectual production' (1978: 32), and to dislocate its concerns from any sociohistorical or political context. Theirs is a critique with which most sociologists would sympathize. Thus Giddens:

> I believe that sociologists must always be conscious of the social context within which theories are formulated. But to stress this does not entail acceptance of a wholly relativistic position, according to which the 'validity' of a given conception is only limited to the circumstances which give rise to it.
>
> (Giddens 1971: x)

The problem arises, however, in the execution of these intentions.

With notable exceptions, for example Nisbet, Lukes and some phenomenologists,[1] most sociological reconstructions of the discipline's past also display analytical reductionism.[2] On those occasions when the development of ideas is treated historically, as in the case of Aron's examination of Weber (1964), the influences are viewed internally, i.e. in terms of the history of ideas developing within the discipline rather than in its interaction with the environment. Thus, Durkheim's evolutionism is typically treated as a continuation of Spencer's and not as part of a European tradition of evolutionism, and a justification for colonialism, of which both Durkheim *and* Spencer are a part.

The point can be illustrated more precisely with reference to Julien Freund's justly influential *The Sociology of Max Weber* (1972). Freund makes little reference to Weber's biography nor to his commitments and preferences. In the chapter 'Weber's vision of the world', Freund talks of Weber's passion for 'defining the concepts he used and distinguishing between orders of problems and different levels of any one problem' (1972: 4) without giving much idea of why Weber should have a 'passion' about such an odd thing.

To avoid making Weber appear nothing more than a tiresome pedant, we would need to know why he came to believe that such a cautious categorizing was important, and the kinds of intellectual and social issues he hoped thereby to address or counter. Instead, his ideas are presented as the insights of a genius who rose above the uncomprehending mediocrity.

In Parkin's study of Weber we find a similar view of the relevance, or irrelevance, of biography:

> There is hardly anything in the main body of the text about Weber 'the man' – his career, his family life, his political doings, of his occasional bouts of madness. For those interested in these things I have provided a brief [two and a half page] biographical sketch.
>
> (Parkin 1982: 11)

Parkin considers Weber 'the man' irrelevant and treats his background as something of a joke. The single focus, as with Russell, is on the 'substance' of his ideas: the methodology, the theory of action, and his analysis of authority, stratification, etc.

Although our orientation towards past texts has become largely interpretative rather than practical, this attitude actually hinders even adequate interpretation. While the pragmatic use of texts may appear cavalier to those for whom accurate and scholarly interpretation has become an end in itself, in one sense it is still truer to the intentions of the classical authors. If we do not understand that their concerns were practical and engaged, then no amount of scholarly examination of sources will enable us to understand the intentions behind the texts, and hence the meaning of the texts themselves. If we treat the biography of the author, his/her social situation and values, including political engagements, etc., as externals, then we cannot hope to approach an understanding.

The unconscious nature of adoption of the philosophical attitude in such writings is probably something of a blessing: it at least excluded its explicit ideological justification. Nevertheless, there are substantive consequences. Once the ideas of the classical thinker are found to be coherent, all the practising sociologist has to do is learn, internally digest and then apply them. The possibility of an active dialogue between substantive sociological research and the 'sociological tradition' and its guardians, is thus foreclosed. Weber, Marx and Durkheim's engagement with comparative history and sociology is at an end. Sociologists become theoretically timid and assume that a conceptual analysis of *past* sociological concepts is the same thing as active theorizing.

The past in the present II: sociological timidity

The treatment of the works of classical sociologists, at once reverent and modernizing, affects not only how we understand our discipline, but also how we practise it. Having conducted conceptual analysis of such sociological concepts as 'mechanical' and 'organic' solidarity, 'modernity', 'postmodernity' and 'tradition', and so on, there is little attempt to assess their historical or descriptive accuracy. Instead they are treated as the building blocks of the sociological method and a permanent framework for sociological knowledge.

This attitude is exemplified most profoundly in the socialization process of new sociologists. Students are taught to learn these concepts as if they were received wisdom. There is something almost masonic about both the way we treat the basic concepts of sociology, and how we use these concepts to initiate new generations. Students are taught theory and to criticize; but criticism is understood largely as the pitching of the arguments of one 'founding father' against those of another. Criticism is in any case exclusively conceptual. For the student, the boundaries of the discipline do not appear to be defined by its subject matter, but by what those thinkers who are designated to us as 'classical sociologists' have written. While we may question the ideas of classical sociologists, the historical assumptions which lie behind those ideas (e.g. Marx's assumption that capitalism is the highest stage of (pre-communist) society) remain for many largely unexamined. One effect is that students treat his ideas as received wisdom. However, such wisdom can carry assumptions from nineteenth-century theories of evolution and remain caught in that intellectual and political timewarp. For those who go on to become sociologists, they learn to become intellectually timid.

John H. Goldthorpe sees this timidity exemplified in the way we constantly invoke classical sociologists. 'How,' he asks, 'is this intellectual piety to be accounted for?' (1968: 10). The answer perhaps lies in the fact that the arguments of the classical sociologists are held to *constitute* sociological theory. In this spirit Ronald Fletcher purports to find a 'core of truth' in the 'midst of extravagance' within Comte's work (Fletcher 1966: 3). It is as if all our efforts since Comte, or Marx, or Simmel, or whichever thinker the commentator happens to be advocating, had been wasted. In fact, all we need is to be found somewhere in the works of that thinker. In the case of Fletcher's Comte, Comte is credited with having already advocated Popper's hypothetico-deductive method and Parsonian social system's theory. 'Comte's problems,' we are told, 'are our problems' (1966: 17).

As Skinner observes, historians of ideas stick closely to the text in order to isolate those 'timeless elements' in the form of 'universal ideas', or even a 'dateless wisdom' with 'universal application' (1969: 4). If this attitude is carried over into the treatment of sociological texts, what is forgotten is why we read, and need, those texts in the first place: not to provide us with 'dateless wisdom', but to aid *us* in *our* attempts to theorize.

Several types of justification are used to legitimize the reverence in which classical texts are held. Pitirim Sorokin, in his foreword to Tönnies's *Gemeinschaft und Gesellschaft*, appeals to the notion of the timeless concept. The Gemeinschaft/Gesellschaft distinction, Sorokin argues, can be found in some form in thinkers from Plato through Tönnies to himself, and thinkers as culturally diverse as Confucius and Durkheim:

> After all, among the fundamental categories and concepts of the social sciences there is hardly one that was not mentioned, developed, and used by the social thinkers of antiquity and past centuries.
>
> (Sorokin 1955: vi)

In contrast, H. Stuart Hughes identifies himself, and the humanities as a whole, with one particular period: the Enlightenment:

> My own position is quite consciously 'eighteenth century'. I believe that we are all . . . children of the Enlightenment, and that it is from this standpoint that civilized members of Western society – the heirs to a humane tradition more than two centuries old – almost necessarily judge the political and social movements of our time.
>
> (Hughes 1974: 27)

Quoting Ernst Cassirer approvingly, he urges us to be self-critical in our age too by 'holding up to it that bright clear mirror fashioned by the Enlightenment' (Cassirer quoted in Hughes 1974: 27). While admitting that some useful work has been done since, Hughes believes that the ethical postulates and rational solutions of the Enlightenment represent 'an abiding legacy of overriding importance: as a guide to intellectuals' (1974: 28).

Whether we appeal to timeless concepts, or to some golden age of intellectual glory, the effect is to induce awe towards the classical texts and a timidity in our treatment of the ideas they contain. Furthermore this has substantive consequences for how we go about our work. A researcher who believes himself or herself to be holding up the 'clear mirror fashioned by the Enlightenment' is bound to run into problems in interpreting non-European cultures or feudalism. The eighteenth-century salon becomes the yardstick against which all else must be measured, and against which all other standards fall short.

To avoid the parochial reading of sociology's past, and the resultant timidity, sociology must develop a comparative theory of rationality and science with which it can counter the pervasiveness of the philosophical attitude. For without this, we cannot *do* sociology. We shall be developing simply bad history of ideas and futile exegesis. It is to the alternative conception of rationality that we now turn.

TOWARDS A SOCIOLOGICAL INTERPRETATION OF RATIONALITY

The view of rationality which underlies the philosophical attitude is one that appeals to anthropological universals. For Bennett that will be defined as 'whatever it is that humans possess which marks themselves off, in respect of intellectual capacity, sharply and importantly from all other known species' (Bennett 1964: 5).[5] This is both too broad and too narrow a definition. Such definitions are selective; they rarely mean *all* those intellectual capacities which mark off humans from animals. Typically they mean those characteristics held to be culturally and historically universal: the uniform principles of a philosophical anthropology. Nietzsche characterizes such approaches thus:

> [They] involuntarily think of 'man' as *aeterna veritas*, as something that remains constant in the midst of all flux, as a sure

measure of things . . . Lack of historical sense is the family failing of all philosophies.

(Nietzsche 1977: 29)

If we reject this formalist view, as we clearly do, an alternative account may be found in the work of Wittgensteinians like Peter Winch for whom:

> Rationality is not *just* a concept *in* language like any other; it is this too . . . It is a concept necessary to the existence of any language: to say of a society that it has a language is also to say that it has a concept of rationality.

(Winch 1970: 99)

This binds rationality firmly to a social and cultural context, but remains ahistorical. The relativism of which Winch has often been accused[4] does not stem, we would argue, from his relativizing rationality to cultural context, but from his static conception of that context. Among other things, what has disturbed Winch's critics is the recognition that linguistically and socially competent subjects are capable of performing shockingly 'irrational' actions, such as gratuitous acts of violence. Any concept of rationality which does not enable us to distinguish the rational and irrational *within* language (except in the minimal sense of falsely executed actions according to local rules) is bound to trouble us and appear impoverished. This recognition has tended to drive Winch's critics back towards universalistic conceptions of rationality of the type described at the start of this section. We shall argue that a conception of rationality as a cultural and historical learning process enables us to avoid both absolutism and ethical relativism.

Our view of rationality is based upon the idea of the progressive institutionalizing of learned standards. This sociological view of rationality must remain historically and contextually bound, but it need not imply cognitive and ethical egalitarianism: i.e. that one view is as good as another. However, as Barry Barnes (1983) points out, even writers influenced by the sociology of knowledge are not fully aware of the 'precise implications' of a socialized theory of knowledge. For Barnes, the social nature of knowledge appears to most sociologists as an 'optional extra' or as 'something which stands in opposition to the character of knowledge as representation of reality' (1983: 20). Drawing back from relativism does not require this retreat into objectivism.

A sociological view of reason has to abandon the Kantian idea that reason is the only reliable guide for history and social life and remains conceptually separate and above human action and community. Reason *is* a criterion which guides human action, but it is transcendental only in the sense that it is derived from previous actions and reflections. Reason arises out of an *awareness* of human history, while it also helps to determine and set limits to the process of deciding a new consciousness. But it no more sets absolute limits to human action than it is anthropological.

An appeal to reason is an appeal not to trans-cultural standards but to institutionalized or even internationalized cultural knowledge. Individuals are rational when they appeal to reason to adjudicate *aspects* of their lives and clear up individual conflict and confusions. They become irrational when they believe that those embodied standards are absolute and static, or believe that there is an absolute distinction between reason and their own interest-bound decision-making processes.[5]

The view of rationality we are recommending here focuses on the institutionalization of three types of standards: (i) historical; (ii) sociological; and (iii) aesthetic. These standards are contained *within* cultural traditions. To act rationally by this conception is, in the first place, to engage with traditionally developed conventions and knowledge within our own culture. This appropriation of 'institutionalized cognition' (Barnes 1983) is what we mean by 'historical' standards of rationality. The second, sociological, standard consists of the awareness of, and willingness to communicate with, alternative cultural traditions, and a sensitivity to the limits of our own traditions. Finally, by the 'aesthetic' standard we mean the process of learning symbols, linguistic concepts (including formal ones), and learning the social skills of argumentation, competition and reaching compromises which are embodied in human cultural formations.

We do not have in mind here the Habermasian or Apelian notion that reaching agreement (*Einverständnis*) is a transcendental condition of understanding (*Verständnis*) within some idealized community of communicating subjects, and in the absence of power and strategic action. Rather, we assume that compromise is a sociological fact of our living-with-others which must be institutionalized within, and between, actual human communities, and the learning of which is a precondition for individual socialization, and for social progress and understanding.

This presupposes neither an idealized, conflict-free community, nor the absence of power and strategic action which we would view as an integral part of the processes of (rational) social negotiation and not, in the manner of Habermas, as a barrier to it. Reason is a social/inter-societal compromise brought about by known and negotiated facts and perceptions.

We stress that rationality is both *conventional* and *negotiable*. While *conventionalist*, this is not *relativist*. Our position does not imply that 'anything goes', but identifies 'rational' from 'irrational' action in quite a strict way. For example, it is, in our view, irrational for an individual to reject *tout court* the conventions of his/her society, as it is equally irrational not to recognize that they *are* conventions. On this view, reaching compromises is not a mere regulative principle against which we measure our achievements, as 'reaching an understanding' is for Habermas and Apel. It is rather an on-going social project imposed upon individuals and whole communities by the necessity of living with other individuals and other cultures. In the absence of the possibility or desirability of eliminating cultural otherness, though both have been tragically attempted, negotiation and compromise and the institutionalization of new results are forced upon us. But being forced upon us, it is no less valuable; they give meaning. Such negotiation is not an end, transcendental and without meaning. It is a fact of social existence and human action.

In order to flesh out this 'conventionalist' view of rationality, we shall examine its components in more detail.

Historical standards of rationality

By 'historical standards' of rationality, we mean the institutionalized form of past compromises. The impact of these standards is fully felt when they are established in linguistic and social wisdom. 'Interest' in struggle helps to establish these standards, but these standards cannot be reduced to utilitarianism. Interest here does not only signify selfish desire: those who pursue their interests may wish to safeguard their honour (as they understand it), their traditions (as they value them) or reduce inequalities (as they see them). In pursuing interests, they use common-sense, bestow generosity, exploit others and defend what they believe to be creditable ideals. The context is as diverse as it is confused and complicated. People use common-sense arguments, 'logical' arguments and 'illogical' arguments to resolve conflict, end a struggle or reach a compromise. The actions associated with this process can be restrained or wild until some equilibrium which avoids self-destruction is achieved.

The long-term results of these ideological and social struggles, however, are not as arbitrary as this description may at first suggest. Arbitrary solutions (those which fail to satisfy some of the demands – and all solutions are in part arbitrary in this sense) only ensure the revitalization of the struggle at a later date. Real differences reappear, even if short-term agreements are reached or imposed. Historical standards of rationality, therefore, are in part the settlement of theoretical, social and cultural difficulties, confusions and struggles. The hope, though not always realized, is that once these standards are agreed, the settlement is once and for all, until, that is, they are raised again.

Historical standards of rationality are arbitrary only in the sense that they do not meet rationalistic standards of validity: they are validated in social practices, morals and knowledge. They are accepted in common-sense not when force is applied, but when in spite of differences or force, some equilibrium emerges. The standards reflect people's needs and interests as they are realized in social compromises: they present realities and knowledge that people have gathered. They are neither consensual (in Habermas's sense) nor are they 'shabby'. They are the product of genuine struggles and resolutions over fundamental differences and inequalities. The periods of struggle during which they are created, are characterized by human creativity and endeavour. What is crucial and rational in this process is that the mechanism which is 'responsible for the compulsive nature of our categorical concepts' (see Gellner 1970: 18–19) is collective and observable; not anthropological in the philosophical sense. Its success depends on its institutionalization, reiteration and adoption. What is discovered is retained in people's minds through ritual, religion, social and cultural practices; it does not arise from a philosophical anthropology.

Historical standards of rationality in no way anticipate or necessarily stop infringements. Clearly, individuals or whole social groups infringe those rules which have become institutionalized through the historical development of the society. That such infringements occur, and individuals or groups can go unpunished for their actions, does not invalidate the rationality of society's institutionalized experiences; for it is against those experiences that such individuals or groups are ultimately judged. What this does suggest is that these standards have not fully been institutionalized in legal, social, political and cultural practices. That too becomes part of the societal learning process. But even when they are institutionalized, that will still not provide a transcendental guarantee.

Comparative standards of rationality

The possession of historical standards of rationality does not in itself make actors rational. Comparative standards of rationality constitute their analytical mechanism. These standards perform two tasks: discursive and investigative. The discursive task is analysed by Winch; the investigative by MacIntyre and Gellner.

In the context of their work, Winch supposes that scientists communicate because they are trained uniformly to engage in similar activities. They are then '*capable* of communicating with each other about what they are doing; what any one of them is doing is intelligible to the others' (Winch 1970: 2–3). Part of what we mean by comparative standards of rationality is this ability to make common *use* of historical concepts.

For Winch's critics, such internal standards of rationality are insufficient and restrictive. MacIntyre and Gellner are concerned with the position of the outsider trying to come to terms with the conventions and rules of a society. They both stress the necessity of a critical attitude towards beliefs and local rules and the possibility that those rules may only be intelligible in terms foreign to the form of life in question. For MacIntyre, ability to follow a rule is not, as it is for Winch, coextensive with understanding the rule: 'sometimes to understand a rule involves not sharing it' (see MacIntyre 1970b). Similarly, for Gellner, some concepts are characterized precisely by their unintelligibility:

> use may depend on its lack of meaning, its ambiguity, its possession of wholly different and incompatible meanings in different contexts, *and* on the fact that, at the same time, it as it were emits the impression of possessing a consistent meaning throughout.
>
> (Gellner 1970: 45)

Clearly, both MacIntyre and Gellner find strictly internalist interpretations restrictive because they exclude any form of ideology critique. The validity of the form of life, and of each rule and concept within the form of life, has to be accepted on Winch's account *before* understanding is possible.[6] For Gellner and MacIntyre, such acceptance *excludes* the possibility of understanding. In this spirit, Gellner warns of the danger of 'excessive charity' towards other forms of life.

This dichotomizing of 'internal' versus 'external' understanding, or 'immanent' versus 'externalist' critique, is misguided. Social formations are not only characterized by homogeneity but also discordance; they are defined both by their internal coherence *and* by divisions and ambiguities, by their insularity *and* contact with other forms of life. Both Winch and his critics appear to treat societies as monoliths which confront each other in mutual suspicion and incomprehension. But contact with other forms of life has been a constant fact of societal existence. Indeed, it is hard to imagine a society which is so simple that there are no competing forms of life within it. We move constantly between internal and external forms of understanding within our own cultures and individual lives. Confrontation with an unfamiliar culture is thus only an extension of this everyday experience. Nevertheless, encounters with other cultures leads, or should lead, to different levels of reflection and in the following discussion we use the terms 'internal' and 'external' to capture this, but the terms are themselves relativized. It is this level of interphase which renders contact and dialogue between the internal and external systems, that inequality is eventually addressed and meaning developed. The issue is exemplified by the placement of bilingual learners in the foreign country of the British classroom (see Gurnah 1989).

In their discursive and investigative tasks comparative standards of rationality have both 'internal' and 'external' reference points. The internal reference point depends on the successful *use* of historical standards for rationality, freely to discuss, analyse, counter, criticize, evaluate and compare knowledge and techniques in any particular cultural unit. Thus, rational legitimacy is increased when historical rationality is made use of internally, through the discursive and investigative processes. Legitimacy is increased by a discursive and investigative relationship between various conventions stemming from different interests within the culture, and between cultures. In this way, various ambiguities in establishment views, as well as objections to them, eventually become part of a new discursive balance. An analytical tension is created on historical standards for rationality, and legitimacy is internally increased by dialogue between versions of historical rationality. Sociological rationality, then, provides an internal check mechanism for society's rational framework. For full legitimacy to be attained, other checks are necessary.

External comparative standards for rationality originate from the *perplexity* felt when we encounter other cultures' internal rational frameworks. Their standards set limits to the view that 'Western man [*sic*] understands another culture better than have other men, and better, in particular, than do the participants in it' (Wilson 1970: xii). These external standards are necessary to ensure that scientific imperialism and voyeurism are avoided and in the future permanently rejected. The issue cannot be managed by Weber's concept of *Verstehen* where we equate the term with empathy. Empathetic psychology is incapable of reconstructing other cultures' perspectives; it provides no external check on the scientist. Without such external checks, a scientist cannot be made aware of the fact that social orders may be explicable in terms of a framework previously unknown to him/her. Empathetic psychology of itself does not sensitize us to the possibility, pointed out by Brian Wilson, that cultural relativism may spring from the assumptions of the investigator who believes that 'by ordering their concepts, beliefs, activities according to the premises of the traditional Western social science', we can render unfamiliar beliefs intelligible (see Wilson 1970: xii). Comparative, what we call sociological, standards of rationality, should act as a check on such parochialism. The cultural framework of other societies function *for us* as a control on our own assumptions and as a standard with which we can reflect upon our own cultural heritage and therefore enhance it.

Social subjects do not act solely out of a desire to be 'rational'. There are individual vicissitudes and external pressures causing individuals to act out of ambition, egotism, of the necessity of survival and perusing these ends in ways which may appear 'irrational'. Any *sociological* account of action must strive to render these actions meaningful too, rather than to consign them to the realm of the inexplicable and purely irrational. The irrational is the *inability*, exemplified in philosophy, to do precisely that. Western universalism is relativist and irrational because it is unable

to explain or live with these views. Such actions stretch conceptions of rationality into more indeterminate tantalizing but
promising realms. It is only in the longer term with the ability of
the culture to incorporate such actions in properly institutionalized forms that we can finally make a judgement on the rationality
of these actions. When they are properly institutionalized into
legal and political sanctions and rules, the historical and comparative standards will help define social from anti-social acts.

Aesthetic standards of rationality

The problem facing social science when it confronts other cultures
is essentially this: to what extent can a social analyst understand
'outsiders'' perspectives without being privy to their rational standards? Conversely, if the analyst is only able to gain superficial
knowledge of others, how much can we trust his/her account? In
the previous section, we proposed a sociological mechanism for
dealing with this problem. But while that proposes a practical
procedure, it still does not resolve the issue of meaning. It is to this
that we now turn. For there to be meaning there must be sharing;
when there is sharing this must be *recognized* as such. Lévi-Strauss,
more than any other sociologist, has provided us with the means
by which we can explore the issue of aesthetic standards of
rationality.

The way the problem is normally set up in this debate reproduces eighteenth-century antinomies. We argue that only a
sociological theory of rationality is able to take account of the
difficulties and still resolve the theoretical polarization between an
authentic understanding and mere observation.

It is, in our view, impossible to bridge the gap between authentic
understanding and observation by invoking formal rules or methodological procedures. Different groups, classes and individuals
have different perceptions and interests, and are constantly engaged in defining, struggling and negotiating the best ways of
representing them and achieving them. Interpretation, including
social scientific interpretation, is to be understood as part of this
process; a process which cannot be circumvented, though it can be
disguised, by formal methodological procedures. That such pro-
visional understanding can be attained is part of the answer to the
question: 'How is social life possible *and* successful?'

Meaning is found in these successful relationships, by using socially constructed standards of judgement. But we have argued that this perspective has not been extended to theories of rationality and science sufficiently to bridge the gap between understanding and observation. Realist and positivist theories of knowledge are incapable of evaluating these social relationships so as to engender meaning into them and so avoid teleology, abstraction and racism. To do so we need to evoke the third, aesthetic, standard of rationality implicit in social relations.

'Aesthetic standards' complement historical and comparative standards. If the historical standards arise out of struggle and comparative ones out of critical comparisons and internal consolidations, these aesthetic standards represent the third stage of social communication and evaluation. Aesthetic standards perform the following tasks:

1 They convert the historical and comparative knowledge into representational and symbolic forms which achieve greater permanence and are a more powerful and instantly recognizable symbolic expression of cultural learning.
2 They make and represent cultural truth claims which embody sociological truth.
3 As Lévi-Strauss, when at his best representing empirical universals, demonstrates, new symbolic forms now enable us to make internal truth claims. In other words, cultural production makes symbolic universals possible.
4 Aesthetic standards order and categorize representations, and probably at some level signal greater historical order in things. They therefore stand a greater chance of representing truth. For example, people come to do things and order them in a certain way because they work in this way, or it implies accumulated knowledge and/or rationality.
   The fact that mistakes are made does not invalidate the fact that a preponderance of what has become routine in culture does work, and indeed to such a degree that we are often no longer conscious of it: e.g. don't breathe under water – water suffocates; don't touch fire – fire burns.
5 Aesthetic standards are the empirical realization of our ability to classify.

The role of aesthetic standards is to interrogate and clarify the meaning of new rational consciousness by conducting a close examination of linguistic and scientific concepts. These reflections open up a new dimension which, in the name of science, realists and positivists have excluded. In other words societies process claims to know, including those of science, through their already existing cultural symbols, and thus integrate new knowledge into a modified framework.

These cultural frameworks are not, nor can they be, closed systems. They are of necessity open to comparative and historical learning, and are moulded within this process. Culture is not, as has sometimes been suggested in discussions of 'rationality', a closed system. The 'ultimate goal and value' of human rational standards, as Wilson observes, may 'not fit the instrumental means–end–means schema of self-perpetuation circle that characterizes formal rationality'. To reduce ritual acts, for example, to Western categories would be to make a category mistake and would 'render the categories employed by the ritualists eventually untenable' and destroy an internally coherent 'code of meaning . . . derived from its own social context' (Wilson 1970: xvii).

I.C. Jarvie and J. Agassi concur with Wilson and argue that religion and cults are rational (1970). While Jarvie falters in the last analysis in favouring modern science, he nevertheless makes the essential points: 'in the sense that religious beliefs are theoretical explanations of things and events in the world, they are as rational . . . as other (say scientific) explanation' (1970: 59). He also rejects the argument that there is an 'incompatibility between wants and their satisfaction' in non-Western societies due to low levels of technology:

> When natives want crops they don't just chant: they chant *and they plant seeds*; they chant and they cast their fishing nets; they pray and go out and hunt. That they indulge in magic does not mean they have no science; they fully realize that the two must go together.
>
> (Jarvie 1970: 53)

Robin Horton makes a similar point. He suggests that because it 'puts together in causal context', African thought too is theory in spiritual language:

> To say of the traditional African thinker that he is interested in the supernatural rather than natural causes makes little more sense . . . than to say of the physicist that he is interested in nuclear rather than natural causes. Both are making the same

use of theory to transcend the limited vision of natural causes
provided by common-sense.

(Horton 1970: 136)

As Winch has suggested, a distinction needs to be made between
meaning and function. However, unlike Winch and the cultural-
ists, on the one hand, and positivists on the other, aesthetic standards of rationality refer to both meaning *and* function. Authentic
understanding and observation cannot be divided, as observation
is itself grounded in symbolic structures and categories. Within
this circularity, detailed content analysis of pre-given historical and
comparative standards takes place. The impact of new struggles
and new sociological analysis ensure that aesthetic standards
remain circular only for the duration of any particular discourse.

Aesthetic standards are thus able to remedy a crucial deficiency
of realism, without trivializing its concerns. As Gellner points out,
when a social anthropologist is faced with the problem of translation he/she cannot just turn to 'reality' as a third mediator, for
that would merely introduce one more level to be translated and
thus invite in 'an elusive ghost' (1970: 24). Expressions are conceptual and many do not refer to physically located 'objects'.
Without the mediation of 'reality', learning about another people
consists in learning their language, concepts, behaviour and
assumptions. The only source of information for us is the analysis
of their 'meanings' as *they* present them, and through this
reflection on our meanings as *we* present them. Investigation has
to rebound on the investigator and involve the questioning of
his/her own society and standards. Being 'rational' means more
than being appropriately socialized into Western culture.

In our account, rationality has its foundations neither in
Western logic and philosophy, nor in intuition or human nature.
It is grounded in a continuous critical engagement in an international and historical context. Rationality has no determinate
foundation; there are no prescribed inner or outer truths, and
most definitely no formal theorized liberal rules in our definition.
Rationality is merely a title for acceptable and successful rules
constructed from past traditions, struggles and wisdom and
present analysis. Each element is a product of social negotiation
and struggle. Rationality has to be a system of thought which
exhibits an *internal* nexus between history and theory of 'rational'
development of social structures, concepts and meanings within

and between societies in response to their everyday needs, desires, common-sense, hopes and perceptions. Thus, we do not by definition reject the idealist view that rationality distinguishes people from animals. But we do argue that human rationality is the product of social life as a whole. Rationality is grounded in the cultural nature of human beings and in the pragmatically developed rules of cultural existence.

The history of rationality is also the history of the people. To be rational in the context of modern societies is to engage in struggles to defend and extend gains in the areas of equality, whether economic, racial or gender-based, and democracy. Rationality mobilizes social and political reform, initiates new laws, mobilizes people to resist state abuse and legitimizes arguments for democracy, civil rights, etc. It is most powerful when it becomes institutionalized.

SYSTEMATIC KNOWLEDGE AND ITS VALIDATION

Our discussion of rationality implies a view of science and of the understanding of the validation of scientific knowledge. In his seminal *The Structure of Scientific Revolutions* (1970), Thomas Kuhn emphasizes the social character of scientific knowledge in a way that undermines both the realist and positivist view of science. Treating science sociologically reflects a general tendency within the sociology of science. This includes the 'increasing awareness of the relevance of language' and a methodological concreteness which rejects 'theorizing which is detached from close empirical study of complexities of social action' (Knorr-Cetina and Mulkay 1983: 13). The implications of the sociological interpretation of science for sociology, however, has not been fully worked through. Again it is the fear of relativism, exemplified by writers like Lévi-Strauss and Habermas, which has foreshortened reflection on these matters.

But is this fear of scepticism and arbitrariness on the part of major modern sociologists justified, or does scepticism only appear to be a threat because of formalist assumptions? As Rorty observes in another context: 'nobody would want "human knowledge" . . . justified unless he had been frightened by scepticism' (1979: 229). In the following sections we shall argue for a sociological interpretation based upon an aesthetic and sociological criteria of rationality.

The problem of scepticism

The sociological interpretation of science has become associated with Pyrrohonian or Humeian scepticism; with the belief that there are no rational grounds for judgement and no basis for judging between competing cognitive claims. Thus Popkin represents Hume as believing that 'there are no rational grounds for our judgements, and that we have no ultimate criterion for determining which of our conflicting judgements are true or preferable' (1968: 57). Hume is convinced that our values, statements of facts, and even mathematical concepts are merely contingent, since our sense data are insufficient for rational selection.

As a critique of the assumptions of rationalism, there is much in Hume's view which should indeed be acceptable to sociologists. Where we depart from Hume's argument is in its nihilistic conclusions. Having disposed of the possibility that the isolated ego could provide a rational foundation for judgement and truth claims, Hume was not about to turn to actually existing human communities for an explanation. In our view it is such a sociological turn that enables us to accept Hume's critique of rationalism, while resisting its sceptical conclusions. For Hume, the only conceivable alternative to a judgement rationally grounded in a solipsistic subject is judgement which is purely psychological: i.e. prejudice, habit, and predilection. The possibility of a socially and historically grounded rationality, that is neither absolute nor fully arbitrary, is beyond the ambit of Hume's solipsistic assumptions:

> The intense view of these manifold contradictions and imperfections in human reason has so wrought upon me, and heated my brain, that I am ready to reject all belief and reasoning, and can look upon no opinion even as more probable or likely than another.
>
> (quoted in Popkin 1968: 56-7)

Rather than deny the possibility of alternative bases for the rationality of belief, sociology turns to the practical context of human cultural existence. It replaces a rationalist or empiricist with a sociological epistemology. Sociology's appeal is to the historical, sociological and aesthetic standards of rationality immanent to human culture. Like Hume, we too are not convinced of apodictic standards; but unlike him, we do not draw sceptical implications about the arbitrariness of human judgement and belief.

A sociological view of science: for people

A sociological view of scientific knowledge must start from, but not end with, a political economy of scientific practice:

> Scientists who had begun by feeling that 'their' science had been betrayed in the defoliation campaign in Vietnam, or that 'their' scientific community was a hollow myth, began to ask such questions as: Whose science is it? Who pays for it? Who decides it? Who benefits from it?
>
> (Rose and Rose 1976: xiii)

A political economy of science too argues that social factors are important to concept formation, valuation and action within the following respects: (i) social factors are inherent in technical analysis; (ii) science is therefore political; (iii) treating scientific claims as purely technical is itself ideological in that it serves the narrow interests of the scientific community; (iv) the recognition of the social nature of the production of scientific knowledge has an emancipatory promise.

With respect to concept formation, both Marxist and non-Marxist sociologists acknowledge the role of social ideology in science. It is argued, first, that issues identified as 'purely technical' are in fact social, i.e. they involve policy and political decision in the selection of ends and methods of implementation. The technical is said to 'display those characteristics which have traditionally been attributed to social phenomena' (Knorr-Cetina and Mulkay 1983: 11). 'Technical' decisions are, according to any sociology of science, taken within the context of general societal interests and the attempt to maintain their status as purely technical can itself be strategic, e.g. a tactic of exclusion from decision-making processes.

In addition, Marxists place scientific production within the broader social context of capitalist production: 'the vaunted internationalization of science was a function of [capitalism's] mode of production, just as much as contemporary capitalism demands the existence of the multinational corporation' (Rose and Rose 1976: xvi).[7] Science is not, as some positivists and orthodox Marxists have maintained, above class (or other social) struggle (see Levidow and Young 1981). As Norman Desmond observes: 'the concepts with which scientists organize data and formulate theories, show that science is inherently political' (1981: 32). For critics like Desmond:

> How we organize data in science as in every sphere of consciousness embodies an overall outlook which derives from our social existence. Underlying and structuring all our thoughts is our understanding of our society and our reactions and adaptations to it. Scientific concepts are thus inherently political, continuing to express and reaffirm socially based world-views.
>
> (Desmond 1981: 38)

In a similar spirit, others have examined the links between the organization and funding of science and major social interests such as the military:

> As research money [in the USA] becomes more difficult to obtain, universities are turning increasingly to the Pentagon to make up for the loss. As a result . . . military funding for research increased from 10.8 to 16.4 per cent of the total research budget of US colleges and universities between 1980 and 1983, rising in current dollars from $455 million to $813 million over the three-year period.
>
> (Dickson 1984: 109)

Dickson gives a detailed account of the complex web of connections existing between even 'pure' scientific research, the university system, and what C. Wright Mills (following Eisenhower) called the 'military-industrial complex'. The later 'Star Wars' initiative reinforced the dependencies Dickson describes.

The social ideology of science also serves the interests of the scientific community as a community of 'experts'. The distinctions between 'laity' and 'expert', 'technical' and 'emotive' arguments, 'facts' and 'prejudices', etc., maintain the boundaries of a privileged and authoritative discourse and legitimize the place and privileges of those laying claim to that discourse.

Nevertheless, a sociological interpretation of science has to go beyond a political economy of the organization, funding and utility of science to include social criteria for the validation or authentication of scientific claims. If we remain at the level of the political and political economic analysis our criticisms will remain external to the actual activity of 'doing science'. To engage science at this level sociology must show how organizational, and thus seemingly 'external', factors affect the form and content of science as a cognitive and explanatory enterprise. It must, in other words, demonstrate that 'beyond the social determination of the field of inquiry, the *constitution of the scientific object of knowledge of inquiry is linked to the prevailing social and technical division of labour*' (Aronowitz 1988: 320).

Such a sociological approach questions realist notions of 'objectivity', and hence asocial, reality as well as positive notions of objective methodology which excludes social interest and power factors. For these reasons the sociological view of science has in some respects been more contentious than the political economy of science. For example, it undermines the rigid distinction between subject and object common to most theories of science. We have, essentially, a socialization of the Kantian claim that the object is dependent on consciousness. As Levidow and Young observe:

> Only as nature becomes socially mediated does it have any practical existence for humanity. All attempts to characterize nature, to know it and to shape it to human purposes, are constituted by the prevailing social priorities of a given epoch.
>
> (Levidow and Young 1981: 1)

Thus, though concepts are correspondent in the sense that they relate to objects, they also have a 'definite operational validity' and are not 'exclusive ways to organize data' (Desmond 1981: 42).

Following Kuhn, Mulkay, Desmond and others, our view implies that the social aspects of science are not extraneous to it. As we have already suggested 'the very distinction between "social" and "technical" is produced through the scientist's own interpretative practices' (Knorr-Cetina and Mulkay 1983: 13). Unless we accept at face value the claims of science, we are not persuaded that scientists are privileged with a qualitatively different form of knowledge from social knowledge, or a special procedure for acquiring it. They assume, as Kuhn points out, that 'the scientific community knows what the world is like', or are at least capable of finding out from a position of privileged methodology. Thus, the success of science 'derives from the community's willingness to defend that assumption . . . often suppressing fundamental novelties because they are necessarily subversive of its basic commitments' (Kuhn 1970: 5).

While science is clearly a very specialized form of symbolic knowledge, so are other forms of knowledge and belief: indeed, that is the definition of all 'knowledge'. Science and belief are not to be distinguished because they are qualitatively different in the claims they can legitimately make to validity, but because they define and deal with 'reality' in different ways. Science itself does not constitute a single, stable, cognitive system. Further, we do not accept that there are fixed methodological criteria for qualitatively distinguishing scientific from other beliefs. Contra the Popperian view, beliefs, like scientific knowledge, can be 'falsified' in terms of their own standards of validity. Contra the realists' view, science cannot lay claim to privileged access to unchanging reality *an sich*. For a believer to persuade a scientist, or a scientist a believer, there must both be shared grounds *and* respect of each other's systems, or at least willingness to listen to each other's views with some respect. That is not the realm of 'objectivity', but of social knowledge and negotiation.

On a sociological account, science, like any other form of belief, must receive its vindication in a societal discourse: in humanity's practical and cultural existence. It too must satisfy social needs and demands. If it is to do more than serve the interests of the scientific community and the interests of those whom community itself serves, science must address socially situated questions and knowledge, and not maintain that its own esoteric discourse and findings are *always* more truthful, and qualitatively different from those concerns.

The sociology of science has come in for considerable criticism, notably, the charge of relativism. The main focus of recent criticism has been on the so-called 'Edinburgh School' of Barry Barnes and David Bloor (see especially Hollis and Lukes 1982). Some discussion of these issues should clarify our own position. We shall argue that while this debate raises difficulties for a determinist approach to the sociology of science, the rationalist case against a comparative sociology of knowledge has not been established. The attempt to argue that there is a core of thinking which is not historically revisable creates difficulties for a strong rationalist critique of sociology the moment we ask what the content of that core is. Thus, while sharing some of its critics' doubts about the determinism of a 'strong programme' for the sociology of science, we defend the central contention that beliefs, including scientific beliefs, are socially situated.

Barnes and Bloor's 'strong programme' for the sociology of knowledge combines a staunch defence of relativism with a commitment to rigorous scientific method. In the spirit of – no doubt conscious – paradox, they argue that it is science's own empirical mode of reasoning which demands an empirical explanation of science. The sociologist, as scientist, cannot but heed the call:

> [The sociologist's] ideas therefore will be in the same causal idiom as any other scientist's. His concern will be to locate the regularities and general principles of processes which appear to be at work within the field of his data.
>
> (Bloor 1976: 3)

The novelty and challenge of this lies in its provocative combination of an interpretation of science as a product of societal interests with a realist methodology. As Peter Manicas points out, Barnes and Bloor combine 'relativism' with realism to produce a programme for the sociological *explanation* of scientific practices and claims: 'being capable of making apt responses to the causal inputs from this world, humans learn, and collectively they develop social patterns which, in turn, become causal factors in their reproduction' (1987: 262). 'Science' is itself merely one such 'social pattern' which emerges as one response to external 'causal inputs'.

The central tenets of the strong programme are (i) a realist view of causality, and (ii) symmetry of treatment for all human beliefs. In other words, they are committed to the view that beliefs require *causal explanation* and that 'true' beliefs are no less in need of causal explanation than 'mythical' or 'false' ones.[8] On the basis of these principles, Barnes and Bloor have undertaken empirical investigations linking scientific beliefs to the social structures in which those beliefs are 'located' and to which they are causally related (see especially Barnes 1977 and Bloor 1976).

Both planks of the strong programme – determinism and symmetry – have come in for criticism. Against determinism, Martin Hollis (1982) has argued that in treating social structure and location as *causes* of beliefs and ideas, sociologists fail to see the constitutive role beliefs and ideas play:

> Deeper problems are set by the presupposition that social and intellectual systems can be separated and then related as cause and effect. This seems to me a dangerous piece of rot. Ideas

cannot, I submit, be described in isolation from the social world, which they let actors describe to themselves; nor can the social world be furnished without the aid of actors' ideas.

(Hollis 1982: 70)

What is at stake here is not, we would contend, the validity of sociological accounts of science as such, but rather the appropriate nature of such accounts.[9] Hollis is objecting to an account of human belief which first separates beliefs and social structure, and then tries to re-establish the link by invoking 'societal interests' as a causal mechanism. This causal treatment of beliefs and ideas proposed by the Edinburgh School, however, is not shared by all sociologists of science:

> It is especially important *not* to rely on any science of society or science of man to impute interests because ... sciences are one of the most convincing tools to persuade others of who they are and what they should want. A sociology of science is crippled from the start if it believes in the result of one science, namely sociology, to explain the others.

(Latour 1983: 144)

Bruno Latour's influential analysis of scientific practices, and especially of Pasteur's laboratory, does not display the simple determinism of which Hollis is critical because such externalism is for Latour poor sociology. In his work the constitutive role of ideas is central to the *sociological* analysis of science as a source of social power:

> *in his very scientific work, in the depth of the laboratory, Pasteur actively modifies the society of his time and he does so directly* – not indirectly – *by displacing some of its important actors.*

(Latour 1983: 156)

Rather than view laboratory practices as passive 'reflections' of social structure or sociopolitical interest, Latour treats them as a generator of those structures: '*Microbiology laboratories are one of the few places where the very composition of the social context has been metamorphosed*' (1983: 156). Here is a quite distinct research programme which inverts the relationship between 'social' and 'intellectual systems' posited by an externalist sociology of science. Rather than the causal explanation of the role of social structure in determining beliefs, Latour shows how one human cognitive practice (science) reproduces social relations beyond that practice.[10]

The view of science for which we would wish to argue here is closer to Latour's than it is to Barnes and Bloor's. Scientific beliefs cannot be 'read off' social structure precisely because they play an increasingly important role in constituting that structure. It is precisely this which makes the sociology of science an especially urgent task. We share Hollis's reservations about a model which would propose that 'some interests are indeed structurally generated and ultimately attributed to social-structural categories' (Barnes 1977: 58). The attempt to link beliefs to structure via the category of objective interests is both instrumentalist and ahistorical (see also Scott 1988). But what of the question of relativism?

Rather than restate the standard objection that relativism is self-defeating (see, for example, Popper 1944), Hollis develops a more positive argument to the effect that common standards are the precondition for rather than the outcome of cross-contextual com- munication. In the act of translating 'their' concepts into 'our' language, how do we know that our translations mean the 'same thing' as the original? Only, the answers goes, by pre-supposing a common rationality; a 'massive central core of human thinking which has no history' (Strawson, quoted in Hollis 1982: 75). In Hollis's version of this argument, such a 'bridgehead' requires (i) the presupposition that the distinction between rational and irrational, and truth and falsity, is common to all human com- munities; and (ii) the ascription of rationality to the agents whose utterances, beliefs, etc., we are interpreting. On the basis of this 'plea for metaphysics' (1982: 84) and an assertion of the 'epistemological unity of mankind' (1979: 230), Hollis criticizes the sociology of knowledge for trying to remain neutral with respect to the truth or falsity of the material it interprets.[11]

What should we make of the claim that there is a 'massive central core of human thinking which has no history', beyond perhaps pointing out that this may do less to facilitate communi-cation than to render it redundant? First, we can argue, as the original targets of the criticism have done (see Barnes and Bloor 1982: 35–6), that the existence of this core is asserted rather than established by the critics of the sociology of knowledge. Hollis's argument, for example, has a Kantian and quasi-transcendental structure. His concern is with the conditions of the possibility of accurate translation: what universal categories must be present in order that successful translation is possible? Hollis is aware that this mode of argumentation can produce an answer which is merely formal: 'the plain snag here is that such reflections yield at most an existence proof' and 'it is tempting to respond by making the core all form and no content, by assigning to it the formal properties of coherent belief, and leaving all particular beliefs about what there is to empirical enquiry' (1982: 84). We have argued, with respect to Habermas, that quasi-transcendental arguments can only produce such formal delimitations of the core, and that questions of common content are indeed empirical and historical.

Much also hangs on the nature of the bridgehead alleged to be necessary before translation can commence. The rationalist would want to claim that the bridgehead must be fixed and beyond history, a conclusion which would indeed be embarrassing for the sociologist. Because the strong rationalist case appears to run into difficulties when trying to specify the substance of the 'core', a weaker form of the argument has been proposed in which the bridgehead is viewed as a movable rather than a fixed item (see Lukes 1982).[12] The suggestion of a bridgehead which is itself, even in part, historically and experientially revisable is already enough in our view to subvert rationalism and once more opens up the space for an historically informed sociology of knowledge. If all we are being asked to accept is that social actors are rational, or at least should be thought to be so in the absence of firm evidence to the contrary, without the content of that rationality being specified ahistorically or asocially, then a comparative sociologist is unlikely to object.[13]

The dilemma for sociology's rationalist critics appears as sharp as any they seek to identify: either to hold the ground but at the cost of identifying at best a merely formal 'common core', or to concede too much to sociology by cutting the bridgehead loose from its asocial moorings. But the dispute between the Edinburgh School and its critics also disguises some common assumptions.

Both the scientistic sociology of science *and* rationalism are interested in communication/translation as first and foremost a one-way journey: *their* beliefs into *our* language. For Barnes and Bloor the causal language of one of the partners (the sociological community) is privileged over that of another (the scientific community in general). But this unidirectional flow of communication is assumed by their critics too.[14] The philosophical discussion of translation, in contrast to its actual practice, appears to leave the target language unaffected. A concern with 'correct translation' fails to address the question: 'What must change in our language that we may understand their beliefs?' Those willing to let the bridgehead float (Horton 1982 and Lukes 1982, but see also Winch 1970) recognize this limitation. Furthermore, the debate is cast largely in ahistorical terms.

Our argument has been that questions of validity can be addressed neither through science nor philosophy, but are themselves historical. A sociology of knowledge in a non-determinist mode needs to focus on the interaction between 'communities' or 'societies' *over time*; it needs, we argue, to examine processes of mutual understanding and misunderstanding. Nor should this social learning be conceptualized in purely cognitive terms. The 'intellectual' life of a society cannot, for the sociologist, be divorced from its practical life. We must neither, à la Habermas, sunder power from knowledge, nor, as Foucault sometimes appears to do, collapse the one into the other.

Our criticisms need not distract from the central point which the sociology of science seeks to establish: knowledge cannot be secured once and for all in the categories of a transcendental ego or communication community, nor in scientific methodology. The disputes between the philosophy of the subject, positivism, universal pragmatics, etc., remain trapped within a Western foundationalist discourse. For sociology, the substantive consequence of foundationalism is formalism: a methodological procedure which inhibits learning and self-reflection. In this final chapter we have, in contrast, stressed the continuity between sociological and 'common-sense' (lay) knowledge. Specialist scientific knowledge, of which sociology is one type, embodies the character of all societal learning: namely sensitivity to history and other cultures. Sociological knowledge too is thus a form of what Paul Connerton (1989) has recently called 'social memory', but it is also a framework for learning. The recognition of this demands a sociological recasting of notions of rationality and science. Finally, the recognition of the social aspect of science is also potentially emancipatory. The identification of scientific practices as *social* practices may make it possible to open up those discourses and liberate populations from technological, 'scientific', control.

CONCLUSION

In this work we have developed a critique of sociological 'formalism'. Although formalism entered sociology through philosophy, it has taken root in the assumptions of both theoretical *and* empirical sociologists who are concerned to ground sociological knowledge in an *a prioristic* and foundationalist logic, and to apply these, in the last analysis local (i.e. 'Western' or 'European'), categories to other societies. This, we argued, has two profound effects; first, it blunts the radical edge of sociological modes of thought which if developed would present a basic challenge to parochial rationalism; secondly, it inhibits sociology's ability to understand other societies, and thus to understand the society in which it itself developed.

In Chapter 1 we argued that positivism not empiricism characterizes sociological practices. The critique of sociology as 'empiricist' thus misses the mark. Empiricism characterizes much historiographic work, but sociology is more typically formalist. The impact of positivism and later structuralist Marxism and realism on sociological research programmes illustrates the attraction of essentially foundationalist and formalist modes of thought with sociology.

Chapter 2 traced the strands of formalism within philosophy and showed how the assumptions developed with Western thought were taken up by and incorporated into sociology. To illustrate the sociological reception of philosophical formalism further, Chapter 3 and Chapter 4 examined the works of two prominent theorists: Lévi-Strauss and Habermas. Of the two we argued that it was Lévi-Strauss who, in his critique of racism, developed the sociological critique of formalism the more fully, but even he was unable to resist the temptation to search for cultural universals to shore up his structural anthropology. Habermas, on the other hand, restricts his critique of formalism to a critique of *positivist* formalism. While he offers a powerful critique of positivism and contrasts it to social theory, when it comes to developing a positive account of what that social theory is he forgets his own lessons and once more defines its project in the universalistic and philosophical language of universal pragmatics. We switch once more from 'epistemology as social theory' back to the status quo of 'social theory as epistemology'; albeit epistemology by other means.

Chapter 5 traces the effect of formalism on the substantive sociological diagnosis of 'modernity'. We argue that there is a degree of continuity between theories of modernization where ethnocentric assumptions are only thinly veiled, if at all, and more recent accounts of 'modernity' and 'postmodernity'. All three approaches are caught in a simple dichotomy in which 'tradition' and 'modernity', or 'modernity' and 'postmodernity', are thought-lessly counterpoised. Not even 'postmodernist' sociologists question the categories themselves. They too treat 'modernity' as an homogenous entity, rather as modernization theory treated 'tradition' as static and homogeneous. In contrast, we argued that there is not, nor was there ever, a single human 'condition', be it 'tradition', 'modernity' or 'postmodernity'.

Finally, in Chapter 6 we argued that a central task for sociology is to wrest concepts of 'knowledge' and 'rationality' from the discourse of philosophy and recast them in the language of soci-ology. This is not to argue for relativism, but for a conception of human knowledge and rationality as a learning process, located (contra-Habermas) in communication within and between *empirical* human communities. Forms of human knowledge are too subtle to be reduced entirely to explicit propositional statements. Knowledge is carried in and through culture: through gesture, expression, reaction, humour, emotion, and even within forms of manipulation and bluff. Any attempted 'rational reconstruction' of the subtleties of cultural knowledge foreshortens the potential-ities for intra- and cross-cultural understanding. We are sym-pathetic to the view of social (and sociological) knowledge which likens understanding to learning another language rather than to the explicit codification of 'cultural grammar'. In our view, sociology constitutes a self-aware form of cultural learning in which the implicit characteristics of all such learning (i.e. his-torical and comparative sensibility) are explicitly embodied in its methodological principles.

If the argument of this book can be wrapped up in one motto then it would be: sociologists must learn to take their own paradigm more seriously and work through its very radical implications. The prohibi-tive and positive consequences of a self-confident sociology stripped of its usual angst can be summed up as follows:

1 Sociological arguments cannot be expounded in philosophical langauge, but rather must take the form of comparative and

historical analysis. This excludes seeking secure foundations for either (a) sociology as a discipline or (b) rationality in general.

2 Likewise, neither 'a' nor 'b' can be secured in theories of evolution which merely substitute pseudo-empirical practices for philosophical argument.

3 In contrast to both philosophy *and* evolutionism, historical and cross-contextual sensitivity must be seen as the precondition for both good sociology *and* human rationality. In other words, sociology implies a view of rationality not as a reconstructable and secure foundation, but as a changing embodiment of human experience: i.e. as culture.

4 Science too (including sociology as a science) must be viewed as a specific form of cultural knowledge, not as a discourse having prior claim to truth by dint of its methodological or procedural characteristics.

Unless sociologists learn to apply a sociological mode of thought rigorously and without self-imposed censorship, they cannot hope to harvest its potential. Sociology will in these circumstances remain a muted voice in social debate. It is not merely anxiety, but also the smugness which accompanies a defensive posture, which has inhibited sociologists from developing the radical implications of their own 'calling'. As long as sociological arguments remain subordinate to philosophical ones, they do not risk exposure to rigorous examination in the arena of societal discourse. It is consistent with our view of rationality as culturally embedded learning that we should argue finally that unless sociology does expose its arguments in this way, its validity will not be put to the rigorous test societies apply to all claims. A sociology in the service of human emancipation, as Critical Theory would have it, is only possible to the extent that sociology is able to emancipate itself.

NOTES

1 But see Bauman's review of *Individualism*, where he laments Lukes's rejection of a sociology of knowledge approach in favour of a more conventional history of ideas (Bauman 1974). Geoffrey Hawthorn (1976) rejects sociological approaches in his interpretation of the rise of the discipline because of their relativism.

2 For examples of this neglect of biography in the case of Weber alone, see Parkin 1982; Aron 1964; Freund 1972; Wrong 1970; and Lachmann

1970. On similar treatments of Simmel, see Lawrence 1976 and Wolff 1964. Rhes 1981 treats the whole sociological tradition in this way.

3 For similar views, see Gardner 1974; Dray 1966; Finnegan and Horton 1973; and Benn and Mortimore 1976.

4 See the various articles in Wilson (ed.) 1970, especially those by Lukes, Hollis and Gellner.

5 Paradoxically, Habermas's attempt to defend reason against decisionism would lead to irrational behaviour. To take literally the absolute distinction Habermas implies between reason and decision would produce compulsive actions and individuals who lacked a sense of their own responsibility for their actions; that responsibility being displaced on to rules of rational action.

6 It may be possible to argue that Gellner and MacIntyre misrepresent Winch's views and that the participants in this famous debate are in fact talking past each other in many respects. Thus, Winch does for example allow for the possibility of parasitic practices (e.g. Black Masses) which may be criticized externally (though how one identifies such practices as parasitic is itself an issue). Our concern here is less with whether there are misunderstandings in this debate, than in the assumptions which the participants share.

7 For an application of sociological analysis to science in a non-capitalist context, see Aronowitz 1988, chs. 7–8.

8 Even Mannheim, the chief object of opprobrium for an earlier generation of the critics of the sociology of knowledge, is taken to task for attempting to limit sociological explanation to non-scientific beliefs. Barnes and Bloor's work also breaks with the historical-sociological paradigm developed by Robert Merton. One of Merton's major concerns was to identify the sociohistorical preconditions for the development of science. It was never his intention to develop a sociology which challenged the claims of science. See Merton 1973.

9 At this point the debate between the sociology of science and its critics is a re-run of the 'Methodenstreit' (dispute over method) which so occupied German social theory around the turn of the century. In terms of that earlier dispute, Barnes and Bloor take the view that there is a unity of scientific method (for the natural and social science), while Hollis is siding with the broadly hermeneutic position that the social world, as the active creation of social actors, demands a distinctive *interpretative* approach.

10 Latour's approach to the sociology of science is much influenced by Foucault, and particularly by the latter's concept of 'power/ knowledge'.

11 A similar ambiguity arises within the sociology of science with respect to relativism as does with the case of scientism. The alternative to the rigorous scientism of the Edinburgh School is the more ethnomethodological approach adopted by, for example, Gilbert and Mulkay 1984. This approach can be viewed as a concession to the kind of criticism Hollis is levelling against the sociology of science. It recognizes that we cannot constantly assert the *Zeitgebunden* (time-bound) nature of science without also recognizing the implications of this for

which abandons a 'single, coherent account of the patterns of action and belief in science' (187) and restricts itself to descriptions of accounts scientists give of their activities and the methods used in constructing those accounts. By abandoning the traditional sociological project, discourse analysis embraces the paradox of relativism. In so doing it is in a sense more consistent than the sociology of science in its scientistic mode. Gilbert and Mulkay attempt to soften their relativism by holding fast to 'the assumption that interpretative regularities could be discerned behind the babble of tongues, if a suitable analytical approach could be devised' (187). Such a move lends support to Skorupski's observation that 'realist scepticism . . . tends to go over into anti-realist relativism, which affords a more comfortable resting place' (1978: 96, footnote 14). But need a sociology of knowledge be laid to rest with either realist scepticism (read, the Edinburgh School) or anti-realist relativism (read, ethnomethodology)?

12 Like Hollis, Lukes takes relativism to be self-defeating in so far as it denies any bridgehead: 'without such a common core, the entire enterprise of interpretation and translation cannot get started' (1982: 266), but he is willing to see the bridgehead 'float': '*what* that foundation is, what must be proposed for the interpretation of belief systems to proceed is in a sense an empirical matter, or at least revisable in the light of experience' (1982: 272).

13 In fact the injunction to treat beliefs as rational can be found too in the work of sociologists of knowledge and science. See, for example, Latour 1987, ch.5.

14 Perhaps the rather unfortunate term 'bridgehead' is itself indicative of this assumption. 'Bridgehead' is a military term meaning '1) an area of ground secured or to be taken on the enemy's side of an obstacle; 2) a fortified or defensive position at the end of a bridge nearest to the enemy' (*Collins Dictionary of the English Language*). Bridgeheads then are not 'presupposed'; they are 'taken' (usually by force). If we were literally to translate the language of 'bridgeheads' into the sphere of communication, the aim could not be understanding but victory: the absorption of the enemy's conceptual territory into our own.

Bibliography

Abrahams, J.H. (1973) *Origins and Growth of Sociology*, London, Penguin.

Adorno, T.W., Albert, H., Dahrendorf, R., Habermas, J., Pilot, H. and Popper, K.R. (1976) *The Positivist Dispute in German Sociology*, London, Heinemann.

Alexander, J. (1986) 'Habermas's new critical theory: its promise and problems', *American Journal of Sociology* 91, 400–24.

Allen, V. (1977) 'On the differentiation of the working class' in Hunt (ed.) *op. cit.*

Althusser, L. (1969) *For Marx*, London, Allen Lane.

Andreski, S. (ed.) (1971) *Herbert Spencer*, London, Thomas Nelson.

Apel, K.-O. (1980) *Towards the Transformation of Philosophy*, London, Routledge & Kegan Paul.

Aron, R. (1964) *German Sociology*, NY, Free Press.

Aron, R. (1967) *18 Lectures on Industrial Society*, London, Weidenfeld & Nicolson.

Aron, R. (1968) *Main Currents of Sociological Thought*, 2 vols., London, Penguin.

Aronowitz, S. (1988) *Science as Power: Discourse and Ideology in Modern Science*, Minnesota, University of Minnesota Press.

Badcock, C.R. (1975) *Lévi-Strauss: Structuralism and Sociological Theory*, London, Hutchinson.

Banks, O. (1971) *The Sociology of Education*, London, Batsford.

Barnes, B. (1977) *Interests and the Growth of Knowledge*, London, Routledge & Kegan Paul.

Barnes, B. (1983) 'On the conventional character of knowledge and cognition' in Knorr-Cerina and Mulkay (eds) *op. cit.*

Barnes, B. and Bloor, D. (1982) 'Relativism, rationalism and the sociology of knowledge' in Hollis and Lukes (eds) *op. cit.*

Baudrillard, J. (1983) 'The ecstasy of communication' in H. Foster (ed.) *Postmodern Culture*, London, Pluto Press.

Bauman, Z. (1974) 'Extended review of Lukes's "Individualism"', *Sociological Review* 22,1, 157–61.

Bauman, Z. (1989) 'Sociological responses to postmodernity', *Thesis Eleven* 23, 35–63.

Benn, S.I. and Mortimore, G.W. (1976) *Rationality and the Social Sciences*,

London, Routledge & Kegan Paul.

Bennett, J. (1964) *Rationality: an Essay Towards an Analysis*, London, Routledge & Kegan Paul.

Benton, T. (1977) *The Philosophical Foundations of the Three Sociologies*, London, Routledge & Kegan Paul.

Berger, J. and Offe, C. (1982) 'Functionalism vs rational choice: some questions concerning the rationality of choosing one or the other', *Theory and Society* 11, 521–6.

Berlin, I. (ed.) (1979) *The Age of Enlightenment*, Oxford, OUP.

Bernal, J.D. (1969) *Science and History*, 2 vols., London, Watts.

Bernstein, R.J. (1979) *The Restructuring of Social and Political Theory*, London, Methuen.

Bloor, D. (1976) *Knowledge and Social Imagery*, London, Routledge & Kegan Paul.

Bock, K. (1979) 'Theories of progress, development, evolution' in Bottomore and Nisbet (eds) *op. cit.*

Bottomore, T. (1962) *Sociology: a Guide to Problems and Literature*, London, Allen & Unwin.

Bottomore, T. and Nisbet, R. (eds) (1979) *A History of Sociological Analysis*, London, Heinemann.

Bronowski, J. and Mazlish, B. (1963) *The Western Intellectual Tradition*, London, Penguin.

Bubner, R. (1981) *Modern German Philosophy*, Cambridge, CUP.

Bubner, R. (1982) 'Habermas's concept of critical theory' in Thompson and Held (eds) *op. cit.*

Buchdahl, G. (1961) *The Image of Newton and Locke in the Age of Reason*, London, Sheed & Ward.

Buchdahl, G. (1969) *Metaphysics and the Philosophy of Science*, Oxford, Blackwell.

Callinicos, A. (1990) 'Reactionary postmodernism' in R. Boyne and A. Rattansi (eds) *Postmodernism and Society*, London, Macmillan.

Carr, E.H. (1961) *What is History?*, London, Penguin.

Cassirer, E. (1944) *An Essay on Man*, New Haven, Yale University Press.

Chattick, N. (1965) 'The "Shirazi" colonialization of East Africa', *Journal of African History* VI (3): 275–94.

Chin, R. (1966) 'The utility of systems models and development models' in Finkle and Gable (eds) *op. cit.*

Connerton, P. (ed.) (1976) *Critical Sociology*, London, Penguin.

Connerton, P. (1989) *How Societies Remember*, Cambridge, CUP.

Cooke, P. (1989) *Back to the Future*, London, Unwin Hyman.

Copleston, F. (1959) *History of Philosophy*, vol. 5, London, Burns Oates & Washbourne.

Coser, L. (1981) 'The uses of classical theory' in Rhes (ed.) *op. cit.*

Davis, K. and Moore, W.E. (1969) 'Some principles of stratification' in L. Coser and B. Rosenberg (eds) *Sociological Theory: a Book of Readings*, 3rd edn., NY, Macmillan.

Desmond, N., (1981) 'The politics of scientific conceptualization' in Levidow and Young (eds) *op. cit.*

Dewey, J. (1938) *Logic: the Theory of Inquiry*, NY, Henry Holt.

Dickson, D. (1984) *The New Politics of Science*, NY, Pantheon Books.

Dray, W. (1966) *Philosophical Analysis and History*, NY, Harper & Row.

Dunn, J. (1968) 'Identity and the history of ideas', *Philosophy* 43, 164, 85–104.

Eisenstadt, S.N. (1966) *Modernization: Protest and Change*, Englewood Cliffs, NJ, Prentice-Hall.

Eliot, S. and Stern, B. (eds) (1979) *The Age of Enlightenment*, 2 vols., Milton Keynes, Open University Press.

Faurot, J.H. (1970) *Problems of Political Philosophy*, San Francisco, Chandler Publication.

Fay, B. (1975) *Social Theory and Political Practice*, London, Allen & Unwin.

Field, G.C. (1961) *The Philosophy of Plato*, Oxford, OUP.

Filmer, P., Phillipson, M., Silverman, D. and Walsh, D. (1972) *New Directions in Sociological Theory*, London, Macmillan.

Finkle, J.L. and Gable, R.W. (eds) (1966) *Political Development and Social Change*, NY, John Wiley.

Finley, J.N. (1970) 'Kant and Anglo-Saxon criticism' in L. White Beck (ed.) *Proceedings of the 3rd International Kant Congress*, Dordrecht, Holland, D. Reidel Publications.

Finnegan, R. and Horton, R. (1973) *Modes of Thought*, London, Faber & Faber.

Fletcher, R. (1966) *Auguste Comte and the Making of Sociology*, London, Athlone Press.

Foucault, M. (1977) *Discipline and Punish: the Birth of the Prison*, London, Penguin.

Frank, A.G. (1972) 'Sociology of development and the underdevelopment of sociology' in J.D. Cockcroft, A.G. Frank and D.L. Johnson (eds) *Dependency and Underdevelopment*, NY, Doubleday.

Frankfurt School of Social Research (1973) *Aspects of Sociology*, London, Heinemann.

Freund, J. (1972) *The Sociology of Max Weber*, London, Penguin.

Frisby, D. (1981) *Sociological Impressionism*, London, Heinemann.

Gardner, P. (ed.) (1974) *The Philosophy of History*, Oxford, OUP.

Garforth, F.W. (1971) *The Scope of Philosophy*, London, Longman.

Gay, P. (1967) *The Enlightenment: an Interpretation*, 2 vols, London, Weidenfeld & Nicolson.

Gellner, E. (1964) *Thought and Change*, London, Weidenfeld & Nicolson.

Gellner, E. (1970) 'Concepts and society' in Wilson (ed.) *op. cit.*

Giddens, A. (1971) *Capitalism and Modern Social Theory*, Cambridge, CUP.

Giddens, A. (1979) 'Positivism and its critics' in Bottomore and Nisbet (eds) *op. cit.*

Gilbert, N.G. and Mulkay, M. (1984) *Opening Pandora's Box: a Sociological Analysis of Scientists' Discourse*, Cambridge, CUP.

Goldthorpe, J.H. (1964) 'Social stratification in industrial society' in P. Halmos (ed.) 'The Development of Industrial Society', *The Sociological Review Monograph* 8, 97–122.

Goldthorpe, J.H. (1968) 'Introductory chapter' to Raison (ed.) *op. cit.*

Goldthorpe, J.H. (1971) 'Theories of Industrial Society: reflections on the recrudescence of historicism and the future of futurology', *Archives européennes de sociologie* 12, 263–88.

Gurnah, A. (1989) 'After Bilingual Support', in M. Cole (ed.) *Education for Equality*, London, Routledge.

Habermas, J. (1971a) *Towards a Rational Society*, London, Heinemann.

Habermas, J. (1971b) *Knowledge and Human Interest*, Boston, Beacon Press.

Habermas, J. (1974) *Theory and Practice*, London, Heinemann.

Habermas, J. (1979) *Communication and the Evolution of Society*, London, Heinemann.

Habermas, J. (1981) 'Modernity versus postmodernity', *New German Critique* 22, 3–14.

Habermas, J. (1984) *The Theory of Communicative Action*, vol. one: *Reason and the Rationalization of Society*, Cambridge, Polity Press.

Habermas, J. (1987a) *The Theory of Communicative Action*, vol. two: *Structure and Lifeworld: the Critique of Functionalist Reason*, Cambridge, Polity Press.

Habermas, J. (1987b) *The Philosophical Discourse of Modernity*, Cambridge, Mass., MIT Press.

Hagen, E.E. (1966) 'How economic growth begins: a theory of social change' in Finkle and Gable (eds) *op. cit.*

Halfpenny, P. (1982) *Positivism and Sociology*, London, Allen & Unwin.

Hall, S. (1977) 'The "political" and the "economic" in Marx's theory of classes' in Hunt (ed.) *op. cit.*

Hartung, F.E. (1970) 'Problems of the sociology of knowledge' in J.E. Curtis and J.W. Petras (eds) *The Sociology of Knowledge: a Reader*, London, Gerald Duckworth.

Harvey, D. (1989) *The Condition of Postmodernity*, Oxford, Blackwell.

Hauser, P.M. (1966) 'Some cultural and personal characteristics of less-developed areas' in Finkle and Gable (eds) *op. cit.*

Hawkes, T. (1977) *Structuralism and Semiotics*, London, Methuen.

Hawthorn, G. (1976) *Enlightenment and Despair*, Cambridge, CUP.

Held, D. (1980) *Introduction to Critical Theory*, London, Hutchinson.

Heller, A. (1982) 'Habermas and Marxism' in Thompson and Held (eds) *op. cit.*

Heller, A. and Fehér, F. (1990) *The Postmodern Political Condition*, Cambridge, Polity Press.

Hindess, B. (1973) *The Use of Official Statistics in Sociology*, London, Macmillan.

Hindess, B. (1987) *Politics and Class Analysis*, Oxford, Blackwell.

Hindess, B. and Hirst, P.Q. (1975) *Pre-Capitalist Modes of Production*, London, Routledge & Kegan Paul.

Hollis, M. (1979) 'The epistemological unity of mankind' in R.S. Brown (ed.) *Philosophical Disputes in Social Science*, Brighton, Harvester.

Hollis, M. (1982) 'The social destruction of reality' in Hollis and Lukes (eds) *op. cit.*

Hollis, M. and Lukes, S. (eds) (1982) *Rationality and Relativism*, Oxford, Blackwell.

Honneth, A. (1985) 'An aversion against the universal: a commentary on Lyotard's "Postmodern Condition"', *Theory, Culture & Society* 2, 3, 147–57.

Honneth, A. (1990) *Die zerrissene Welt des Sozialen: sozialphilosophische Aufsätze*, Frankfurt am Main, Suhrkamp.

Honneth, A. and Joas, H. (eds) (1986) *Kommunikatives Handeln: Beiträge zu Jürgen Habermas' "Theorie des kommunikativen Handelns"*, Frankfurt am Main, Suhrkamp.

Horton, R. (1970) 'African thought and Western science' in Wilson (ed.) *op. cit.*

Horton, R. (1982) 'Tradition and modernity revisited' in Hollis and Lukes (eds) *op. cit.*

Hoselitz, B. and Moore, W.E. (eds) (1963) *Industrialization and Society*, Paris, UNESCO-Mouton.

Hughes, H. Stuart (1974) [1958] *Consciousness and Society*, London, Paladin.

Hull, L.W.H. (1965) *History and Philosophy of Science*, London, Longman.

Hume, D. (1961) [1777] *Enquiries Concerning Human Understanding and Concerning the Principles of Morals*, Oxford, OUP.

Hunt, A. (ed.) (1977) *Class and Class Structure*, London, Lawrence & Wishart.

Huyssen, A. (1986) *After the Great Divide: Modernism, Mass Culture, Postmodernism*, Bloomington and Indianapolis, Indiana University Press.

Ingram, D. (1987) *Habermas and the Dialectic of Reason*, New Haven, Yale University Press.

Jarvie, I.C. (1970) 'Explaining cargo cults' in Wilson (ed.) *op. cit.*

Jarvie, I.C. and Agassi, J. (1970) 'The problem of the rationality of magic' in Wilson (ed.) *op. cit.*

Jay, M. (1988) *Fin-de-siècle Socialism*, London, Routledge.

Joas, H. (1986) 'Die unglückliche Ehe von Hermeneutik und Functionalismus' in Honneth and Joas (eds) *op. cit.*

Kant, I. (1929) [1781] *Critique of Pure Reason*, London, Macmillan.

Kant, I. (1953) [1783] *Prolegomena*, edited by P. Gray-Lucas, Manchester, Manchester University Press.

Kant, I. (1974) [1798] *Anthropology from a Pragmatic Point of View*, The Hague, Nijhoff.

Keane, J. (1988) *Democracy and Civil Society*, London, Verso.

Keat, R. and Urry, J. (1982) *Social Theory as Science*, 2nd edn., London, Routledge & Kegan Paul.

Kellner, D. (1988) 'Postmodernism as social theory', *Theory, Culture & Society* 5, 2/3, 239–369.

Kline, M. (1954) *Mathematics in Western Culture*, London, Allen & Unwin.

Knorr-Cetina, K.D. and Mulkay, M. (eds) (1983) *Science Observed: Perspectives on the Social Study of Science*, London, Sage.

Knorr-Cetina, K.D. and Mulkay, M. (1983) 'Introduction: emerging principles in the social study of science' in Knorr-Cetina and Mulkay (eds) *op. cit.*

Kolakowski, L. (1972) *Positivist Philosophy*, London, Penguin.

Kroner, R. (1956) *Kant's Weltanschauung*, Chicago, Ill., University of Chicago Press.

Kuhn, T. (1970) *The Structure of Scientific Revolutions*, Chicago, Chicago University Press.

Lachmann, K.M. (1970) *The Legacy of Max Weber*, London, Heinemann.
Laclau, E. and Mouffe, C. (1985) *Hegemony and Socialist Strategy*, London, Verso.
Lash, S. and Urry, J. (1987) *The End of Organized Capitalism*, Cambridge, Polity Press.
Latour, B. (1983) 'Give me a laboratory and I will raise the world' in Knorr-Cetina and Mulkay (eds) *op. cit.*
Latour, B. (1987) *Science in Action*, Milton Keynes, Open University Press.
Lawrence, P. (1976) *Georg Simmel*, London, Thomas Nelson.
Leach, E. (1974) *Lévi-Strauss*, 2nd edn., London, Fontana.
Lessnoff, M. (1974) *The Structure of Social Science*, London, Allen & Unwin.
Levidow, L. and Young, B. (eds) (1981) *Science, Technology and the Labour Process*, CSE Books, Highlands, NJ, Humanities Press.
Lévi-Strauss, C. (1952) *Race and History*, Paris, UNESCO.
Lévi-Strauss, C. (1964) *Totemism*, London, St Martin's Press.
Lévi-Strauss, C. (1966) *The Savage Mind*, London, Weidenfeld & Nicolson.
Lévi-Strauss, C. (1967) *The Scope of Anthropology*, London, Jonathan Cape.
Lévi-Strauss, C. (1968) *Structural Anthropology: 1*, London, Penguin.
Lévi-Strauss, C. (1978) *Myth and Meaning*, London, Routledge & Kegan Paul.
Locke, J. (1964) [1689] *An Essay Concerning Human Understanding*, edited by A.D. Woozley, London, Fontana.
Losse, J. (1972) *A Historical Introduction of Philosophy of Science*, Oxford, OUP.
Lukács, G. (1971) *History and Class Consciousness*, London, Merlin.
Lukes, S. (1970) 'Some problems about rationality' in Wilson (ed.) *op. cit.*
Lukes, S. (1982) 'Relativism in its place' in Hollis and Lukes (eds) *op. cit.*
Lyotard, J.-F. (1989) 'Universal history and cultural differences' in A. Benjamin (ed.) *The Lyotard Reader*, Oxford, Blackwell.
McCarthy, T. (1982) 'Rationality and relativism' in Thompson and Held (eds) *op. cit.*
McCarthy, T. (1985) 'Complexity and democracy, or the seductions of systems theory', *New German Critique* 35, spring/summer, 27–53.
MacIntyre, A. (1970a) 'The idea of a social science' in Wilson (ed.) *op. cit.*
MacIntyre, A (1970b) 'Is understanding a religion compatible with believing it?' in Wilson (ed.) *op. cit.*
Manicas, P.T. (1987) *A History and Philosophy of the Social Sciences*, Oxford, Blackwell.
Mannheim, K. (1936) *Ideology and Utopia*, London, Routledge & Kegan Paul.
Manning, D.J. (1976) *Liberalism*, London, J.M. Dent.
Marcuse, H. (1955) *Reason and Revolution*, 2nd edn., London, Routledge & Kegan Paul.
Marcuse, H. (1968) *Negations: Essays in Critical Theory*, London, Allen Lane.
Martin, E.B. (1978) *Zanzibar*, London, Hamish Hamilton.
Marx, K. (1975) [1844] 'Economic and philosophical manuscripts' in *Karl Marx: Early Writings*, London, Penguin.
Merton, R.K. (1973) *The Sociology of Science*, Chicago, Ill., University of Chicago Press.

Nagel, E. and Brandt, R. (1965) *Meaning and Knowledge*, NY, Harcourt, Brace & World.

Nietzsche, F. (1977) *Nietzsche: a Reader*, edited by R.J. Hollingdale, London, Penguin.

Nisbet, R. (1967) *The Sociological Tradition*, London, Heinemann.

Ottmann, H. (1982) 'Cognitive interests and self-reflection' in Thompson and Held (eds) *op. cit.*

Parkin, F. (1982) *Max Weber*, London, Tavistock.

Poole, R. (1964) 'Introduction to Lévi-Strauss' in Lévi-Strauss *op. cit.*

Popkin, R.H. (1968) 'David Hume: his Pyrrhonism and his critique of Pyrrhonism' in V.C. Chappell (ed.) *Hume*, London, Macmillan.

Popper, K. (1944) *The Poverty of Historicism*, London, Routledge & Kegan Paul.

Prins, A.H.J. (1961) *The Swahili Speaking People of Zanzibar and the East African Coast*, London, International African Institute.

Pye, L.W. (1966) 'The concept of political development' in Finkle and Gable (eds) *op. cit.*

Raison, T. (1968) *The Founding Fathers of Social Science*, London, Penguin.

Ree, J., Ayres, M. and Westoby, A. (1978) *Philosophy and its Past*, Brighton, Harvester Press.

Rhes, B. (ed.) (1981) *The Future of Sociological Classics*, London, Allen & Unwin.

Robertson, R., Gallagher, J. with Denny, A. (1974) *Africa and the Victorians*, London, Macmillan.

Rorty, R. (1979) *Philosophy and the Mirror of Nature*, Princeton, NJ, Princeton University Press.

Rorty, R. (1985) 'Habermas and Lyotard on postmodernism' in R.J. Bernstein (ed.) *Habermas and Modernity*, Cambridge, Polity Press.

Rose, G. (1988) 'The postmodern complicity', *Theory, Culture & Society* 5, 2/3: 357–71.

Rose, H. and Rose, S. (eds) (1976) *The Political Economy of Science*, London, Macmillan.

Rossides, D.W. (1978) *The History and Nature of Sociological Theory*, Boston, Mass., Houghton Mifflin.

Rostow, W.W. (1963) *The Stages of Economic Growth*, Cambridge, CUP.

Ryan, A. (1970) *The Philosophy of the Social Sciences*, London, Macmillan.

Schmid, M. (1982) 'Habermas's theory of social evolution' in Thompson and Held (eds) *op. cit.*

Scott, A. (1987) 'Politics and method in Mannheim's "Ideology and Utopia"', *Sociology* 12, 1, 41–54.

Scott, A. (1988) 'Imputing beliefs: a controversy in the sociology of knowledge', *The Sociological Review* 36, 1, 31–56.

Scott, W.R. (1970) *Social Processes and Social Structures*, NY, Holt, Rinehart & Winston.

Sjobergt, G. (1966) 'Folk and "feudal" societies' in Finkle and Gable, (eds) *op. cit.*

Skinner, Q. (1969) 'Meaning and understanding in the history of ideas', *History and Theory* 8, 3–53.

Skorupski, J. (1978) 'The meaning of another culture's beliefs' in

C. Hookway and P. Pettit (eds) *Action and Interpretation*, Cambridge, CUP.

Smart, B. (1976) *Sociological Phenomenology and Marxian Analysis*, London, Routledge & Kegan Paul.

Smelser, N. (1966) 'Mechanisms of change and adjustment to change' in Finkle and Gable (eds) *op. cit.*

Sorokin, P. (1955) 'Foreword' to Tönnies *op. cit.*

Staniland, H. (1972) *Universals*, NY, Doubleday.

Stedman Jones, G. (1972) 'History: the poverty of empiricism' in R. Blackburn (ed.) *Ideology in Social Science*, London, Fontana.

Sutton, F.X. (1966) 'Analyzing social systems' in Finkle and Gable (eds) *op. cit.*

Taylor, C. (1986) 'Sprache und Gesellschaft' in Honneth and Joas (eds) *op. cit.*

Theodorson, G.A. (1966) 'Acceptance of industrialization and its attendant consequences for social patterns of non-Western societies' in Finkle and Gable (eds) *op. cit.*

Therborn, G. (1971) 'Jürgen Habermas: a new eclectic', *New Left Review* 67, 69–83.

Thompson, J. and Held, D. (eds) (1982) *Habermas: Critical Debates*, Cambridge, Polity Press.

Tilley, C. (1990) 'Claude Lévi-Strauss: structuralism and beyond' in C. Tilley (ed.) *Reading Material Culture*, Oxford, Blackwell.

Tönnies, F. (1955) *Community and Association*, London, Routledge & Kegan Paul.

Walsh, W.H. (1963) *Metaphysics*, London, Hutchinson.

Walsh, W.H. (1975) *Kant's Criticisms of Metaphysics*, Edinburgh, Edinburgh University Press.

Weber, M. (1930) *The Protestant Ethic and the Spirit of Capitalism*, London, Unwin.

Williams, R. (1973) 'Base and superstructure in Marxist Cultural theory', *New Left Review* 82.

Wilson, B. (ed.) (1970) *Rationality*, Oxford, Blackwell.

Winch, P. (1958) *The Idea of a Social Science*, London, Routledge & Kegan Paul.

Winch, P. (1970) 'Understanding a primitive society' in Wilson (ed.) *op. cit.*

Wolff, K. (ed.) (1964) *Essays on Sociology and Philosophy*, New York, Harper.

Wright, G.H. von (1941) *The Logical Problem of Induction*, Oxford, OUP.

Wrong, D. (1970) *Max Weber*, Englewood Cliffs, NJ, Prentice-Hall.

Index